Praise for Susan Shapi...

"Barash skillfully channels her interviewees' experiences and convinces that these real and raw friendships are the norm."
Publishers Weekly on *Toxic Friends*

"A gutsy look at a controversial subject."
—Liz Perle, author of *Money, A Memoir,* on *Little White Lies, Deep Dark Secrets*

"A thoroughly well-researched and solidly reported exploration . . . She skillfully illuminates the extraordinary variety of women's experiences in their most complex and demanding role and relationship."
—Jane Adams, Ph.D., author of *I'm Still Your Mother* and *When Our Grown Kids Disappoint Us,* on *You're Grounded Forever . . . But First Let's Go Shopping*

"This in-depth exploration of female friendships and useful, self-help guide will interest women readers, students, scholars, and others. . . . Highly recommended."
—*librariansreviewofbooks.blogspot.com* on *Toxic Friends*

"*Toxic Friends* teases out the nuances of female friendships in unprecedented detail. Susan Shapiro Barash shines a light on the complicated feelings and questions we seldom discuss but feel so powerfully. You will see yourself and the friends who most beguile you in these pages."
—Rachel Simmons, author of *The Curse of the Good Girl,* on *Toxic Friends*

"A helpful starting place for any woman wondering if it's possible to get what she wants without hurting or being hurt."
—*Publishers Weekly* on *Tripping the Prom Queen*

Also by Susan Shapiro Barash

✳

Toxic Friends:
The Antidote for Women Stuck in Complicated Friendships

Little White Lies, Deep Dark Secrets:
The Truth About Why Women Lie

Tripping the Prom Queen:
The Truth About Women and Rivalry

A Passion for More:
Wives Reveal the Affairs That Make or Break Their Marriages

Sisters: Devoted or Divided

The New Wife:
The Evolving Role of the American Wife

Second Wives:
The Pitfalls and Rewards of
Marrying Widowers and Divorced Men

Mothers in Law and Daughters-in-Law:
Love, Hate, Rivalry and Reconciliation

Reclaiming Ourselves:
How Women Dispel a Legacy of Bad Choices

Women of Divorce:
Mothers, Daughters, Stepmothers—The New Triangle

The Men Out There:
A Women's Little Black Book
(with Michele Kasson, Ph.D.)

You're Grounded Forever...

But First
Let's Go Shopping

The Challenges Mothers Face with Their Daughters and Ten Timely Solutions

Susan Shapiro Barash

St. Martin's Griffin
New York

A NOTE TO THE READER:

References in this book to Web sites and other resources as potential sources of additional information do not mean that either the author or the publisher endorses anything that might be said in such material. Neither the author nor the publisher has control over, or is responsible for, the content or policies of this material.

www.stmartins.com

Design by Kathryn Parise

The Library of Congress has cataloged the hardcover edition as follows:

Barash, Susan Shapiro, 1954–
    You're grounded forever—but first let's go shopping : the challenges mothers face with their daughters and ten timely solutions / Susan Shapiro Barash.—1st ed.
        p. cm.
    Includes bibliographical references.
    ISBN 978-0-312-59564-7
    1. Mothers and daughters—Psychology. 2. Developmental psychology. I. Title.
    HQ755.85.B3565 2010
    649'.133—dc22

                                                        2010029182

ISBN 978-0-312-61422-5 (trade paperback)

First St. Martin's Griffin Edition: October 2011

10 9 8 7 6 5 4 3 2 1

To my mother and to my daughters

Author's Note

✳

This book is based on extensive personal interviews with women and experts in the field of psychology and counseling. Names have been changed and recognizable characteristics disguised of all people in this book except the contributing experts. Some characters are composites.

Contents

❀

Oh, my son's my son till he gets him a wife,
But my daughter's my daughter all her life.
—DINAH MARIA MULOCK CRAIK

Susan with her daughters in 1990.

Preface
What Do We Do Wrong with Our Daughters?

The Facts About Mothering Girls

- Ninety percent of mothers today believe that mothering daughters is much more loaded than mothering sons.
- More than 80 percent of mothers wonder if they can do better with their daughters.
- Seventy percent of mothers say they haven't set enough limits with their daughters.
- More than 70 percent of mothers question whether they are teaching their daughters proper values.
- More than 50 percent of mothers admit their hands-on approach to mothering smacks of overkill.

"My twenty-four-year-old daughter's life hasn't turned out the way we both thought it would," sighs Terri, forty-nine. "She's lagging behind her friends at work, with boys, and it's all because of

her anger toward me. She hates me and she's never listened to
anything I say. She figured she'd find things out for herself.
She's always thought that I didn't know anything, and this has
been going on since second grade. She relies on me emotionally
but she doesn't respect me, and I only hear from her when there's
a problem—her love life, her job, her roommate. I'm there to put
out the fires and to support her while she is mean and awful. I
jump for her every time. I feel so responsible for everything. . . . I
try to convince her to assume some responsibility, if it's not too
late. I wonder, What am I really doing and what have I done?
Why am I still spoiling her and why is my daughter such a heavy?"

The Tricky Game of Mothering Daughters

As the mother to two daughters, twenty-nine and twenty-two, I,
like most of us, have caved in to their needs, jumped through
hoops, and wished I had a magic wand to set the world straight
for them. I opted to be a mother who said yes rather than
no, and I believed that this would instill independence and
trust. From the start I was aware that I treated my daughters
differently than I treated my son. This was not only because I
identified with them so strongly in that mother-daughter way,
but also because I knew too well through my own research how
females of every age often fight to be heard, to hone their place,
and doubt themselves along the way. And so with my girls I re-
canted more often, worried more, and shopped with them more.
My aim was to please, and in this quest I did not, unfortunately,
become more seasoned as my younger daughter grew up, and
enough times I remained at a loss. There were occasions when I
racked my brain for why this feeling of helplessness on my part
surrounded my relationship with both daughters; it seemed to

me it had begun as early as kindergarten or even preschool with each of them.

Over time, I began to second-guess my style of mothering, and what I expected to be the best approach fell short. Throughout these challenges, I was hearing comparable concerns not only from close friends but also from women at the gym, at business lunches, at social gatherings, in women's groups, and from my pool of interviewees for other projects. For years, I have listened to mothers express concern about issues with daughters of all ages—from first grade through adulthood.

Many of the women's stories were eerily alike; an eight-year-old daughter who manages always to get her way, a sixteen-year-old daughter repeatedly swearing at her mother, a twenty-three-year-old daughter quitting her job after three weeks, a daughter whose anorexia surfaces in grad school, a daughter who is obsessed with her appearance, a daughter who endures a failed romance by leaning on her mother, an engaged daughter who morphs into bridezilla, a recently married daughter whose mother describes herself as walking on eggshells.

What was universal in the voices of the mothers with whom I spoke was their despair, their sense that it should be different, that their efforts seemed in vain when they considered the results. And the haunting questions: Had they done what they could for their daughters? Had their decisions and guidance been helpful or a hindrance in the long run?

With each year that passes, the bar is raised and the expectations for the mother-daughter bond are greater, set as they are now against the backdrop of a technological, media-saturated, celebrity-driven culture, where traditional values are entwined in the latest trends. Past generations' rigid rules for mothering girls have been replaced by rules encouraging a mother who is more of a pushover—cushy, with a coddling mentality. Even the mothers who think that they can micromanage their daughters' lives and seem to have an edge struggle to achieve boundaries. While these mothers *appear* tougher or collected to the outside world, they share the same frustrations and insecurities as mothers everywhere. Thus the template of mothers who have the best intentions, greatest determination, and highest hopes—but suffer for their mistakes with their daughters—has become a phenomenon.

Essentially, instead of relishing the joys of mothering daughters (who doesn't recall the thrill of giving birth to a baby girl and how special it is to be a mother to a daughter?), these mothers reported feeling regretful, uneasy, and misguided when it came to determining what is best for their daughters. Weren't we all resolute when it came to raising our daughters to be autonomous, goal-oriented, with strong values and a solid sense of self? Except few of us knew how to do this—What would work? What would backfire? How would our daughters react?—and consequently we made some major errors along the way. Could it possibly be that each of us, in order to provide a brave new world for our daughters, was actually getting it wrong?

Of the three hundred women who came forward for this study from large cities, suburban areas, and small towns across the country, from various social strata, religious beliefs, and ethnicities, their emotional sensibility was strikingly similar. These women blamed themselves. Some felt guilty, some hopeless, distraught, furious, and as if they'd missed the mark with their daughters. Many said they had been hesitant to talk about it with other mothers, that they felt disenfranchised rather than united. As they described their experiences, it seemed that each woman realized the complexity of the mother-daughter bond, but few felt advised or prepared to make any changes.

And so the ten most common scenarios for twenty-first-century mothers have been culled, and these troubling—sometimes haunting—scripts are each examined, chapter by chapter. What is valuable is that we understand what we do, why we do it, and how this affects the mother-daughter relationship, from childhood through adulthood. My intention is that once we are enlightened, our attitude and responses can change, and the situations be remedied.

I invite mothers of daughters of all ages everywhere to join me in advancing ourselves, asserting ourselves, investing in personal dominion and confidence, and establishing healthy parameters. In this fashion, the ongoing mother-daughter dance becomes a remarkably positive experience. It's never too late to confront the matter, adapt our behaviors, and embrace the solutions.

You're Grounded Forever . . .

But First
Let's Go Shopping

✳

Chapter 1

*

I'll Just Say You Aren't
Feeling Well

Making Excuses/Endless Explanations

- Do you always find a way to make things work for your daughter?
- Do you defend your daughter rather than address the problem?
- Do you avoid confrontations with her at any cost?
- Do you figure out a way to make your daughter look good?
- Are you rewriting her story so she seems in the right?

If so, you are absolving your daughter, regardless of circumstances.

THIS PAST WEEK was particularly taxing. Your fifteen-year-old daughter was caught cutting school and your nineteen-year-old daughter, a college student, e-mailed you her midterm warning from the dean that she is behind in her work. In the past, your ability to find your daughters faultless and to generate a universe where others are at fault has worked. This has made life smoother and allowed you to believe that you are doing what's best. After all, what mother doesn't want positive results for her daughters? Our ties are so strong with our girls, our hopes so profound, and our memories of our own conflicts so vivid, that any way to assuage pain seems appropriate.

So while you know deep in your heart that both daughters need to buckle down—and frankly, they can be so aggravating—you immediately take action. First you call the high school principal, promising it will never happen again and expressing concern about your daughter's group of friends. Next you call the dean to say that your older daughter is a perfectionist and simply couldn't deliver mediocre work. As usual, you push very hard and it seems to work. And so, another day, another crisis averted for both daughters.

Unconditional Love = Many Clever Excuses

As we can see from the above composite, making excuses for our daughters is often a coping mechanism for the mother. By going to great lengths to make the excuse, we don't have to face who our daughters are or who we are as mothers. Since much of what we do for our daughters, right or wrong, has evolved from the excuse mode we began when they were in nursery school, it sets the tone for how they are prepared for the world. The idea that we can mitigate circumstances, calm them down, and soften the blow if we whip up some creative truths compels us. Surely that's more tempting than confronting our daughters' issues, which from an early age include their social lives, academics, financial requirements, sibling relationships, and female friendships. The mother-daughter love fest, fraught with complications and best intentions, practically *demands* excuses, and our skills are impressive. We excuse our daughters so readily and seamlessly, these patterns may become lifelong behaviors.

Our daughters tug at our heartstrings it's the intensity of the connection that churns up excuses at every turn. When we consider the amount of baby lust in our culture and how strong the desire to have a child is (the American Society for Reproductive Medicine reports that fertility attempts in the United States increased by 68 percent from 1996 to 2005), it reminds us that once we have our children, we'll do just about anything to help them out. For mothers of daughters, it's riveting; one excuse leads to another, with our explanations more convincing than ever before. As a mother remarked, "Who knew that I'd be whitewashing my daughter's math grades to my husband, her father, but I had to do it." With the knowledge that our daughters' struggles exceed anything we ever encountered at their age, the stakes are raised on a daily basis. The axiom "Bigger daughters, bigger problems" holds true, but oddly enough, the *way* that we, as mothers, have been excusing our daughters is eerily the same whether they are five or twenty-five. Only the circumstances have changed.

Bad Habits = Top Five Excuses

The goal of ensuring that a daughter isn't uneasy, judged, or burdened is a worthy cause that clouds our vision. Frequently, mothers admit, it's simply better to give tacit consent to a bad habit rather than face it head-on. In this way, the mother and daughter are in two-step, a complicit dancing duo. This occurs in the following realms:

Mothers and Daughters in Cahoots: Substance Abuse and Smoking

In her book *Mother-Daughter Wisdom,* Christiane Northrup points out the dangers and negative effects of substance abuse for adolescent girls and also acknowledges that millions of teenagers use marijuana and alcohol. The majority of mothers are aware of what Dr. Northrup reports—the impairment of brain function from marijuana use and the increase in risk of breast cancer associated with alcohol consumption. Yet many mothers, even those informed of these dangers, are willing to look the other way when it comes to their daughters' choice to use drugs or to drink. This manifests in *not* confronting the daughters, despite the mothers' worry about their daughters' health and well-being. Katia, forty-five, a stay-at-home mother in Ohio, confesses that her daughter, now twenty, was "obsessed" with getting high with her friends throughout high school.

If this wasn't behind me, I couldn't talk about it. I have always found a way to not face the problem. I didn't want to have a daughter who wasn't right. I had this sneaking suspicion that she was high and she always smelled of cigarette smoke, too. My own mother accused me of not taking charge, but I couldn't handle it once I started, so I backed off. I see what these mothers do and I do it myself. I think it's part of being a mother who seems to be in charge but isn't. It was better to have a stoned daughter, deny it, and wait. I'm lucky it worked that way or I'd still be making something up when it comes to the pot. As for cigarettes, I still say to myself, "Oh, all young women today smoke, aren't they foolish," when I see her smoking.

Lazy Daughters

By the time that mother and daughter are in high-gear excuse form, the daughter is disdainful and acts too tired to care about what is expected of her. Mothers are at a loss with teenage daughters when they are unkind, uninspired, and acting against how they've been raised. This produces a daughter who rejects responsibilities around the house or who ignores her schoolwork or disrespects family life. For example, Audra, forty-four, who lives in Michigan and works as an office manager, has a sixteen-year-old daughter who has become a "nasty, perfect stranger."

I always knew this daughter was tough and had to have her way. When she was three years old, she could blow me over. I used to say to my friends that she was very headstrong and a show-off. Then when she hit fourteen, she'd call me on things and say, "Why don't you tell the neighbors the truth, that I won't go to their boring barbecue, instead of saying I have homework?" Or she'd say, "Why don't you tell Grandma I don't want to sleep there anymore, I'm too old, instead of saying I have a sleepover with a friend?"

These days she uses my laptop and can't bother to charge it. She leaves dishes in the sink, she erases my phone messages when she's searching for her own on our home line, she takes cash from my wallet rather than go to an ATM. But I've done it this way for so long that I just add ways to make her look better than she is.

Life Overload

Although it doesn't bode well for a daughter's performance at school or in her career (more on this in Chapter 9), there are mothers who allow and encourage their daughters to not live up to their potential or strive for success. The excuse here is that the requirements are too great and the rewards too few. This applies to school, where a mother wants her daughter to do well but also willingly forgives bad grades. If the mother has made excuses for her own abbreviated accomplishments, she may try to protect her daughter by cutting her some slack. Consider Nora, forty-five, who lives in Ohio and fills in at her husband's accounting firm when asked. She is concerned about her eighteen-year-old's preoccupation with getting into the right college.

My daughter had a terrible week when she failed a math test, and it had already been a month from hell. Her friends were torturing her and she was writing her essay for her college applications. I told her it's okay to get a bad grade, it's okay to not get into the first school on your list. And friends will make life miserable, no matter what. I said that we've all been through it and none of this is a reflection of her but just the way life goes.

Purchasing Power

In our capitalistic society, a constant bone of contention among mothers and daughters centers around shopping, lifestyle, and the right purchases. Although we'll delve into this in Chapter 3, what we buy for our daughters, despite our value system and budget, warrants mention at this juncture. More than 70 percent of mothers report that they will spend money on their daughters in ways they wouldn't spend for themselves, and that doing so actually straps them financially. There are all sorts of excuses surrounding what money can buy, but the truth is that few mothers feel strong enough to say no to their daughters.

These mothers lavish allowance money and subsidize their daughters' living expenses, explaining that until the economy grows strong again, they feel this is an act of necessity. The majority of mothers remarked they would go to great lengths not to disappoint their daughters. Consider Maggie, forty-seven, who works in the food industry and lives in Massachusetts. She has just overspent on her twenty-three-year-old daughter's wedding because she felt she had to.

I didn't want my daughter to think we were counting pennies. I tried to convince her to buy a used gown, but she wouldn't hear of it. Then I tried to get her to do an afternoon wedding, but she wanted a night wedding. My husband wasn't happy, but I made up all these reasons why we had to do it this way for her sake. If business was busier for both of us, we wouldn't have minded. But my daughter wasn't going to adjust— I could see that—so I worked hard to please her and it meant appeasing her father, saying all kinds of things. We had over a hundred guests because I kept saying that she should have all her friends there— it was her wedding. Now that I look back on it, we probably should have given them the money for a down payment on a house. But how could I do that to my daughter?

Social Status

Mothers suffer when a daughter ends up in uncomfortable social situations. In such cases, the mothers' excuses offer a soothing element and lessen the blow for the daughters. Mothers tell me they defend their daughters, even if the daughters are capable of churning up lies, leading peers astray, and bullying. If a mother is too lenient and pardons her daughter, she's not helping her in the least. Frequently, mothers excuse their daughters out of fear and desperation, unable to face these prospects. "I'm always saying my daughter, who is thirty, is a career woman rather than that she can't find the right guy or that she ruins every relationship she has," remarks an interviewee. Victoria, fifty-two, who lives in California, where she works in a lab, rationalizes why her youngest daughter is so agitated that she alienates people.

I'm just unable to deal directly with my daughter, who is nineteen, and who has been a huge headache for ages. I say to my friends that she's fine—just edgier than her older sisters. Every time she skips out or steals the car or screams obscenities at us, I say she's my "dicey one." She's so good at telling me she isn't "out there" and that everyone is like this, that I want to believe her. The weird thing is that being in this any deeper frightens her as much as it frightens me. So we both make excuses for her and I know it isn't working. I know in my heart she's a misfit and can't be a real friend or fit in anywhere.

The danger for a daughter is that her mother feels helpless and disrespected. She observes her mother use excuses as a tool to get through the morass of life and picks up on her mother's sense of helplessness. If mothers are able to gain authority in any predicament, the excuses will lessen.

The Blame Game

The majority of mothers with whom I spoke admitted that part of why they make excuses for daughters is that they dread being blamed and judged. In our culture, it feels satisfying to point a finger at someone after an incident, and mothers are acutely aware of this. In his book *Credit and Blame,* Charles Tilly notes that when something happens, finding blame satisfies people, and parent blame is a part of the equation. Mother blame is taken to another level, however, because motherhood is highly touted and scrutinized.

Because mother blame is rampant in our society, a mother is deeply indoctrinated into the system and blames herself for things that go wrong in her daughter's life. This can chip away at a woman's self-esteem, and the mother becomes a poor model for her daughter. Daughters are then led to believe that when mothers fall short, it is because the mothers themselves are deficient. "What kind of mother is she?" people whisper. The mothers are unnerved and the daughters are influenced by this. Under such conditions, why would a mother admit if her daughter has poor grades, struggles at college, feels unpopular, has no boyfriend, no job, or a drinking problem, an eating disorder, a troubled love relationship, or anxiety issues? After all, she'll be the one blamed, judged, and whispered about as a result. As evidenced in Cindy's narrative below, the situation can become overwhelming. Cindy, forty-three, manages a restaurant in New Jersey and lives with her pregnant nineteen-year-old daughter.

My daughter got a scholarship to college and I was so proud of her I told everyone in our neighborhood. She was there for a year and one day she came home and told me she was pregnant. I decided to wait until she was showing before I told friends and family. I asked her if the father of her child would marry her and said that it's what I want. I never got a straight answer, but I tell people it's the plan because it sounds better. Who knows . . . I keep thinking of how hard it will be on all of us financially to have this baby and how it will affect the family. I smile and act

pleased and as if it's just what I wanted for my daughter. What
else is there to say? Should I wear my heart on my sleeve? Should
I betray my daughter by saying how upset this makes me? And
the truth is, it all comes back to the mother. When people whisper,
they're basically calling me a bad mother and figuring that this
somehow happened because of me.

In September 2008, the Republican vice presidential candidate, Sarah Palin, announced that her seventeen-year-old daughter, Bristol, was five months pregnant. According to People .com, Palin announced to the press, "Bristol and the young man she will marry are going to realize very quickly the difficulties of raising a child, which is why they will have the love and support of our entire family." According to *OK! Magazine,* when actress Jamie Lynn Spears announced that she was pregnant, her mother expressed surprise. "I didn't believe it because Jamie Lynn's always been so conscientious," Lynne Spears said. "She's never late for her curfew. I was in shock. I mean, this is my sixteen-year-old baby."

Everyday women can surely relate to both Governor Palin and Lynn Spears because for mothers everywhere, a teenage pregnancy poses tremendous obstacles. And while the world read the Web sites and newspapers that reported these events with a perverse fascination, there was the nagging question: *Where was the mother in all of this?* As Paula J. Caplan reminds us in her book *The New Don't Blame Mother,* "The most poignant instances of mother-blaming within the family are those in which the mother blames herself for whatever goes wrong."

The common scenarios are the following:

The Shame Factor

If being blamed for what goes on with our daughters isn't dis-
comfiting enough, another component of why we make excuses
has to do with shame. For mothers who find a way to support
their daughters' conduct, there is, on enough occasions, a component of shame and blame threaded into the excuse. Shame,
as defined by *Merriam-Webster's Collegiate Dictionary*, is "a
painful emotion caused by consciousness of guilt, shortcom-
ing, or impropriety." Although mothers find ways to absolve
their daughters, they can't always escape a sense of shame.
An unfortunate side effect of this is how it filters into the
daughter's life. If a mother shows her daughter she is ashamed
of herself or her daughter, she copes by making excuses to her
circle of friends and to family. This has a direct effect upon
her daughter.

- My daughter is this way because I'm a single mother in a
  community where everyone is married.
- My daughter didn't have my attention when she was small
  because I had to work a night shift.
- My daughter compares our lifestyle to her friends and feels
  denied.
- My daughter feels that my job loss has ruined her social
  life and mine. We can't afford as much now.

Mothers who describe themselves as feeling constantly judged
churn up whatever relief is on hand. Sara, forty-three, who lives
in Oregon, has been concerned about her fifteen-year-old daughter since her divorce last year.

I don't believe I've done the right thing for my daughter, but I'm not sure I know what the right thing is. I know my divorce has upset her so much and it bothers me that I can't do anything about it. On top of the divorce, she's started tenth grade at a new school and it's bringing out the worst in her. I get to meet with the administrators to tell them repeatedly that she's always been a good student with lots of interests and this is just a hard time for her.

I know they think I'm an awful mother, but I'm more worried about what will work best for my daughter than about what they say about me. I'm just at my wits' end. I go to these special meetings where they tell me what's wrong with her, describing all these days that she did something she shouldn't have done. So I just forgive her and hate them—at every stupid meeting. My daughter knows this, too, that I don't respect the school or the principal, and that can't really be helping her.

Since mothers believe that everyone is watching them, it requires courage to stop taking their own actions and their daughters' actions so personally. Those mothers who face problems head-on are able to discard blame and shame and stop hiding behind excuses.

Seeking Perfection

A mother who has narcissistic tendencies, meaning she is egotistical, self-important, and grandiose, causes her daughter to suffer the consequences. The problem is complicated for a daughter of any age because it is so difficult to please a mother who operates this way. This type of mother can be angered by reality, including an inevitably flawed daughter whom she views as a reflection of herself and for whom she has to make excuses. If the daughter pulls away from her mother in adolescence, which is developmentally appropriate, the mother's excuses are ratcheted up. How else can she explain what is happening?

Consider Pamela, forty-eight, who lives in Southern Florida and has two daughters, twenty-five and eighteen, and twin twenty-three-year-old sons. Pamela laments her younger daughter's lack of accomplishments to date.

My younger daughter is going to college in the fall and she won't get a scholarship like her brothers and sister did. She isn't that kind of student and she wasn't advised to apply. She'll end up at the local junior college and it's more about having been sidetracked and not working on college applications than anything else.

If this hadn't happened, she could have aced something. . . . I feel like everyone is wondering how I ended up in this mess with her, as if I have a less smart child somehow, especially after the older three are known around town for being so smart. And what's worse is that she doesn't seem to care, she really wants to have fun in her senior year and she hardly listens to me anymore. While I'm worried and telling anyone who will listen what went wrong, she's off partying, probably drinking too much. We come from the middle of nowhere and I have better ideas at the town meetings than anyone else. We're known as a smart family. It feels like I'm always telling someone how messed up this got and how surprised I am. Meanwhile, I'm annoyed by the whole thing.

If a mother has an inflated ego or is too caught up in how she is perceived as a mother or pushes her daughter to be more than she ever was, it can harm her daughter and cause tension between mother and daughter. A mother who has been an acrobat for her daughter, saying whatever it takes for the daughter's benefit or closely running her life, is hurt if the daughter pulls away. So while Pamela takes pride in being the mother of intelligent children, her younger daughter's status isn't all about her as the mother. Her daughter seems happy enough, despite Pamela's fantasy of how it should be and her desire to explain what happened. Not that some of us haven't felt this way when it comes to our daughters, but there is no need to prove our excellence in mothering. Handling our daughters in a way that sustains them rather than confuses them should be the goal.

Part of the issue today is how driven mothers are to fix what went on in their own childhood by getting it right with their daughters, according to Jeanette Friedman, a psychologist who treats young women. "What happens is that the mother has difficulty with the notion of facilitating her daughter's growth," she remarks. "If the mother can stop making excuses that sanction her daughter, the daughter will flourish and the mother's sense of self will improve."

Stress and Excuses

Few of us would question that the high stress levels in our lives these days contribute to easy explanations. For a family that has "issues," this route is all too familiar. It certainly is the case in the 2007 film *Georgia Rule,* starring Jane Fonda as Georgia, the mother of Lilly, played by Felicity Huffman, and the grandmother of Rachel, played by Lindsay Lohan. In this multigenerational tale, the three women converge when Lilly, at her wits' end, takes Rachel to stay with her tough-minded grandmother for the summer. By the time they arrive at Georgia's, Lilly is so worn-out by Rachel's attitude that the viewer can only imagine what's in store. We get the impression right off the bat that Lilly has been making excuses for her daughter for years. In fact, as the story progresses, Rachel announces that she's slept with her stepfather and Lilly has to acknowledge that this might be the case. But in the initial scones, it's enough to observe Rachel's belligerent behavior and assume that she's had to cook up a few excuses herself. The genesis of all this rationalizing comes from Georgia, who, while in command, appears to have gotten through life with an improvisation or two.

As pathological as the film ends up being, the part that is identifiable is how excuses ease the pain while glibly rolling off one's tongue. It isn't that those mothers misread the culpability factor, but that *they actually excuse themselves for making excuses.* By pardoning ourselves and our daughters, we have less guilt about what we might not have done or about our own inadequacy.

There are also those mothers who dispute that their excuses come from any weakness. Rather, they feel vindicated in the steps they've taken and the choices they've made as a method to avoid anxiety. Consider June, sixty, a telemarketer who lives in Virginia. She has two married daughters and two unmarried sons.

I've always been a crowd-pleaser and my daughters get it, although they deal with it differently. The older one is in the moment, and she's carved an amazing life for herself. The younger daughter is more ambitious and in both cases, when they were in high school, I defended them. Mostly I defended the younger one for her eating disorder and the older one for her academic shortcomings. This had to do with showing the crowd how fine it really was, which made me feel slightly crazed.

I look at it as if I had to work around what was really going on, and I did. It was never their problem, never my problem when things weren't going well. I couldn't have it that way. So I rationalized everything and they learned to do the same, and now that I look back on it, I think it worked. I would say to my closest friends that my older daughter had a slight learning disability and a flare for the arts, when it came to math, but she was actually flunking high school. I'd say that my younger daughter, who has weight issues, was the beauty and it was never something that was a problem—it was all good.

A mother who reserves the right to vindicate her daughter as circumstances dictate also encourages her daughter to deal with life in this manner, and is comfortable with her system. In these instances, the mother feels successful, empowered by excuses. However, according to Dr. Ronnie Burak, a clinical psychologist with a primarily female practice, "Mothers are just too overwhelmed without having some sort of story to back them up." The danger here is that an adult daughter will feel she has little choice but to make excuses herself when the going gets tough.

A Disservice to Our Daughters

Ultimately, we, as mothers, should understand why we make all these excuses. Benedict Carey, in his *New York Times* article "Some Protect the Ego by Working on Their Excuses Early," writes that those who make excuses do it before "pursuing a goal or delivering a performance." This disclaimer comes in handy for a mother who has low expectations or who needs to find a way to justify the results when it comes to her daughter. This knee-jerk reaction to our daughters gives them tacit approval to clarify all sorts of occurrences, taking their cues from their mothers, as witnessed in the above interviews. There are also mothers who realize the inherent danger in a nimble defense of a daughter's life and are attempting to avoid the pattern. Consider Reneé, thirty-seven, a stay-at-home mother who lives in Maryland and has begun to notice her eight-year-old daughter's "teenage" attitude. Renée has made the conscious decision to face it head-on.

I already see my daughter is trying to be independent, and she now pretends to be shy or she pretends to not hear me. I see her watching her older cousins and it worries me. I don't want this for my daughter and I don't want her to play games with people. My first message is that she can't do it with me, that I'm not fooled by some story about a stomachache or being too tired to go to church. I've decided to stop [it] immediately. She watches her friend throw a tantrum and she thinks why not, especially since her friend's mother is giving in, making excuses for her daughter. My hope is to give her the tools that will guide her and to let her know that there is a cause and effect for her actions.

I'm aware that peer pressure leads girls astray and maybe that's why I'm such a strict mother. And I have two other small daughters and they are watching their older sister closely. If she gets away with something, they'll believe that they can, too. So I'm really getting set for all three of my girls and they'll know that the right thing is what matters, not excuses which only get them into trouble in the long run, as easy as it would be to do.

Although her daughters are young, Renée's determination represents the possibility that if a mother doesn't cave in, both mother and daughter can benefit. "Daughters become strong by example," Dr. Claire Owen, a psychologist specializing in women and their relationships, tells us. "And part of that means not bending every which way to please them."

Working Through Excuses

Do not enable your daughter to cope through the excuse. Understand what your own motivation is, since a mother who constantly cooks up a rationale for her daughter gives the wrong message.

Address what it is in your life that incites excuses. It is best to try to eliminate the situations and lessen your excuse patterns first; then you can honestly suggest the same to your daughter about her own life.

Be aware of what you are teaching your daughter. If you expect her to be reliable and there for others, set the right example. It isn't good for you or your daughter to be known for breaking plans or for disappointing friends.

Warn your daughter of social excuses. Although these appear reasonable, making excuses keeps your daughter from learning how to fend for herself honestly and can hurt people's feelings.

Encourage your daughter to be independent and to solve her own problems. If she faces complications head-on rather than avoiding them, she'll have the right skills to sort out an issue.

Steer clear of ongoing excuses. Beware that excuses can be insidious; the risk is that your daughter will not become a responsible person in school, in the workforce, or in interpersonal relationships.

Chapter 2

❊

Of Course You Can Drink When You're Home with Me

Lacking Boundaries and Rules

- Do you feel that you have no limits with your daughter?
- Are you engulfed by your responsibilities as a mother?
- Is your daughter aware of the demands placed upon you financially, emotionally, physically, and timewise?
- Does your daughter defy you—at times gleefully?
- Have you become the family punching bag, and do you feel despair?

If the above questions apply to you, there is confusion over who is in charge—mother or daughter.

ALTHOUGH IT'S NOT EASY to admit, you've felt that your three daughters have been taking advantage of you since they were quite small. It haunts you that you've been so permissive. You even allowed your youngest, who is now seventeen, to have her ears pierced at a jewelry store when she was seven against your better judgment because she was screaming at you on the main street of your hometown. Your older daughters, twenty-one and twenty-three, were outrageous as teenagers, using your credit cards, drinking together in high school, and blatantly lying to you when they were caught. At the time, you were overworked at the office and outnumbered at home. Secretly you felt beleaguered and powerless. The worst part about it is that whenever you have confronted them, all three girls, with the eldest coaching the younger two, always say what you like to hear.

Not only that, but all three girls have accused you of being overbearing, while you feel they've walked all over you for years. Recently your youngest daughter has declared that she wants to travel to India with her boyfriend, which worries you. When you say you are against the trip—it's too far away, too expensive, she's too young—she carries on until you doubt yourself. It's that same sick feeling in the pit of your stomach: Will this business of having rules that no one respects ever end?

Losing Ourselves to Our Daughters' Wishes

The delicate balance of giving in to our daughters rather than being in command plagues modern-day mothers. Although it's rarely a mother's plan to infuse her daughter with too much power, this invariably becomes the downside of not having rules. By junior high, it's apparent which daughters are difficult to manage, but most of the mothers in my study confess that there were red flags as early on as third or fourth grade. There are mothers who describe themselves as lightweights—exhausted, depleted, and concerned for their daughters even as they succumb to their demands. These situations run the gamut from serious matters to the daily minutiae of life. One mother describes her sixteen-year-old daughter as skipping school daily. Another confesses that her daughter, at fourteen, is already lying about her sleepovers on weekends in order to be with a boy. Another mother believes that her thirty-year-old daughter has a drug problem. What about a daughter in graduate school who has an abusive boyfriend despite her mother's protestations, or the daughter who is married and depends upon her mother emotionally and financially? In each of these cases, the mothers are troubled because they feel they somehow missed the mark; they didn't instill parameters, and their daughters suffer for it.

As conscious as mothers are of the inherent dangers lurking for young women today, a dearth of rules is pervasive. "My thirteen-year-old daughter is impossible to reason with," one mother states, while another reports that her sixteen-year-old thinks she "knows it all." A third mother says, "My instincts tell me to say no to my daughter, but she just begs and begs to be out past curfew every weekend." Mothers who are reluctant to say no end up weak, and problems with their daughters mushroom. The daughters may later resist rules beyond their home and may not be able to decipher healthy choices for themselves.

Sissy, fifty-six, who lives in Atlanta, regrets how ineffectual she was with her twenty-seven-year-old daughter when she was in high school and college.

I always knew my daughter was spoiled, but I also thought I had given her some limits. She had to follow my decisions in our household and she would lie about things to get around them. My daughter started telling me what she thought I wanted to hear when she was about fifteen. But it took me years to figure this out—I wasn't smart enough to realize it then. And her father saw her as a child who could do no wrong. So by the time she got to college, she was making me look like the bad guy, and she was coming up smelling like roses. I never knew what to do and all these years later, we're at an impasse. I never knew how to discipline her and she knew how to play me and how to play me against her father to get what she wanted. My idea of how my daughter should be raised and what is and isn't allowed has not worked—it wasn't even on the table.

Similar to Sissy's experience is Lisa's ongoing concern about her twenty-one-year-old daughter. While Sissy describes being undermined by her husband and her sense of helplessness, Lisa believes that her divorce—and the divisiveness that followed—only accentuated her lack of influence. The plight of a mother who feels she isn't heard or recognized can transpire with or without a father in the mix. These mothers are acutely aware of the importance of rules, but they are unable to execute them.

Lisa, forty-nine, lives in Philadelphia, where she works as a freelance designer.

There is such tension in my relationship with my daughter because I can't make her be who I want her to be. I think that my divorce has affected her and her younger sister. But this is the daughter who suffers. There were rules that didn't work, not for a minute, and I kept trying to fit the square peg into the round hole. My daughter rebelled against what I expected and what I told her to do, and she became a very out-there kid—it was scary to me. I couldn't make her do things, but I kept trying.

And now I'm pushing her to find a career, to figure out how to get on with her life. But it's all blurred. I don't think we've established enough good for me to have any real say in her future.

Maybe she thinks I'm overbearing, but it feels to me that I never made anything clear and she sort of walked all over me in some ways, especially when she was in high school and I was holding down two jobs and not around. Then she could do anything she wanted in our house and she did. In a strange way, I can't let go. I doubt she respects how I mothered her and I doubt I made her feel safe.

It is obvious that a mother who skips regulations chooses to avoid conflict, but in the end, she's causing her daughter to feel unprotected. "Instead of implementing rules early on, when her daughter is a baby, a mother will try out the rules with a twelve-year-old. This won't work, and the mother gives in quickly. But the daughters actually want rules," remarks Brenda Szulman, a therapist who treats women of all ages.

Withering Control

The late Betty Friedan, author of *The Feminine Mystique,* certainly had it right when she pegged motherhood as both revered and reviled. Mothers today know that the reviled part is a kind of secret, not something they can be open about. They are judged according to the end result, and producing successful, stable, attractive, high-functioning daughters is what counts. With this mind-set directed at mothers everywhere, it's little wonder that such attention has been paid to actress Lindsay Lohan's escapades and to her mother, Dina Lohan. The amount of speculation as to how Dina's mothering has affected the actress's hard times (including substance abuse, an arrest for drunken driving, and walking off the set) is explored in Stephen M. Silverman's 2007 article "Dina Lohan: 'I'm Not a Party Mom'" on People.com. Silverman reports that although Dina Lohan has been clubbing with Lindsay in New York City, and "sips Montrachet in front of her daughter," she seems cognizant of what rules could do for her daughter. For example, Dina Lohan has "led a couple of interventions for Lindsay in the past."

Enough everyday women who begin on a high note (approximately half of my interviewees believed they were emphatic with their daughters until their daughters were ten years old and then things began to disintegrate) report their diminished command as discouraging. The types of mothers who feel at a loss fall into several categories:

The Pushover. To sustain a daughter's affection, this mother dreads any rift and prefers not to discipline. To this end, she hasn't much say and fancies herself in her daughter's good graces. An example of this is shown to us in the film *Mean Girls,* in which Amy Poehler plays the mother of Rachel McAdams (meanest of the mean girls). Not only has she no rules, but she's clueless as to what her daughter is up to or even that her daughter is in charge. For instance, Julia, forty-seven, who lives in Maine and works as a nurse, is concerned about her sixteen-year-old daughter.

My daughter and her friends get high in my garage while I'm on my shift at the hospital. What can I do about it? I've asked her, but I won't accuse her. And she just denies it and I don't say, "This isn't okay, I won't put up with this." Instead, I tell her I believe her, and that way we're okay, the two of us.

The Revisionist. These mothers want to do it better than their own mothers, who were too strict. The result is that the daughters have no rules because the mothers felt they were immobilized by their own mothers' stipulations. Bonnie, fifty-eight, who lives in Vermont and is a social worker, is mother to a thirty-three-year-old daughter.

I never pressured my daughter like my passive-aggressive mother did me. She always told me how things had to be done, and I decided to do the opposite with my daughter. The only reason that I lucked out is because my daughter is smart and she wanted to have her homework finished and not go to parties late on weekends. I probably would have allowed anything just to prove I wasn't like my mother.

The Single Mother. Frequently these mothers say they are beyond cautious when it comes to instructing their daughters. They worry about alienating them in any way and losing ground in terms of time and trust. The shadow of the divorce, the absent father, or widowhood hovers over single mothers and informs their decisions. As this applies to divorce, the mother's perception is that if she allows her daughters more leeway, it will ease the tensions of going between two families and curry favor for the mother. Elle, forty, who lives in the Northeast and is a stay-at-home mother, has two daughters, ages fourteen and eleven.

I was never big on tough love, and once I was divorced, there wasn't much I could do right anyway. So why would I make life harder for my daughters by insisting on things? I once came home with my boyfriend and both girls had come back to be with me on their father's night. I told the boyfriend to go when I probably should have just taken them the three miles to their father's and let them know that on his night the girls can't show up on my doorstep.

The Strung-out Mother. This is the working mother who finds herself immersed in the "second shift" and who admits to cutting corners. It also applies to the stay-at-home mother who has several children and is absorbed with community service. Both types of mothers find themselves very busy and opt for a lack of discipline. Many times it's the second or third daughter who experiences this kind of upbringing, since the mother becomes more worn-out as the years go by. Consider Jacqueline, forty-nine, who lives in Georgia and works in real estate and is the mother of twin fifteen-year-old daughters and an eighteen-year-old son.

I can't do it all, so I do the best I can. I will carry on about bedtime and schoolwork and weekend curfews, and it doesn't matter a bit to the girls. I ask questions but I don't push. If they say their work is finished, I say good. That's it, and I can't take it any further than that. I tell myself this is how it's going to be, and everyone will get through.

A dearth of rules is often accompanied by a mother's ability to excuse herself (as explored in Chapter 1) and to excuse her daughters. If a mother concedes that she is deficient when it comes to providing rules for her daughter, it's half the battle. The next step is to insist upon control and stop worrying that this will offend her daughter.

The Fear Factor

Anthropologist Sarah Blaffer Hrdy notes in her book *Mother Nature: Maternal Instincts and How They Shape the Human*

Species that there are "conflicting self-interests between parents and offspring, between mothers and fathers, within families, between families." The threat of a daughter becoming remote, cooling off toward her mother with whom she was once close, or accusing her mother of being hypercritical can be very threatening. The recurring theme here centers on the mother's purpose. The answer, according to the mothers interviewed, is to raise confident, independent, high-functioning daughters. How is it that what a mother does and says can be counterproductive to this end result?

Consider Louisa, fifty-two, who lives in North Dakota, where she practices medicine and has a daughter, twenty-six, who works in finance.

From the beginning I was under the spell that there should be no rules. There was this prevailing sense that my child would speak up and that she'd also listen. I had grown up in the sixties and seventies and there were no rules with my own mother, so I thought this would be okay. She was self-motivated and once I had this wonderful child, I let it influence me in terms of who was in charge. I gave my daughter credit for being able to make decisions she wasn't able to make. I let a first-grader decide when to go to bed because she wanted to.

I realize now that I was so absorbed with my daughter that I was afraid to tell her what to do. When she was twelve, she turned into a beast and told me that everything I did was wrong. I'd started it by allowing her to run her life and the truth is, when this was intensifying, and she'd become so critical, my medical practice was very busy. So she had unlimited freedom while I was at work. There was so much tension. Then when I was home, to make it all okay, I had no rules.

As we can see from Louisa's experience, a mother's stance is usually gauged by her daughter's point of view and how serious the matter is at hand. For Gillian, forty-seven, a nurse practitioner living in the South with two daughters, twenty and twenty-five, the idea that her older daughter has settled down has mitigated circumstances and alleviated some of her fear.

There were some tough times—boyfriends, running away, drugs and alcohol, skipping school, lying about school—you name it and my daughter did it. That's when my heart was always sinking, when I couldn't stop the anxiety and basically, if she came to the dinner table, I was happy. Then she sort of got her act together and I stopped being such a desperate mother. For years I'd done whatever I needed to please her. It was the opposite of rules, it was my girls trampling on me and my hoping to come up for air. I got sick of it and that's about the same time that my older daughter quieted down. It's odd, now that I think about it, but we all stopped pulling these stunts at the same time. I think that both daughters were dumbfounded when I was finally too tired to say okay again, whatever you want. I started to say no because yes was a such a weight for me all the time, every day. It was too much, and that's how I started to make rules, about everything.

While Louisa compromised her position because she operated out of fear and guilt, and Gillian became too tired to put up with her troublesome daughter, Judith Anne, forty-six, who works as a chef in a restaurant and lives in New Jersey, has deliberately *not* been intimidated by her two daughters, ages twenty and seventeen.

My seventeen-year-old fights with me about everything, and keeps thinking, Mom will change her mind, but I won't. Then we'll have

*a battle, and I won't be worried that she'll pull away. Or that
she'll be angry with me because I've always made it known that
I have strong opinions. I know I'm very strict—people always
say so, and I know it's true compared to other mothers. At least
I don't worry that the girls won't be close with me or that somehow I'm putting our relationship at risk if I don't please them.
This is who I am and if they want a relationship with me, then
they have to respect how I want things, as their mother. The
problem is with my younger daughter, over and over again, because my older daughter gets it, and thinks, Why bother with
Mom when she won't say yes no matter what and it won't get you
anywhere, and that's more like it. My younger daughter is fighting the fight, thinking she can outsmart me. Whatever the question, about a boy, about school or work, I keep things under
control.*

Ultimately for those mothers who have operated from fear, a
newfound ability to discipline a daughter is an enormous relief.
This alteration in the relationship proves not only how fluid it
actually is but also the importance of getting it right. Nonetheless, more than 70 percent of the mothers in my study admitted
to being fearful on some level during their daughters' adolescent
years. As time marches on, mothers become less intimidated,
although they're still very conscious of not wanting to be fault
finding or insistent upon a rule or stipulation. According to Susan Campbell's *Psychology Today* article "The Mother-Daughter
Bond," those daughters who "winced at a mother's criticism . . .
still seek" their mother's approval in the later years, and 88
percent of women say their mother had a positive influence on
them.

As loaded and complicated as it can be, especially with a
daughter between the ages of ten and thirty, the bottom line is

promising: For mothers who are willing to speak their minds and to assert themselves, the tyranny of fear and hesitation is lifted—and the mothers gain respect.

Rules and Regulations

The rules that mothers frequently lament not establishing concern curfew, money, schoolwork, dating, drinking and drugs, and shopping. Since these do not always fall into place as the mothers imagine they will (this applies to mothers of adolescent daughters and young adult daughters alike), a mother begins to feel beaten down, as if she isn't heard and isn't respected Meanwhile, setting rules is intimidating, which can pose more unease for both parties. In theory the rules make sense, but in reality, a majority of mothers complain that they worry that their daughters will move away if they say no, not yes, to specific requests.

As Deborah Tannen explains it in her book *You're Wearing That?*, "Mothers and daughters continually integrate the desire to feel connected with the simultaneous desire to feel unencumbered and in control of their lives." When we consider this precept, the idea of setting guidelines is not only appealing to a mother but also sounds simple and solution-oriented. The truth is, for plenty of mothers, it's difficult to attain and sustain. The complexity of the mother-daughter rapport, the depth of emotions involved and the underlying tension, keeps a mother from saying "My way or the highway." A mother is not only concerned about what she communicates to her daughter but also interested in how her daughter responds to her. To complicate matters further, the mother might be filled with doubt about how she is viewed by others. For instance, Penny, forty-five, who lives in Texas and works full-time for a corporation, is the mother of two daughters, eleven and thirteen, and wishes she could be more of an "enforcer."

How great it would be to be one of those übermoms who just blows a whistle and her perfect daughters come running. But I'm not like that at home, and it's partly because I've been working so hard to be where I am at the same time that I've been raising my girls. Lately I've wondered if all this sacrificing is worth it, since people are losing jobs left and right—but I'm hanging in. It isn't as if I'm going to change and the stay-at-home mothers aren't going to change, either. I'll go to a PTA meeting where the stay-at-home moms are basically sniffing at my efforts. I once brought bakery cookies and they whispered about it. Meanwhile, at home with my daughters I can't get them to do a thing, from dishes in the sink to homework.

I feel like I'm in two communities, one at work, where my word counts and coworkers report to me, and the mothering, where I'm lucky that my girls are good students and mild mannered. But who knows what will happen when they get to high school and I'll be sorry I'm not a better enforcer.

In contrast to Penny's situation is that of Alice, fifty, a stay-at-home mother living in Maryland who has wrestled with guidelines for her daughter, twenty-four, for many years.

I thought that since I was at home, I would be better at getting my daughter to do things, things she should have done, things she knew to do. If she wasn't home by one A.M. and she didn't call, I worried. I begged her to call, just like I begged her to do her schoolwork. She never wanted to live by the rules, and I worried myself sick, but I couldn't get anywhere. I always said it was her immaturity that made her someone who wouldn't do what she was supposed to do, but I don't know . . . maybe it was me. . . . The other mothers in town, they had daughters who were better off and it was torture. . . . I found myself always begging my daughter instead of being the boss. . . . There was no punishment that worked, nothing I might take away or, if I grounded her, nothing that mattered. That was part of it, I had nothing over her, nothing. It's still like that.

Summoning up the courage to insist upon rules and guidelines has worked for some mothers. Consider Tammy, forty-four, who lives in New Jersey, where she is a stay-at-home mother to a twelve-year-old daughter and two younger sons.

My mother was a single mom who didn't have the luxury of spoiling us, and that impressed me. We all had to pull our own weight because she had two jobs and worked long hours. When I married my husband, we talked about how to raise our children and we agreed that it would be a strict home and that we wouldn't spoil these kids in any way. With my daughter it's harder than with my sons because I've been tempted to say yes to her, to give in, and I do. I remember how it was growing up and how other girls treat you, and I want it to be easy for her. So lately, I've been sympathetic to her and I've cut her some slack. Then, recently I realized I wasn't doing her a favor and if I want my daughter to be independent and capable, that means that she has to respect what I ask of her. She has chores and homework, so I decided to flat-out refuse a social life during the week. That's the way it is.

So when the other girls get together after school, she isn't allowed to see any girlfriends after school on weekdays. On weekends, she's not allowed a sleepover at someone's house unless I know the mother and the mother is at home that night. This all works fine except on those days when I want to just say, "Sure, of course you can do this or that." Then I remind myself that I want to raise my daughter to understand responsibility. I know the other girls have it easier, but my daughter is a solid citizen, already at twelve.

For those mothers who have resisted implementing rules, the backlash becomes apparent with the years. So while it's enticing to say yes (the strictest mothers are tempted, too), it isn't productive. Dr. Ronnie Burak notes, "If the mother is constantly giving in and unable to stand by her rules (or hasn't any), the daughter will not adjust well to restrictions in life. It all begins with what her relationship is with her mother."

Boundaries Versus Rules

Although boundaries and rules go hand in hand, the concept of establishing boundaries with our daughters exists on two levels: the daughter's knowledge of the mother's rules and values and how the daughter responds (is she okay with this, or is she a rebel) and the daughter's attitude toward her mother's rank (as an adult, as a parental guide). In the best situations, a mother has supremacy and the daughter honors this, but frequently the rules don't exist because the mother hasn't put them into play. The outcome is that the mother becomes uncertain about her role as a disciplinarian and then loses her own sense of self once this happens. As one mother remarked about her twenty-seven-year-old daughter, "I feel like I haven't been able to advise my daughter in twenty years and that I have always said yes, no matter what she wanted. I feel useless when I know so much. There wasn't any way to keep me the mother and her the child."

Porous Boundaries

What takes many mothers by surprise is our daughters' desire and need to become their own people with their own personality, style, and dreams. When asked, the majority of mothers will declare their daughters' independence to be a good thing, yet mothers are also frustrated and ill-prepared in enough instances, when the daughter stakes out her own identity. Waking up and realizing that boundaries are essential in spite of how fluid the relationship has been in the past is a solid start. This has been important to Marilyn, forty-six, who lives in Arizona and is a single mother with two daughters, nineteen and seventeen.

I grew up in a highly dysfunctional family and I won't let that happen to my daughters. I think I'm a pretty hip mother and I've had lots of different boyfriends since my divorce and I've been very open with it. But I'm also watching them as teenage girls and know they need guidance. So I won't do that "jean shopping together with the girls," where we're all sort of the same, and we don't compare notes after a weekend. That doesn't mean I don't dress as if I'm young or that I look like a fifties mother, but it means I resist making it that we're alike.

I can be strict, and on occasion I've surprised them with this. My older daughter had a party while I was away and I found out about it. I grounded her and I told her she couldn't borrow my car for two months. I think she was astonished, since I've always been someone who wanted to make her happy.

The three types of mothers who frequently attempt to strike an appropriate balance with their daughters are the following:

Merging Mothers. It's important for a mother to establish an appropriate distance with her daughter and to allow the daughter to have her individuality. Merging mothers encourage their daughters to be just like them, which affirms the mother's worth but is not healthy for either party.

Last-ditch Mothers. A last-ditch mother yearns for a second chance at her youth or is reluctant to age gracefully. She prefers a friendship with her daughter rather than a traditional hierarchy or being in the shoes of a regulator. Watching the daughter's life is both a vicarious thrill and a reminder of lost opportunity.

Competitive Mothers. The Merging Mother + The Last-ditch Mother = The Competitive Mother. These mothers will compete with their daughters rather than define the differences that come with age and experience. Not only does the daughter *not* have a mentor if her mother is competing with her, but also she can't trust her mother to be there for her. Her life is then complicated by her mother as a rival when her female peers already are filling that role.

If the mother hasn't sorted out her own feelings about her life, this can affect the daughter in terms of boundaries. So while the assumption is that the daughters don't honor boundaries, it can also be that the mother isn't insisting upon them at her end. Psychologist Claire Owen remarks that "most daughters crave boundaries, although some mothers aren't up to the task. This becomes taxing on both mother and daughter."

Separating from Our Daughters

For the past few decades our awareness has been raised regarding the concept of individuation for parents and children. Individuation is described by psychologists as the ability for a child to express her own needs. When my older daughter was a toddler she would hold her breath in her stroller when she had to leave a store or was told that she couldn't have another cookie. While an expert might say this was a healthy way for a two-year-old to express her own desires that didn't mesh with mine, I found it much easier when she was six or seven, and I could reason with her if our agendas were at odds. Yet for most of us, reasoning with our daughters exists for a brief period of time before the open communication shuts down during adolescence. Once this happens, daughters straddle the thorny issues of their own belief system versus the rules imposed upon them by their mothers.

A daughter's sense of the world and of herself may be contradictory to what her mother represents, despite her mother being the person with whom she has been most connected. A rite of passage for many a teenage daughter in order to separate from her mother includes rejecting her ideas and returning to them later when she has a more defined self-image. What is disturbing about both Sissy's and Lisa's situations, cited earlier in this chapter, is that both women feel stuck, as if they can't get to the good part. The good part is when daughters reach their early to mid-twenties and rediscover their mothers, remembering their role in the early years as wise, caring, and maternal.

Why It's So Cagey for the Mother

Occasionally a mother who is divorced or widowed will lean on her daughter in inappropriate ways, asking too much in terms of time and energy. This also keeps the daughter from her own agenda, which is so critical during this period. Consider Joanie, forty-seven, who lives in North Carolina, where she works in sales. Her husband's abrupt exit four years ago set her reeling. Although this didn't change her relationship with her college-age sons, it altered her rapport with her daughter, who was thirteen at the time.

I suddenly had these Saturday nights free and so did my daughter. She might have gone to a movie with a girlfriend or had a sleepover, but instead she stayed home with me. I also made her into my confidante and I know that wasn't fair. I was angry that my ex had gone back with his college girlfriend, and I let my children know. The boys didn't say much and managed to befriend the girlfriend, but my daughter was very upset. I told her too much about the marriage, my sadness, and how worried I was about the future. I don't think it was the right thing to do and she began to worry about me. She felt guilty if someone invited her somewhere on a weekend, and on her visits to her father's house, she'd call me every few hours to see how I was doing. I'm not proud of what I did, and I see now that she's a senior in high school, she wants to go away to college and I don't blame her. Why not escape the suffocating train wreck that I was?

As reported by the U.S. Census Bureau, approximately 13.6 million single parents in America are raising 21.2 million children in our country. Of this population, 84 percent of custodial parents are mothers. Thus Joanie is not alone in her plight, and the demands of being a single mother to adolescent daughters are very real. The boundaries in these circumstances can blur, as we're shown in the novel *Anywhere But Here* by Mona Simpson. Adele, the mother of Ann, is a single mother who is not only overbearing but also believes that her daughter will be a famous actress and that this will benefit both mother and daughter. The question here is never about how much the mother loves her daughter, but how she conducts herself with her daughter and how entwined they are.

The Danger in Unhealthy Connections

As we discussed in Chapter 1, the mother who exhibits narcissistic traits doesn't always factor her daughter's best interests into the equation, and the narcissistic mother who lacks boundaries may not be able to separate in a balanced way from her daughter. According to Karyl McBride's *Will I Ever Be Good Enough?*, this separation from the mother is "crucial to psychological growth, but the narcissistic mother does not allow her daughter to be a distinct individual." McBride tells us that this kind of mother "usually has no clue how wrong this is, and how unhealthy it is for her daughter" to see the daughter as "simply an extension of herself." Consider Dalia, forty-eight, who works in advertising in a Southern city and has a twenty-one-year-old daughter who is following her path.

I'm of two minds when it comes to my daughter's career after she graduates from college. I would help her at my firm, but I worry that it won't be good for either of us. I don't want to be compared to my daughter, who is a younger version of me, and I don't want to be so physically close to her when she's following in my footsteps. My work was a source of tension when she was in high school and she always accused me of being at work. So I guess I should be flattered that now she wants to do exactly what I do.

The thing is, we look alike and sound alike and for years I looked better. Not that she couldn't have looked better, but she's very thin and her clothes hang on her. She wasn't into fashion the way I am, and I worked more at being glamorous than she did. I go back and forth between thinking we should be together and thinking that it's best not to be. It's hard to believe the years have gone by and now my daughter is doing what I do. No matter what, she can't escape my level of achievement and how I look.

A narcissistic mother might not realize how much her daughter yearns for a mother who knows her place. "The move from maiden to mother can be difficult for egotistical women," remarks Dr. Barton Goldsmith, psychotherapist and author, "and these mothers find the reality of aging to be difficult, as well as the idea of mothering older daughters. These daughters do well with mothers who have boundaries, and the novelty of a mother who doesn't insist on this wears thin."

Setting Guidelines

The 2001 Harvard School of Public Health study *Raising Teens,* by A. Rae Simpson, Ph.D., reports that parents "contribute" to their children's healthy adolescence in five ways: by offering affection and "connection"; by overseeing their behavior; by providing guidance, including "setting limits"; by helping them to understand, discuss, and steer themselves for a "larger world"; and by offering advocates, i.e., adults who can guide and care for them. The study emphasizes that these are the needs of the adolescent, not younger children, and encourages parents at this juncture to "strengthen their skills."

This list includes the prickly issues of the mother-daughter relationship in adolescence and those topics that continue into early adulthood. The suggestions in the Harvard study that apply to the mothers' attachment to their daughters concern handling criticism, ways to negotiate, tackling problems, listening to your child, and delegating responsibility. Indeed, Marguerite, sixty-two, who has been widowed for more than thirty years and lives in Dallas, where she runs a small business, believes that being a mother to three "beautiful" daughters, ages thirty-seven, thirty-three, and twenty-nine, has been "mostly easy and natural."

I have always believed in my influence. I remember being such a lucky young woman with my three darling daughters, and then my husband died. I knew then that everything was different. I was no longer the queen. I was a minority woman with three small children and I had to be practical. I controlled my daughters' environment and who their friends were, and I ran a tight ship. As far as rules and respect, it was a must. If there was a problem, we discussed it and came up with a solution. Their friends came from church and school and I didn't allow any funny business—no drugs, no leisure time—all this because I had no husband and they had no father. It changed everything; it made me tougher and smarter, and I didn't get sidetracked. If there was a problem, I stopped it at once.

And it's only now that they're older that I would take a step back and I know I don't have to be a drill sergeant anymore. I didn't have the luxury of doing that when they were younger and it worked out well. All three daughters have gone to good schools and have good jobs. If they bicker, if there's a problem, all that I taught them when they were younger kicks in, and I don't stress over it anymore—I did my job right.

What's Best for Our Daughters

Be understanding but firm. A mother who relinquishes her power becomes a wet noodle, and her daughter knows too well how to manipulate a situation. If a mother can be empathetic but insist on the rules, her daughter will benefit.

Do not assume that your daughter will take charge or can handle a situation without guidelines. So often we give our daughters more credit than they deserve or expect more than they can handle. It's best to pay attention to your daughter's age and not imbue her with an emotional maturity she doesn't have.

Explain to your daughter the importance of guiding her. Those mothers who repeatedly remind their daughters of the dangers inherent in society might seem negative and a drag, but they are training their daughters to be cautious and to appreciate their mother's refuge.

Have the confidence to insist upon your system. A mother who has a strong sense of self is able to handle new issues in a daughter's life as she grows older. This offers the daughter a striking role model and persuades her of the value of rules.

Have the flexibility to change as circumstances change. In any situation, a mother who remains collected, in charge yet able to reconsider, provides her daughter with the right tools. This also instills self-esteem in her daughter as she realizes she can manage any curveball herself and that boundaries are an asset.

Chapter 3

❋

What Color Would You Like That Prada Bag in?

Indulging Daughters Materially/Fostering Entitlement

- Do you find that your daughter acts entitled, as if she's royalty?
- Do you end up buying the "right" thing for your daughter so she can keep up with her friends?
- Have you taught your daughter the perks of a material life?
- Do you feel that your daughter deserves an easier time than you had?
- Has it occurred to you that you are too indulgent with your daughter?

If you answered yes to two or more questions, your currency with your daughter is through possessions and indulgences.

WHEN YOUR DAUGHTER got into college, you were so excited that you bought her a knockoff Gucci purse. Instead of being pleased, she was offended. Who knew she was serious about saving money from her babysitting job to get a real one? It's hard to believe how much this all matters to her, but of course, you are also a label buyer and someone who rewards with purchases—except a good copy will suit you. And then you wonder how this all happened, and fondly recall those days when she was satisfied by shopping at the Gap— or how long ago it was that she didn't care about wearing the "right" things and getting her hair highlighted at the "right" salon.

It isn't that you don't appreciate material goods or don't fantasize about what life would be like with an assistant and live-in maid. But what your daughter desires and her attitude about having it is shocking. It's as if she doesn't recognize that you've made plenty of sacrifices so she can live a certain lifestyle. The phrase "do without" hasn't entered her stratosphere, and it's your own fault. The reason that every step your daughter takes requires money is because you don't want your daughter to suffer in any way and not have what the other girls have. To this end, you deny your daughter nothing.

The Far-Reaching Material World

Remarkably, the dangers of indulging our daughters in a material world plague mothers of various economic strata, whether the temptations are designer products or the trappings of a designer life, including private schools, travel, scalped tickets to rock concerts, or meals at hip restaurants. In case we wonder where it all begins, the tabloids and weekly entertainment magazines feed the frenzy, adding to the social pressures our daughters endure. With the recent surge of rich and famous film stars giving birth to daughters, mothers and daughters alike have the opportunity to contemplate their unique universe, shown in glossy spreads. We are suffused with information about the lives of this rarefied group, among them Angelina Jolie, mother to Shiloh, Vivienne, and Zahara, Katie Holmes, mother to Suri, and Jennifer Garner, mother to Violet and Seraphina.

The March 30, 2009, issue *of OK! Magazine* is practically an ode to motherhood, with Katie Holmes quoted saying, "[Motherhood] is the most important job in the world," as she stands glamorously beside her husband, Tom Cruise, in Tokyo. We also observe a photo of her alone with her daughter, Suri, in Beverly Hills. Both mother and daughter are sporting black attire, and Holmes is quoted saying of her daughter, "She's really such a special girl." A few pages earlier, there's a candid picture of actress Nicole Kidman with her baby daughter, Sunday Rose, and a spread on the country singer Martina McBride, who says, "Being a mom is hard work." The photo for this piece shows her with her husband and their three daughters, all posing with the Jonas Brothers (not something most daughters can expect in a family shot).

The message here is twofold: that motherhood is demanding, sure, but magical and luxurious as well—and that privilege is a given. So while in theory mothers and daughters who are not stars know that this isn't their destiny, it all has an impact. Spreads about famous mothers of adult daughters include Sharon Osborne, mother to Aimee, twenty-seven, and Kelly, twenty-six, Goldie Hawn, mother to Kate Hudson, thirty-one, Blythe Danner, mother to Gwyneth Paltrow, 38. We read about the daughters, their love lives, babies, personal circumstances, and, of course, their lifestyles and wardrobes.

Whatever is ahead for these daughters of all ages—who will want for nothing—how can they *not* take it into consideration? As one mother put it, "When I mention the economy to my sixteen-year-old daughter, she just flips the pages of her magazines and tells me she needs a new iPod."

Passing on the Baton?

Celebrity culture goes hand in hand with fashion, and few of us can avoid the allure of designer clothes and accessories when we are bombarded with brand names 24/7. Not only are luxury goods paraded before us constantly—on billboards and in ads in magazines and newspapers, and on the Internet—but there are the beautiful women who sport them (more on our daughters and beauty in Chapter 4). Mary Pipher, Ph.D., notes in *Reviving Ophelia*, "Mothers are expected to protect their daughters from the culture even as they help them fit into it." As this applies to materialism, many mothers want to say no to their daughters' requests for designer labels, to avoid giving tacit approval to superficial choices, exorbitant prices, and herd mentality. However, these very same mothers confess to humoring their daughters along these lines and feeling hopeless as what their daughters covet spirals out of control. To complicate it further, the mothers themselves are immersed in a materialistic world. For example, Wanda, forty-nine, who works in a family business in upstate New York and has a twenty-five-year-old daughter, has emphasized that choices matter.

I've raised my daughter to know the good life because that's how I've lived and what I want her to have. Whether it's a car, a dress, an apartment, or theater tickets, I wanted my daughter to have the best. Sometimes I'd think to myself, This isn't so smart, she's getting too much, but since she was small I've been spoiling her, and I don't think I can stop now. It changes as she gets older. Now it's not about the doll or a school bag or a pair of boots in high school for a party, it's about putting yourself together in every way, from scarf to shoes. I'd be a hypocrite to stop now.

Lee, forty-four, who lives in Portland and works in the art world, has a sixteen-year-old daughter whom she has taught to strive for luxury.

What is the point in struggling? I have been struggling to raise my daughter for many years. She goes to religious school and I pay for it, and the kids there have more than she does. I tell her to get friendly with the families that have more so that she can be invited away on vacations or so she can be invited to the right parties. Why should she not only have less but also never get to see what life would have been like if her father was around? I save money to buy good things on sale and I try not to bother her with costs. I've worked so we can live in the right part of town and I've managed. But my daughter has to know that it's either hard work or someone else's hard work that brings you a happy life, free of stress and with beautiful things. Not only things, but comfort, and I encourage her to go after it since it's worth having.

Conflicting Messages from the Mother

The perils of constructing a universe where daughters do not comprehend the cost of possessions is skewed not only by keenly observing celebrity lifestyles, but also by the air they breathe. There are mothers who encourage their daughters when it comes to a material life, and those who feel that their daughters are "too materialistic," despite their own interest in designer brands and the power of money.

The majority of mothers feel that their own experience in how they were raised has made them more determined either to be judicious or to spoil their daughters. There are mothers who grew up in humble households who would like to monitor spending and warn against the adage that money buys happiness. Others in the same position want their daughters to have what they never had. An example of a daughter who is preoccupied with the best and most stylish goods while her mother isn't the least bit interested is shown to us in the feature film *Confessions of a Shopaholic*. Isla Fisher plays Rebecca Bloomwood, a young woman working in New York City. Her character is obsessed with shopping, and her credit card debt climbs to such astronomical proportions that she's being chased down (not that she's so unique, since a Stanford University study reports that one in twenty adults shops compulsively for all sorts of items). In contrast to Rebecca is her mother, Jane Bloomwood (Joan Cusack), an unassuming woman who clearly does not live outside her means. Her calm and quiet life is quite a contrast to her daughter's; this mother aspires to travel the United States in a Winnebago with her husband, played by John Goodman. Cusack's character is stupefied by her daughter's spending and penchant for expensive attire.

The film reminds us that a daughter who isn't surrounded by prosperity isn't inured to it, and, in fact, may find it very tempting. Daughters meet people who have better wardrobes and a more elegant lifestyle than their own at every turn, be it in high school, at college, socially, or at work. And according to most mothers, their daughters are quickly drawn in.

For those mothers who grew up without concerns about money, the predominant message is that their daughters will be raised in the same manner. Mothers who have lost their wealth or never had any may feel guilty, as if they've let their daughters down. In any case, mothers should beware that an exaggerated interest in a material life can give the daughter false values and expectations.

Morphing into Conspicuous Consumers

Mothers across the board recognize the consequences for themselves and their daughters when the daughters not only want the goods but also feel entitled to them. More than 60 percent of the women interviewed for this chapter confessed to having "snobby daughters," "spoiled daughters," or "impatient daughters." This manifests in the following ways:

A Shared Language. The currency of shopping is potent stuff, and mothers report that their early shopping days together are a part of the mother-daughter bond. In some families, shopping is as important as sports or family get-togethers. A mother of three daughters remarks, "We go to the mall on Saturdays. I used to do it with my mother, and I wouldn't miss the chance to do it with my girls. It's expensive, but we love being together this way."

Increased Stakes. A common lament among mothers is that what once satisfied the daughters no longer has an effect. A mother describes how "out of control" it is for her daughter who, at fifteen, reaches for expensive items that the mother wishes she had. One mother of a twenty-six-year-old daughter recalls, "From Hello Kitty we went straight to North Face. And from there to Kate Spade purses. Today my daughter wears Manolo Blahnik shoes that her boyfriend buys her, thankfully."

A Sense of Entitlement. Whether a daughter is four, four-teen, twenty-four, or thirty-four, her expectations make it harder for the mothers to say no, thus perpetuating entitlement. "I feel almost guilty," begins a mother of a seventeen-year-old daughter. "All those years I've tried to please her, I ended up spoiling her. But that was never my plan, and I can't stop now, not with something as simple as buying her what she wants."

Mothers are wise to pay attention to what materialism does to their daughters. On the one hand, it provides a sense of self, and having attractive, chic clothes boosts self-esteem and positions daughters socially. On the other hand, it provides a false sense of confidence—as if to say, Without this, I'm not as important or as popular or as attractive.

Hand in Hand: Materialism + Conceit

What is striking is how a mother's love of possessions and society is passed on to her daughter. Consider Roy, forty-five, an artist living outside of Boston who has two daughters, eighteen and twenty.

My mother came from a poor family and when she married my father, she had it made. He was very successful and he wanted her to have it all. So that's what I've taught both my girls—to always hold on to money somehow, and how important it is to have money. My daughters look at it as I do—they don't feel safe without these options. They also know it takes hard work to be financially secure and that they're not heiresses. My daughters have made money on their own and the twenty-year-old dates someone who is very ambitious. That's all part of my message: Make money and be with someone who makes

*money. Use the money to have a good life because it's awful
without it.*

A mother who tempers her daughters, despite her own dependency on a material life, is Carolyn. At forty-nine, she lives
in Mississippi and has two daughters, twenty-three and twenty-
seven, and one son.

*It doesn't matter so much about my son if he might want some-
thing, because he isn't going to push me if I'm against it and it
isn't going to matter financially if I buy it or not. But my daughters are another story. I have always tried to instill values in
these girls, and I haven't stood a chance. It's not only their
friends and our community, where everyone is spoiled and has
the latest thing, but my husband. He done very well and he wants
the girls to have it all. He is probably frustrated with me since
I've never gotten used to having the kind of money we do, not the
way that I grew up. I find it all foolish, the amount of money
that it costs to have this one cell phone, to have a fancy computer or car, and I don't get involved. I'm not a clotheshorse, and
he is the one who usually shops for me for my better clothes. He
loves it—he wants to show off. Since I'm a lost cause, he buys
and buys for our girls. And they lap it up. He just bought them
each a brand-new car.*

While Carolyn is concerned with the danger of belongings for
her daughters, Kim, forty-five, who lives in Denver, where she
works as an office manager, is worried that her seventeen-year-
old daughter cares too little about possessions.

*I can't get my daughter to buy a thing, and if she'd only let me,
I think she'd be more popular. I'm relieved that she isn't sucked*

in to the whole scene and at the same time I'm worried about her. I feel like she's so far removed from it. I once bought her this great winter coat, and when she found out the price, she returned it. I admire her, but I worry. I could never have had what she could have, and that makes me almost angry. I'm ready to spoil her and she won't have it. She wants to do everything in a kind of cheap way and is happy if she doesn't fit in. She'd never want to stand out by having anything fancy—from clothes to a big house to a Mercedes. She doesn't want to draw attention to herself and she doesn't want to be part of the "designer" scene. She's lucky she's pretty—I'll say that, because despite my protests, she won't dress well or wear anything that's in. Meanwhile, I love to shop, I'm a shopaholic, and I always wear the latest styles. I wish we had a big house, money, all of it.

In each of the above instances we recognize how a mother's style and point of view directly affect her daughter's take on status symbols. As Seth Shulman, a social worker whose practice addresses women's issues, warns, how a mother treats her daughter in terms of materialism speaks for what is going on in the relationship. "Having nice things is a validation for both mother and daughter. Beyond that, if the daughter has what the mother couldn't have or doesn't want what the mother wants, it causes friction."

Credit Card Effect

Of the mothers interviewed for this study, more than 70 percent had either allowed their daughters to use their credit cards, had given them their credit cards, or had provided a card linked to their account (including debit cards, phone cards, department store charge cards), by the time they were sixteen years old. Interestingly, almost all of the mothers who granted their daughters use of plastic admitted that they had a freer attitude with purchases when they themselves had used a credit card versus paying in cash. As reported by Sharon Begley in her 2008 *Newsweek* column "On Science: Inside the Shopping Brain," "The power of credit cards to numb consumers to the pain of parting with money is one of the more robust findings, and even scientists have been surprised at the magnitude of the effect." As one mother of a seventeen-year-old daughter phrased it: "It wasn't that I wanted my daughter to become a shopper. I was just tired of giving her cash all the time. But after six months with this card, she's shopping up a storm because it's just so easy to do. There's this unreal sense that plastic isn't money out of your pocket."

Despite our explanations and justifications for offering our daughters a credit card, mothers often don't realize how this gesture will play out, and credit card dependency is ubiquitous among females and males of all ages and stages of life. Moreover, a mother who gives her daughter a credit card may be holding up her own penchant for spending and shopping as the model. When it comes to the specific way that credit card use plays out with daughters, mothers end up being complicit. At first mothers lead their daughters, and soon after, the daughters are completely facile on their own, often indulging in the following:

Shopping to kill the pain. Known as retail therapy, this is a concept familiar to women of all ages and walks of life. Daughters easily pick up on their mothers' habit of shopping to self-anesthetize or, if the mother isn't a shopper, they adopt the behavior on their own. This works when a boyfriend balks, a college rejection arrives, a daughter is excluded from a party, or after she fights with a close friend. This technique of dealing with emotional pain extends to careers and social lives after high school.

Shopping for special occasions. This is taught to the mothers by their own mothers and is readily embraced by the daughters. Any reason for a shopping excursion—weight loss, prom night, a friend's wedding, a reunion—has value. On such shopping sprees, mothers who stress repeating the outfit report that their daughters don't like recycling. Half the mothers report that they cave in when the daughter wants to shop again for the next occasion.

Shopping to bond. Through the ages, mothers and daughters have been known to shop together, making a special day of this activity. I admit, I am guilty of this with my daughters. It's as if shopping is a secret language that we share. When given several options (movie, museum, walk in the park), they've always chosen a few hours of shared shopping. While several mothers in this study felt that these hours provide a venue to talk about serious matters with their daughters, shopping also reinforces a pattern of spending and precludes other activities that could be shared since time is at a premium.

Shopping to fulfill social expectations. Time with friends trumps family time, making a daughter's social life— theme birthday parties, graduation parties, lavish vacations— fantastically important. A mother wants her daughter to have the best, but at what price? And how does this work with a reality check? Mothers of all economic strata mentioned taking their daughters out for meals from an early age, and traveling during school breaks. Karen, fifty, who lives in California and works in advertising, has two college-age daughters.

I've watched my two daughters, since they were in high school, order three courses at the best restaurants—wherever we go, as if there's no tomorrow. I was taught to order carefully and never from the most expensive side of the menu. I've mentioned this to my girls, who think I'm from outer space. I bet they've learned this from their friends and I've never had the courage to say no.

The Care and Feeding of the Princess Daughter

Daughters rarely escape the influence of a mother who is thrilled to shop for anything, from clothes to kitchen items to housewares to computer software. In this way, it's a natural progression that the daughters themselves will hone their shopping skills.

The downside of materialism, according to the majority of mothers in this study, is having a daughter grow up with a penchant for material goods *and* for the easy life as if it is hers for the asking. The results of growing up in the lap of luxury are shown to us in the ABC series *Dirty Sexy Money,* which ran for two seasons, from 2007 to 2009. The premise of the show is that the Darling family is the richest family in New York City, one with problems, cover-ups, and a pervasive belief that money cures all and makes any problem go away. Jill Clayburgh stars as Letitia Darling, the matriarch; Natalie Zea plays her daughter Karen Darling, who has been divorced three times; and Samaire Armstrong is Juliet Darling, the youngest member of the family, who hopes to be an actress and is blatantly spoiled. Viewers who tuned in to *Dirty Sexy Money* fueled their curiosity as they watched the machinations brought on by endless money and the vanity it nurturers.

It isn't only during the vagaries of adolescence that mothers are perplexed by what to do to satisfy their daughters, but also earlier on in their daughters' lives. "By kindergarten, my daughter was running me ragged, and it's been that way ever since," one mother of a twenty-nine-year-old daughter recalls. "I've been trying to make sure that she has everything she wanted since then." Although many mothers concur that by the time their daughters reach age six, they are acclimating to the girls' requests, mothers with adolescent or older daughters report that it escalates around eighth grade and from then on is a part of the mother-daughter repartee. The entitlement equation breaks down into the following:

Clueless Mothers. What begins innocently enough with a mother hoping to help her daughter socially can become a pattern. If daughter is unhappy, the mother jumps through hoops to assuage her misery, and the entitlement factor is born. Edith, forty-three, who lives in a suburb and works in a hospital, has one seventeen-year-old daughter.

I can put my finger on the day it all began. My daughter was fifteen and she was in the city shopping with her friends. These girls were more sophisticated and took her to some upscale stores. That was it. She never wanted to go to the Gap or Walmart again. And she only wanted "cool" friends who go to "cool" places.

Intolerant Daughters. The more that we offer our daughters, not just materially but emotionally, the less they're able to work through problems themselves. When they face an issue without a mother coming to the rescue, they're baffled and angry. This escalates when the mother, realizing that her daughter is not effective, tries to intervene or calm her with material things or solutions. Betts, forty, who lives in the D.C. area, has one daughter, who is twelve.

I sort of let it happen because it was so impossible to deal with her. She was angry that her friends had an easier time at school or if they had more than she had. Plus, she felt my disappointment in her, which made it harder for her to deal with school, friends, boys, an after-school job, money. It became this cycle where I'd do everything for her just for us both to breathe better, and she was pouty and miserable anyway.

Shedding the best light. For many mothers, there is a sense that they've stepped into uncharted waters and don't know how to stop aiding and abetting their daughters. Rather than face that their daughters are not benefiting from their efforts and, in fact, are spoiled by the mother's actions, they march on, blinded by love—and filled with excuses, as discussed in Chapter 1. Consider Charlotte, forty-seven, who lives in a Midwestern city, where she works in a library. Her daughter is twenty-one.

I wanted my daughter to be happy, but I also wanted her to be a good student and to be a perfect child. I really didn't understand that it doesn't work that way, and my mother, her grandmother, also wanted a perfect child. So I felt my daughter had to excel for my mother's sake, too. My daughter, who was pressured—and also coddled—became impatient and didn't put up with anything that upset her or was demanded of her. She just walked away.

Navigating the twenty-first century. From having state-of-the-art cell phones, computers, iPods, iPads, BlackBerrys, iPhones, to owning her own car at seventeen (mothers of assorted incomes do this), the daughter is positioned to want for nothing. If any of her equipment breaks down, she is in a snit, unaccustomed to an inconvenience. There are mothers who have backup computers to avoid such an incident. Angelina, who lives in Chicago, works at an airport and in a department store. She has a twenty-year-old daughter.

My daughter has had her own car since the day she passed her driver's test. I work two jobs to make ends meet. Her attitude is that she's the kid and this is how it is. When she has friends over, they all carry iPhones and barely look at me when I speak to them. All of them are rude, including my daughter, but I know I feed into it. I mean, how did she get this way to begin with?

Mothers suffer from guilt in enough cases as they trudge on without questioning the repercussions for the daughter. But the mother isn't doing her daughter any favors. Instead, she needs to be brave enough to face the issues stirred up by these types of indulgences and stop herself. If she levels about her plan to break the pattern, eventually she will win the daughter's respect.

Downturn Mentality and Daughters

According to the National Bureau of Economic Research, the recession officially began in December 2007. The downturn, based on the collapse of Wall Street and the sale of Lehman Brothers and Bear Stearns, among other financial institutions, had reverberations across the country, affecting every sphere of society, including ourselves and our daughters. The December 11, 2008, *New York Times* Styles section took this into account when they devoted the first page of the issue to the article "Even in Recession, Spend They Must: Luxury Shoppers Anonymous." Ruth La Ferla's piece addresses how public displays of luxury goods in "recessionary times" aren't very politic. This isn't to say that shoppers aren't still shopping, however. La Ferla writes, "In the current climate, stealth consumption has gained a more potent appeal, taking place at gatherings with an insiders' feel."

On the same page, in an article by Lauren Lipton, "Get Bobbed, but Don't Get Clipped," women are advised on the pursuit of beauty during these dismal financial times. Lipton informs us that hairstylists will come to your home and do group haircuts for much less money than it costs at a salon. And in the third article, written by David Colman, "The Great Sale of '08," we not only learn that bargains beyond belief are offered at the department stores but also the genesis of happy consumerism in America. Colman describes the "retail consumption" problem as a crash and burn due to "a half-century spree that began when the first credit cards arrived." If we apply this theory to mothers and daughters, it makes sense. For example, Nola, thirty-eight, who lives in Rhode Island, where she is a stay-at-home mother to two daughters, ages thirteen and eight, can't recall a time when her daughters didn't want to shop.

My older daughter plays "Let's Shop" at home with her little sister. It's my younger daughter's favorite game and I make it more fun by giving them my wallet. I've noticed that no one ever goes for the cash, only the credit cards. The girls were programmed this way since they were small, just from spending time with me, watching me reach for my credit card, and poof, the purchase is theirs. But now that my husband lost his job and I want to hold on to our house, I'm trying to teach my daughters something. The rules are you can only buy on sale and only after you've gone through your entire closet and toy chest and bookshelves to see that you really need it and can justify the purchase. But I'm not sure that my older daughter gets it, and I keep repeating myself.

Last year my younger daughter wanted this pair of sneakers and I bought the wrong ones. She had a fit and cried that the other girls had the best kind and that she wouldn't wear what I'd bought. I returned them and drove two towns away to get the sneakers she wanted, and they were much more expensive than the first pair. That's what all the mothers do, so of course I'd do that for my children. That's why this new shopping game counts— half the fathers are out of work.

In these unprecedented financial times, one wonders if either the mothers or the daughters, who have had been given so much so easily, can adjust their thinking. While Nola is cognizant of the economic climate and is making an effort to teach her daughters, her desire to please them when it comes to specific purchases might or might not have altered. For Betty, forty-two, who lives in a Northeastern city and works as a fashion consultant, it's been a learning experience. Betty has two daughters, eighteen and fourteen, whom she describes as veteran shoppers.

I've always influenced my daughters when it comes to clothes— mostly that shopping is a kick and that being well dressed is important. That's my job. What's different is that the girls are looking to me for a solution since money is drying up. Most of the time, they don't care a fig what I have to say. Growing up in a city, they've had lots of friends with money and I've always wanted them to be stylish. We secretly used to buy purses and some of our clothes at the resale shops, and now we do it with pride—we tell people. It's acceptable to have something from a thrift shop and to buy secondhand clothes. I do notice that we shop less and shop in our own closets more, and I told my older daughter to get a part-time job if she wants to shop. We all wear the same size, so we're sharing more. It's sort of healthy for us, and what I appreciate is that we're on the same wavelength— my daughters get it.

As Dr. Ronnie Burak points out, both mothers and daughters suffer from a surplus of riches. "If the daughters know they'll get everything they ask for, they won't want to bother with hard work. A mother who has some introspection and figures out what she is doing might actually change her game plan."

Excuses + Lack of Boundaries = Entitled Daughters

What's been established is how determined a mother can be to make life easy for her daughters. By making excuses, as explored in Chapter 1, and not putting their foot down, as evidenced in Chapter 2, many mothers believe that they offer daughters a universe where they feel accepted and in charge. The mothers lavish opportunity and possessions upon these daughters, but frequently the plan backfires. Mothers end up with daughters who think of themselves as extraordinary *not* because of their achievements, but because of how they've been mothered. More than 70 percent of the mothers in my study attest to the fact that daughters feel entitled—materially and in terms of immediate gratification. Consider Amy, fifty-six, who lives in New Hampshire, where she is a nurse. She claims that she has always given in to her twenty-four-year-old daughter.

My relationship with my daughter has always been spirited, we have had so many ups and downs. I thought that she was growing up too fast, but there wasn't much that I could do about it. She wanted too much control, and I wanted to be in control as the mother. I was always setting limits, and she was always defying them. I basically couldn't stand the fighting, and her attitude was that she deserved it all. This business of deserving things happened because when she was little, I had rewarded her if she felt upset.

I saw a sadness in her that I wanted to make better, and so I'd take her to the mall or I'd say yes to a sleepover or to a movie or something that probably wasn't necessary. I tried to take care of the upsets in her life, and if she sulked, I tried to cheer her up. That meant if she was in a funk, I'd do something to make it better. When she was small, there were smaller rewards, and then she got older and it was about bigger issues and bigger rewards. That's how she came to feel it was all about her.

Although Amy views her function with her daughter as that of the fixer, Amanda, forty-two, who lives in Vermont and is a stay-at-home mother to a fourteen-year-old daughter, views the kind of attention and caretaking she provides for her daughter as inescapable.

Getting used to a teenage daughter who wants to go out with her friends all weekend and fights constantly about curfew, boys coming over, and her allowance is exhausting. My daughter moves on from one reason to beat me down to the next. And she's a good kid, she's a good student and will tell me if something is wrong. I'm sympathetic to what her life is like. I try to be strict with the Internet, where a lot of bad things can happen. Then she feels gypped, so I give in a little—let her stay online longer. I buy her something when she gets a good grade. She reminds me constantly of what other girls do wrong and what her closest friends' mothers say to their daughters compared to how little I say to her—because she is so good. I'm at her service. I fill in if there's a problem, if another mother isn't willing to drive, if she wants our house to host the sleepover.

On some level I think I'm more in control of her life if I'm more involved. On another level, I think I'm nothing but her chauffeur and piggy bank, 24/7. I don't insist on only one weekend night out, because she'll be happier if she can be out both nights. So she feels she can do whatever she wants with me, as long as her grades are acceptable. She's figured out that I'll do whatever I can to help her out with her schedule, schoolwise and socially.

Making life easier, i.e., never refusing a daughter, is the priority for many mothers. According to Dr. Barton Goldsmith, this isn't wise, and fosters a daughter who hasn't any independence. "Suddenly when a daughter goes out into the world, the mother asks herself, 'What's wrong with my daughter?' The mother is the problem, because she didn't prepare her daughter for life."

Age of Entitlement

The idea that mothers should be micromanagers extraordinaire is a trend that has gathered force in the past twenty-five years. More than 80 percent of the mothers in my study stated that they were not raised in this way by their own mothers and were independent at an earlier age and left to their own devices. The "sink or swim" style of the last generation of mothers has given birth to the mother who flutters over her daughters, anticipating every wish, need, or purchase. Moreover, as the mother does this, she diminishes her own power.

In their study, "The Role of the Mother in Early Social Development," Schaffer and Cook note that a child's behavior is altered by "socializing agents." These agents "reflect the values of the society in which we live." The lifestyle of many young women today is short on gratitude and appreciation, long on attitude, excess, and finding the easy way out. Whatever belief system mothers have instilled in their daughters, it can be a faint whisper compared to the loud voice of media messaging, celebrity culture, and peer pressure.

Hissy Fits: Early Adolescence and Mid-Adolescence

Arguing with our daughters is inevitable, but for most mothers in this study, it is the unrelenting quality of the fights that is so unsettling. The daughters are strong willed and able to prolong the battles; their sense of being right is overwhelming—the mother is always wrong. The majority of mothers say that they give in, to a degree, because the fights become exhausting and unproductive. Arguments are frequently age-related and occur during the three stages of adolescence (with each stage yielding its own brand of contention). These stages are defined by KidsGrowth.com as: early adolescence encompassing twelve-to fourteen-year-olds, middle adolescence at fifteen to seventeen, and late adolescence at eighteen to twenty-one. Based on my study, the looming issues for adolescent daughters when it comes to their sense of entitlement are:

Finances. In a capitalistic society, mothers and daughters enter the "allowance" phase as early as grade school. Mothers discover that giving daughters an allowance segues into a situation where daughters expect to be handed cash as teenagers, and do not develop the skills to make their own money, balance a checkbook, or open a bank account. Instead, they anticipate that their mothers will do this for them.

Curfew. Daughters fight long and hard to stay out as late as possible as early as junior high school. Mothers complain they cave in because the other mothers are more lenient and they don't want to appear to be a mean mother. However, mothers, once they've conceded, worry about the late hour and describe the situation as out of control.

Computer and homework time. The more the mother remains a disciplinarian in this category, the better off the daughter is. Again, peer pressure and the mother's perception that the other girls are allowed more computer time and have less academic pressures leads to the daughters winning this round.

Household responsibilities. In today's world, not as many mothers insist upon a daughter having household chores as the past two generations of mothers did. As a result, mothers who insist often find stubborn, taciturn daughters, who point out that they are the only ones of their friends who have this requirement.

Lingering Indulgences: Late Adolescence Onward

Once the daughters have been in college for a year or two, an appreciation of their mothers thankfully seeps into the equation. Notwithstanding this awakening on the daughters' part, John P. Hill and Grayson N. Holmbeck report in the *Journal of*

Youth and Adolescence that college girls fight with their mothers approximately sixteen times per month. (This is an improvement over the early-adolescent or middle-adolescent daughter, who, according to the mothers with whom I've spoken, has a fight on almost a daily basis.) As one mother reports, "Both my daughters woke up the day before their twentieth birthdays and decided I was a great mom. That doesn't mean we didn't have our issues or that they stopped fighting me when they couldn't get their way. But it meant that they were getting to a better place." The issues for daughters in their early twenties to those approaching thirty are the following:

Wardrobe. Our daughters are invested in a personal style and/or herd mentality when it comes to their clothing. This manifests in two ways: either the daughter leans on her mother, as we have seen, to purchase certain goods, or the mother is stylish enough (in the daughter's estimation) that she'll borrow from her mother, always selecting the choice goods, and not returning responsibly. Mothers complain about missing things.

Brand power. In order to own particular products, daughters carry on, instilling guilt in those mothers who resist and insist that buying such items doesn't reflect their value system or that their daughter is too young to have these luxury items. Another problem is the unrelenting quality of this syndrome: A mother indulges her daughter once and believes that's it, while the daughter is simply wetting her toes.

Drug and alcohol use. While we know this is often part of an adolescent daughter's life (allowance money might fund this), mothers report that many daughters have stopped using recreational drugs or binge drinking by their early to mid-twenties. If a daughter is still involved with drinking or drugs and it's worrisome, the only recourse is to confront the daughter and seek professional help.

Friends and boyfriends. If a daughter is involved with a certain crowd or has a boyfriend who is less than optimal, a mother feels she must state her case. Arguments ensue when the daughter claims to know what she wants and that she is capable of choosing her own friends and managing her own love life.

New financial parameters. If the daughter is working, the parents often find themselves subsidizing her anyway. This is, in part, a reflection of the steep cost of living and a knee-jerk reaction of the mother who has always paid for her daughter. Some mothers defend their daughters; others wonder when their daughters will be able to support themselves as they continue to kick in for expenses.

In any of the familiar plotlines above, mothers feel bruised and at a loss when their compliant, delightful young child is replaced by an alien who finds fault with her mother at every turn and has tremendous demands. Since daughters remain confident of their mothers' unconditional love (they'll still bail them out, write the check, lie for the cause), the mother needs to take a stand and be strong enough not to acquiesce to her daughter's every requirement.

The Improvement Plan: Reining It In

If initially a mother doesn't believe that her daughter is spoiled, the indulgences can add up. Still, admitting that your daughter can be unmotivated, pampered, and willful isn't easy, and that raises that nagging question: Who are you in this equation?

Encourage your daughter to be an individual and not to follow the latest trends or be so invested in her friends' status. From the time your daughter is in grade school, have conversations with her about materialism, and remind your daughter that money doesn't buy happiness.

Point out the value of a balanced life. Discuss why it's enjoyable to have possessions and trips, but emphasize that relationships, personal achievements, friendships, and personal growth are substantive.

Take the initiative if you realize, at any point in your daughter's life, that she is too caught up in "things" or has a sense of entitlement. This means saying no, insisting upon rules and upon your value system, despite the larger picture—celebrity culture, peer pressure, lenient mothers in the neighborhood.

Be bold about altering the course of your relationship with your daughter, and communicate this to her. If you have not stated the obvious, it's time to exert more control and be less pampering. This conversation conveys that things have gotten out of hand and are about to change.

Stress that love isn't always saying yes, nor is it about money, possessions, or invitations. Your daughter will benefit from a mother who holds the bar high, is serious, focused, and undeterred. Although it may take some time, ultimately she will respect you for these values.

Chapter 4

Perhaps You Should Wear Makeup

Overemphasizing Beauty

- Do you stress how important looks are?
- Do you worry about how your daughter measures up in terms of her appearance?
- Have you told your daughter that attractive women win the day?
- Do you buy your daughter great clothes so that she'll stand out?
- Have you considered plastic surgery for yourself or your daughter?
- Did you agree to (or suggest) highlights when your daughter was a preteen?

If you've answered yes to any of the above questions, chances are you are making too much of your daughter's appearance.

IT'S TRUE THAT your seventeen-year-old daughter is the prettiest among her friends, and since grade school she has known that she can use her looks to her advantage. You have always stressed that looks matter because you want to be honest and because you have a daughter who can benefit from how the world works. Lately, she has become fixated on her looks and her wardrobe, reading every magazine and trying out every beauty trend. She's on the Internet much too much and watches *American Idol*, paying close attention to teen actresses and performers. She hangs out with handsome boys and attractive girls, and it worries you that it's too superficial, but this is what the popular kids do, you assume. They compare themselves to movie stars and consider themselves superior to their classmates. Although you know that your daughter is one of the most sought-out girls in her twelfth-grade class, you feel it's a slippery slope. You are in on it, too, and when she wasn't looking as good, about a year ago, you took her to have her hair highlighted and to a dermatologist. If she eats one cookie too many, you make a fuss. After all, she has to hold on to her looks to sustain her position among her friends. You're actually all right about being her protector because as dicey as it is to have a good-looking daughter, you'd take it any day over having a less attractive daughter and the misery those mothers endure. You've witnessed that, and it's a whole different kettle of fish.

The Power of Beauty

There are those mothers who find the idea of molding and forming a daughter so that she looks her best to be very enticing. Although more than 90 percent of the mothers with whom I spoke believe in having a well-rounded daughter accomplished in all areas, including looks, brains, and achievement, 80 percent felt that beauty is the calling card for women in our culture. The prevailing attitude among mothers is that daughters who look good are at an advantage. This way of thinking is documented in Hamermesh and Biddle's study "Beauty and the Labor Market." According to their findings, people who appear "plain" earn less than "average-looking people," while those who are "good-looking" earn the most for the same position. The study reports that women who are unattractive are not only paid less for their work than their attractive counterparts but also they end up marrying men with "less human capital."

The emphasis on appearance has escalated in the past few years, beyond its importance at any other time in modern history. In researching this chapter, I came across a multitude of articles on hair, skin, and makeup in newspapers, magazines, and online dedicated to young girls and teenage girls. This includes an article by Camille Sweeney that ran in *The New York Times* on February 28, 2008: "Never Too Young for That First Pedicure." Sweeney describes how a seven-year-old girl celebrated her birthday with her friends, her mother, and her little sister at Dashing Diva, an "international nail spa" on the Upper West Side of Manhattan, with "mani's, pedi's and mini-makeovers with light makeup and body art—glitter-applied stars, lightning bolts and, of course, hearts."

Sweeney reveals that cosmetic companies are targeting products at six- to nine-year-old girls, and tells us that Experian, a market research company, found that 55 percent of girls this age use lip gloss or lipstick and almost two-thirds use nail polish. A few weeks later, on April 3, 2008, *The New York Times* ran another article by Sweeney concerning girls and beauty: "A Girl's Life, with Highlights." Sweeney reports that while "no one tracks how many girls twelve and younger go to professionals" for hair treatments that include lowlights, curl-inducing permanents, and straighteners, Gordon Miller, a spokesman for the National Cosmetology Association quoted in the article, describes young girls as "a lucrative niche market." And how can mothers of these young girls deny the effect of Hannah Montana, when it's just at their fingertips to buy their daughters this very look? It's not only that the girls are in the game very early, but also that their mothers are on board. As Sweeney writes, these young clients are from "across the multicultural spectrum" in wanting to emulate one of their idols "or to create a unique look that's then the subject of instant messages long into the night."

When reading these articles, we ask ourselves where this could possibly be taking girls at a vulnerable age, and how is it that mothers sign on, giving the message that a daughter's childhood should be forfeited for beauty maintenance. It isn't just about makeup, nails, or hair, but about how early young girls enter the scene, becoming part of a slick, beauty-absorbed culture. No matter where one raises her daughter in a large city or small town—by their teens, many young girls are pros at maintaining their appearance and are well aware of how high the stakes are.

So while some mothers say they feel it's "too much too soon," others remark that it's "innocent enough" for daughters to begin to focus on looks and maintenance by first grade. There are mothers, too, who feel that their daughters are simply doing what their friends do, and are disinclined to view this as anything more. Consider the following mothers:

Elise, forty-one, who lives in a Southern city and works in marketing, has concerns about her eight-year-old daughter's interest in beauty products.

Not only does my daughter want makeup and pedicures, but she wants to have her hair Brazilian straightened. She learned about this through a teenage sister of her friend, and she's been asking about it ever since. I told her she has to wait, but how long will that last when girls her age are having spa parties?

Martha, thirty-five, who lives in the Midwest, is a stay-at-home mother. She worried that her seven-year-old twins are too "into beauty" already.

I won't allow my girls to have any makeup in our house. They do makeup and nails at their friends' and are so happy with it that I feel slightly mean-spirited. But they have their whole lives to worry about it and I want them to focus on sports and on being seven, not fifteen. I seem to be the strict mother in their crowd, but I'm trying to get the message across that they shouldn't be worrying about how they look now—it's crazy.

Mandy, thirty-six, who lives in Southern California and works part-time, believes that her three daughters, ages ten, eight, and six, are merely part of the herd.

My girls are impressionable and all of their friends, for all three girls, are interested in manicures and face makeup. I say, let them do it, too, or else they'll rebel if I'm too strict and sneak around to do it. Besides, there are plenty of other things to distract them, and it isn't at the center of their lives—it's one curiosity.

If young daughters are already besieged by beauty products and the importance of being attractive, this is due partly to their mothers, who have been maintaining their face, hair, wardrobes, and bodies to varying degrees for decades. An article by Jake Mooney on February 15, 2009, in *The New York Times*,

"Women, Haircuts and the Price of Self-Esteem," addresses how even while enduring financial straits of a recession, women are not giving up their visits to hair salons and view it as a necessity. Daughters of all ages echo the sentiment, from very young girls to teenage daughters onward. No wonder Anne Kreamer's book, *Going Gray*, her account of summoning the courage to stop coloring her hair and an explanation of why gray hair has been pegged as aging and something men aren't supposed to like, is a brave treatise. There are plenty of women who would support Nora Ephron's take on hair color—that hair dye has changed a woman's life, as she notes in her book *I Feel Bad About My Neck*. Whatever the personal choice a woman makes, what is apparent is that being attractive and youthful is a social imperative.

For our daughters, a mother's take on beauty, as on all issues explored in this book, is of great consequence. But can we teach our daughters to value their individual style and own personal look without succumbing to the dictates of ideal beauty? An article that ran in *Marie Claire*, "Your Changing Ideal of Pretty" by Christine Lennon, sheds some light on how "pretty" is no longer one stereotypic face but can be influenced and bought. Those who wield influence include researchers who define beauty, the evolutionary process (i.e., how we are programmed to recognize beauty from the time we are born), and women themselves, who are exposed to a variety of faces from all over the world. As one mother of a thirty-year-old daughter confides, "No matter what I've done, from downplaying my daughter's frizzy hair to encouraging her to straighten it, to how she should enhance her eyes with makeup, we both feel under the gun."

Dr. Claire Owen warns that a mother's emphasis on beauty doesn't always sit well with her daughter. "Mothers who place such a high importance on their own appearance then take the same approach with their girls when they are young. If the daughters don't feel beautiful, they think that they're failures and spend years trying to shake the feeling."

Beauty Versus Brains

The wicked stepmother in the fairy tale "Cinderella" wanted to keep her stepdaughter, Cinderella, out of sight because she was pretty and good-natured, while her own daughters were not only unattractive but miserable as well. If any of the three young women were highly intelligent, it was of little consequence in ensnaring the prince. While this is a fairy tale, with the most popular version written in the mid-nineteenth century by the Brothers Grimm, in the twenty-first century, women still sign on for the idea that beauty wins the day. In fact, this historical division of women prevails despite the gains of women legally, politically, economically, and socially. And so we recognize those women who are blessed with their appearance or blessed with their intellect. An intersection of the two is a pleasant, sort of distant theme.

Of course there are mothers who want their daughters to be beautiful, talented, *and* brilliant, perhaps sharing their mother's pursuits. Indeed, Joan Rivers, comedienne and television personality, and her daughter, Melissa Rivers, have cohosted the red-carpet interviews for the Academy Award presentations, first on the E! cable network and then on the TV Guide Network. Mother and daughter also costarred in a TV film in 1994, called *Tears and Laughter: The Joan and Melissa Rivers Story*. Other famous mothers whose daughters have chosen their path include actress Blythe Danner and her daughter, actress Gwyneth Paltrow, actress Goldie Hawn and her daughter, actress Kate Hudson, Susan Sarandon and her daughter, actress Eva Amurri. While this is encouraging, the premium on looks remains for many young women today.

A film example of a pretty girl who learns the wisdom of brainpower (although her mother expects her to use her looks to achieve her goals) is Elle Woods, Reese Witherspoon's character in the 2001 feature film *Legally Blonde*. When Elle, president of her sorority, Hawaiian Tropic Girl, and Miss June in her campus calendar, is dumped by her boyfriend, Harvard Law student Warner Huntington III, for being too blond, she decides to win him back and applies to Harvard Law School. Once at Harvard, Elle learns that not only does she not want Warner anymore, but how capable she is of excelling as a law student and future attorney, all while remaining stylish and looking good.

Mothers themselves are confused over the issue, since beauty has long been the recognized calling card. Consider Marie, forty, who works in a bank and lives on the Georgia coast. Her daughter is sixteen.

My daughter is awesome—she's just beautiful and she's been a model since she was small. She knows she's really pretty, but she's learning now that it isn't the answer. I've always thought it's important to know this, but she wouldn't listen to me until recently. I would say that she should do well in school, that she should have friends and have a rounded life.

But for a long time she's had everything she needs—thick, long hair, gorgeous face, perfect figure. She was vain and there wasn't much to say. We both saw where it got her, and it's a big deal—being that pretty. Sure, I want her to go to college and to have a life beyond this, and I always thought it would dawn on her at some point that it isn't the answer. The amazing part is that she's figuring out at sixteen that she has to have more in her life. It's hard when your looks work for you to want to do it another way. I mean, why not go for what everyone knows will work?

While Marie succumbs to the leverage that her daughter's looks have provided, Adra, fifty-two, who lives in Southern California and works in retail, realizes that her three daughters, ages thirty, twenty-seven, and twenty-four, have had very different trajectories based on their looks and academic abilities.

My oldest daughter is the beauty and it's been a breeze. Because I was the beauty in my family, I was familiar with her situation. She married the right guy, has the right life, and always had friends. She did well enough in school, but it didn't matter. I never said much because everything she had was about being beautiful. I told her to be nice to everyone so that no one could fault her.

My second and third daughters have both struggled with weight problems and are much plainer. When they were in high school, it was a bone of contention and we had our moments. I am always suggesting diets. I recommended highlights, long hair, that one of them should consider a chin implant. They know that I believe it's important to be pretty but I've always acknowledged what good students they were and, later on, how much success they've had with work. So they're very smart, and their work is satisfying. I urge these two daughters to work hard and get satisfaction in other ways than being beautiful.

Adra's investment in the power of beauty brings to mind a mother-daughter relationship in Kathryn Stockett's novel, *The*

Help. In this story, which takes place in 1962, at the beginning
of the civil rights movement, Eugenia "Skeeter" Phelan returns
from college to her home in Jackson, Mississippi, without a fi-
ancé. Her friends are mostly married with little children, and
Skeeter's strong-willed mother believes that her daughter is
missing the boat. She is determined that her very tall (too tall)
daughter with unruly blond hair will nab a man only if she
conforms regarding her appearance. Skeeter's mother's disappointment in her daughter has a profound effect upon Skeeter,
as is the case with mothers and daughters in this study. When
it comes to this sensitive topic, mothers are divided into several
categories by mind-set:

Beauty trumps brains. Mothers who believe this often
pressure their daughters into trading on their looks, which can
backfire. The daughters don't develop in other ways, and this puts
them at a disadvantage. As Judge Judy's book *Beauty Fades,
Dumb Is Forever: The Making of a Happy Woman* reminds us,
beauty is only for the young in our country.

Beauty is from the inside out. Mothers rely on this plati-
tude only when required. It works in theory but is not always
the case, nor is it truly soothing for a daughter who has angst
over not being pretty enough and is well aware of the perks of
looking a certain way.

Beauty is only skin-deep. Mothers say this about the ex-
quisite "mean girl" to console their daughters. Yet what both
mothers and daughters know is that a mean girl who is pretty
is a double threat and wields power.

Talent is nothing without looks. This notion dies hard
with those mothers who have a showbiz daughter. Those mothers whose daughters aspire to be actresses or singers have
remarked that their daughters "need" to be attractive for it to

work. The article on Jessica Simpson, "The Jessica Question," by Rich Cohen, that ran in the June 2009 issue of *Vanity Fair* underscores this. "Simpson . . . like all starlets, has been careful to be pictured in just one way: as the skinny, forever-twenty-four-year-old sex bomb."

You can have it all. The fantasy that the daughter is a rocket scientist with looks to boot is alluring to some mothers. Yet as mentioned earlier in this chapter, the concept hasn't quite taken off, and the dichotomy still exists for women. Other mothers view having it all as too much of a good thing, and a dread of a daughter "outdoing herself" exists.

Mothers are submerged in a culture that puts a great emphasis on beauty and views it as a potent currency. They would serve their daughters well by removing themselves from this way of thinking and instead valuing their daughters' achievements, independence, and personal style.

Drinking the Kool-Aid

It is curious that in a study conducted by Fingeret and Gleaves, "Sociocultural, Feminist and Psychological Influences on Women's Body Satisfaction: A Structural Modeling Analysis," neither the strong beliefs of feminism nor self-esteem serves as a "protective mechanism" for women who are influenced by "sociocultural appearance standards." The college women who participated in this study are not remotely interested in feminism and are preoccupied with how they appear and "gender attitudes" toward women.

In the January 23, 2005, *New York Times* article "One Word for What's Happening to Actors' Faces Today: Plastics," Manohla Dargis discusses how cosmetic surgery has affected actors' appearances. "Movie stars have always been put on diets, and had their hair and teeth straightened and bleached. Rita Hayworth's hairline was raised through electrolysis and imperfections were erased from Marilyn Monroe's chin. Noses have been bobbed, breasts enlarged, tummies tucked." Yet the difference today is that mothers and daughters are saturated with the lives of stars through various media to the point where they aspire to look as they do and to seek out the same procedures and emulate their wardrobes and bodies. The line is no longer drawn, and everyday women compare themselves to both movie stars and models and feel they come up short.

Four years after Dargis's article ran, mothers and daughters are once again informed by a *New York Times* piece of the high stakes for celebrity women, translating into high stakes for everyday women. In this article the focus is the costume exhibit opening at the Metropolitan Museum of Art on May 4, 2009. Eric Wilson's title, "A Museum Gala Where High Cheekbones and Higher Hemlines Rule," drives home the impact of beauty and style as he describes Kate Moss as "one of the world's most famous models, wearing what was possibly the world's shortest gold lamé toga."

Women of all ages know instinctively what the fast lane requires, and daughters jump in early. Consider Nita, thirty-nine, who lives in Oregon, where she works for a small company and has a thirteen-year-old daughter. She reminds us that a daughter who conforms to a standard of beauty is better positioned as early as junior high school.

I have always been considered good-looking, and it's gotten me through a lot of tough times. I've gotten jobs because of my looks and I definitely had lots of boyfriends before I was married and now that I'm divorced. My girlfriends hung around me because that's where the boys were. My daughter and I look very much alike. We go to the same hair salon, we both wear our hair long, we like the same clothes and love to shop. She's just starting out and I've been in it a long time. Sometimes I wonder how many more good years I've got left. And I know she's up next.

I don't discourage her because I think she's a realist. I want her to know that being beautiful helps, and I'm not going to downplay it. It isn't that I think it's the only way to get somewhere, it's that this is how the world is. If I had a daughter who didn't have great looks, if I hadn't traded on it for years, I'd probably have another way of getting by.

Mothers who are in synch with their daughters have frequently had the same experience concerning beauty. The drawback is that both mothers and daughters are under the spell of what beauty offers. "People are drawn to beauty." Remarks therapist Brenda Szulman, "We've been trained this way, and for girls it's all the more important, from the time they are babies—with mothers encouraging daughters."

Competition Between Mother and Daughter

SuEllen Hamkins and Renée Schultz note in their book, *The Mother-Daughter Project,* that our daughters are engaged in how they present themselves by the time they are eight years old. The authors write, "The image of the Perfect Girl is now in circulation among eight- to eleven-year-olds, influencing them to turn their attention from jumping rope and climbing trees to focusing on their appearance." With this level of awareness, a daughter who has a "babe" for a mother can feel rivalrous—and mothers with very attractive daughters can feel the same.

What if a "perfect mother" is added to the mix, a mother declared by everyone to look half her age, who is at the gym on a regular basis and happily shares accessories as well as clothing with her daughters? What if the daughter *knows* she should get to the gym at least four days a week and can't muster up the energy or discipline and is acutely sensitive about how she appears? What if having a mother who looks this terrific makes it all the worse? A daughter, whether she's in grade school or fully grown, then asks herself, "When will I ever look like that? Is my mother prettier than I am? Is everyone thinking this?"

There are several complications that haunt both mother and daughter when it comes to a showdown over looks. After all, the mothers are trying their best to hold on to their youth while the daughters are dealing with how they appear and are perceived by their peers. Whatever way it plays out, the competition over looks between mothers and daughters is more covert than overt— it's too loaded to be out on the table. Everyday women in this study report the following mother-daughter combinations when it comes to appearances:

Pretty Mothers/Plain Daughters

Mothers who have depended upon their beauty are frustrated by daughters who aren't signed on for this. Some mothers minimize their own beauty and feel guilty; others pressure their daughters to be more proactive in order to look better. For Nellie, fifty-six, who lives in Montana and has raised three daughters, thirty-two, thirty, and twenty-seven, there has been tension concerning her daughters' appearances and her own.

My oldest daughter has all the physical characteristics of my husband's family and isn't attractive at all. The other two girls look almost like twins, and like me. My third daughter was home-coming queen, the most popular girl all through high school. Meanwhile, I have spent all these years compensating for my unattractive daughter. I've talked about her traits that are good, her legs, her big dark eyes. I've lavished praise upon her in a way that is probably so obvious to people. And I've never once mentioned what she is missing. I make no fuss over the younger two, who look just like I used to look. And since I'm older, it helps my oldest daughter, since I'm not looking like I used to. At least someone in the family isn't overshadowing her anymore.

Finally, everyone is married, the younger two first and then my oldest daughter. I felt more comfortable at the oldest daughter's wedding because I wasn't compared to my pretty girls. Maybe it has been easier on my oldest daughter seeing that I haven't held on to my looks.

In listening to Nellie's take on her three daughters' status, I was struck by the complexity of the issue. She embraces the competition with her two daughters whom she feels are on a par with her and worries about her eldest daughter being odd girl out. Despite her goodwill, she competes against herself, past and present, and with all three daughters due to her own ambivalence about beauty, age, and a mother's place.

Pretty Daughters/Plain Mothers

The converse situation also causes friction between mothers and daughters. If a daughter exceeds her mother in terms of looks, the mother might see her daughter as having opportunities that she never had without the privilege of beauty. For instance, Jill, forty-eight, who lives in a small town in the South where she runs a restaurant, observes her two daughters, twenty and twenty-five, as they are rewarded for their looks.

Sure, my girls are pretty and they know it. They have the right clothes and the right friends and the right lives. I have made them work for it, and they've earned their own money to have nice things. I haven't talked to them much about coloring their hair or buying low-cut dresses, but they seemed to know what to do without me. It wasn't my life, the way they dress and go out, and I haven't made it a priority. I've been strict about doing well in school and I've been an example of a mother who works. I'm sure they wonder how they ended up with a mother who hasn't anything glamorous about her.

But this isn't spoken—it's what I imagine they feel. I don't know what it's like to be them and they don't know what it's like to be me. So we deal on another level—we don't shop or do pedicures together. I'm more the disciplinarian so they don't get caught up in how they look.

Look-alike Mothers and Daughters

There is a population of mothers and daughters who both excel when it comes to their appearance. They share a sense of ease in a universe where beauty rules. The competition is less than in the above combinations; instead the mother and daughter might be clannish and accustomed to preferential treatment. Consider Rosa, forty-five, who works in fashion and lives in a Midwestern city. Her twenty-two-year-old daughter just had the same procedure that Rosa had in her twenties, to take "a bump" out of her nose.

I doubt my daughter needed this surgery any more than I did, but she wanted it and I remember wanting it, too. I look at her and I see how she fusses with her looks and how everything has to be just so. She's a beautiful girl and she didn't need to do a thing, but I can't convince her of this since I did it myself. I'm not in favor of her choice, but I understand it. It's almost as if we have to be perfect. Not everyone understands this, so while I'm not happy that she wanted to do something so unnecessary, I also know better than anyone why she did it.

My daughter and I are close because we're similar. It's based on how we look and put ourselves together. I know what it's like to have the advantage of being considered "hot," and so does she.

It is inevitable that neither mothers nor daughters escape the expectations placed upon them when it comes to their appearance. In some cases the mother is so involved in her physical presence or her daughter's that it becomes a preoccupation or a diversion. As psychologist Jeanette Friedman remarks, "A mother who is extremely focused on controlling how the outside world sees her and her daughter should be careful that the daughter is not merely an instrument of the mother's own needs."

Mothers Missing Their Own Youth

Several mothers have touched on how pressured they feel to remain young-looking as their daughters ascend in the world of youth and beauty. "My daughter can't stand that I'm fighting hard to still look good. She thinks I'm disgracing her somehow," remarks one mother about her eighteen-year-old daughter. "I feel cynical. I want to say to her, 'Watch out, it will pass you by, too.'" In her essay "Ageism and the Politics of Beauty," Cynthia Rich points out, "This slice of mainstream media is jammed with political messages. Old women are ugly. Their view of things can be dismissed as just a way of venting their envy of young women. . . . Images like this accustom younger women to unthinkingly adopting an ageist stance."

Ageism is apparent to both mothers and daughters from an early age. According to the study "Effects of Age and Gender on Perceptions of Younger and Older Adults" by Linda M. Woolf, older women are "defined as socially undesirable." Neither mother nor daughter misses this cruel message. One mother tells me this is compounded by her daughter's radiant beauty: "The more that my face wrinkles and my body sags, the more amazing my daughter looks."

On April 26, 2009, the Sunday Styles section of *The New York Times* ran a feature article, "Yes, Looks Do Matter," by Pam Belluck, focusing on singer Susan Boyle, who came into prominence in the spring of 2009, when she appeared on *Britain's Got Talent*. Boyle, a never-married woman in her late forties, wowed the judges with her voice and stirred up the question of how women are stereotyped by age and appearance. The mothers with whom I've spoken agreed unilaterally that ageism makes it all the more difficult for women. However, this is to varying degrees, depending upon their mothers' personal level of investment in aging. Daughters either pay no attention to their mother's plight (although they might be slightly repulsed) or feel this is their destiny, too. For example, Darryl, forty-eight, who lives in northern Florida and works in the hotel business, feels her twenty-year-old daughter objects to how she is treated.

My daughter sees me struggling to still look good in order to make a living. She doesn't envy me and she also gets how one day it will be her turn, but she thinks that it's light-years away and isn't exactly worried about it. She knows how being young and attractive is the only ticket. Sometimes she and I talk about how being young is everything if you're a woman. But she also thinks that the world can't be like this by the time she's in her forties, and I laugh. What could make it change? What would make it easier for women when they lose their sex appeal?

Complicit Vanity

While it's unfortunate when a mother suspects that her daughter sees her as old and worn, a youthful mother may elicit a daughter's resentment. Consider Ruthie, forty-eight, who lives in Nevada, where she is a teacher, and has two daughters, twenty and seventeen.

As I get older, my girls see me trying out new creams and hair colors. They are happy on the one hand and on the other, they want me to retire, to give it up and look old. Their attitude is, you look good enough and you've had plenty of years to look good. Now it's their turn. They don't have much understanding of what it's like to have to color your hair, to look in the mirror and know you're sort of losing it and you once were great. In some ways, getting older helps with girls because no one says, "Gee, your mom is so young and pretty" anymore. But it's not fair that they don't have some sympathy for what I'm going through. I watch them go out with their friends so easily and have a great time. It's harder each year to meet people and to have a social life. I miss what they have and they don't think I deserve to miss it. So whatever I do—with my hair, with my makeup, with my clothes—they find sort of annoying.

There are those mothers who not only rail against the system and stereotyping of women by age, but who also put their desires into action. A mother's take on plastic surgery, Botox, and fillers often gives the daughter the message that improving one's looks is central to women. On May 12, 2009, *Good Morning America* ran a segment on how a mother yearned to look like her twenty-nine-year-old daughter to the point that she underwent cosmetic surgery to get this result. Janet Cunliffe and her daughter, Jane Cunliffe, look similar because the mother spent close to $15,000 on plastic surgery and lost thirty pounds. On the ABC Web site, an article by Thea Trachtenberg and Imaeyen Ibanga, "Mom Has Plastic Surgery to Look Like Daughter," details how Janet Cunliffe chose to "remake herself" in her daughter's image." Plastic surgery can alter a woman's appearance dramatically, but how does it affect the mother-daughter relationship? What happens when a mother has had cosmetic surgery and her daughter, who is over forty and showing signs of aging, has not?

Many Generation X mothers and boomer mothers hold on to their youth as long as possible. The American Society for Aesthetic Plastic Surgery reports that in 2007, 11.7 million cosmetic procedures were performed, including surgeries and nonsurgical procedures such as injections of Botox and Restylane. The cosmetics industry proves to be a multibillion-dollar industry, as reported by www.indiacom.com. And in August 2009, Lady of America, a leading women's gym franchise, offered free enrollment to new members, claiming to "understand" how important working out is for women. Our daughters, whether they are ten, twenty, or thirty years old, are cognizant of what beauty brings to the table because they have seen our attitudes regarding our own and their appearances. The majority of mothers who spend time and money on their looks believe that their daughters will do the same, on an as-needed basis. Consider Sarie, forty-seven, who lives in Colorado, where she is a stay-at-home mother to a fifteen-year-old daughter. When it comes to skin and hair, Sarie believes that her modeling has worked.

My daughter has watched me all these years. I've had glycolic peels and Botox. I've been coloring my hair for her entire life. She's gone with me to the hairdresser, the dermatologist, and once when I consulted a plastic surgeon. I know she worries about having good skin, and she takes great care of her hair. She sees that I don't go out of the house without looking good, and she does the same thing. I have always made a fuss about how she looks and how I look. And she's my daughter, so she's vain and she believes what I believe—that any attention that we pay does make a difference. We're sort of the same, at different stages.

If mothers are able to separate from their daughters when it comes to appearances and stop believing they have to share a path, the daughter will be less encumbered. A mother who achieves a balance when it comes to beauty and the other parts of her life provides her daughter with a positive role model.

Avoiding Narcissism and Beauty

As we have gleaned from the voices of the mothers in this chapter, whether the mother is high-maintenance, in fear of aging, invested in cosmetic procedures, filled with regret about not being beautiful, or lamenting how it no longer works, the daughters react to their mothers' approach. The mother's message regarding this is significant.

Be careful not to place too much importance on hair, body, and face. This sounds like a no-brainer, but close to 90 percent of the mothers interviewed for this chapter admitted to emphasizing at least one aspect of a daughter's appearance. Most of these mothers had the best intentions and were unwilling to admit that their endeavors only upset their daughters.

Do not compare your daughter's look to yours. If the mother uses her daughter's beauty to her benefit, or believes it is a reflection of herself or rewards her for her looks, the daughter can become narcissistic herself. Avoid asking your daughter to present herself a certain way (because it reflects on you).

Avoid twin wardrobes with your daughter. The "Who looks best in these jeans?" syndrome can be very disconcerting to the daughters. It can affect the daughter's self-esteem if her mother and she are competing over looks and wardrobe.

Don't hold your daughters to too high a standard. A daughter feels she has to attain a specific look among her peers, and if her mother is also expecting a particular standard, daughters can become frustrated and angry. Others rebel if they feel judged or examined by their mothers.

Don't allow your daughters to hold you to too high a standard. If a daughter feels embarrassed by her mother— either she's not fashionable or too chic, too vain or too sloppy— this causes strain in the relationship, and some mothers say they second-guess themselves.

When it comes to youth and beauty, don't live vicariously through your daughter. A mother's desire to appear youthful and attractive is understandable. However, it's best to define a mother's style and her daughter's style as distinctive and age appropriate.

Chapter 5

※

Do You Need to Be
Eating That?

Fixations on Food and Weight

- Have you taught your daughter to count calories?
- Do you tell her she's too fat?
- Does your daughter constantly wonder if she's too heavy?
- Does she watch you yo-yo diet? (And does she do the same?)
- Are you concerned that your daughter has an eating disorder?
- Have you made a big deal about going to the gym or exercising?

If you answered yes to any of the questions above, you are pressuring your daughter and placing too much significance on weight.

YOUR THIRTY-YEAR-OLD DAUGHTER has been heavy since the day she was born. By kindergarten, you were rationing her cookies, censoring her candy at Halloween, and urging her to be athletic. You considered yourself an excellent example, someone who has struggled with weight and overcome it by going to the gym, counting calories, and eating a sensible diet. Your efforts have paid off, and it's maddening that this hasn't sunk in for your daughter. There was a period when she was in college when she seemed almost anorexic—and was actually the thinnest she's ever been. Although you worried she might have an eating disorder at that stage, she gained the weight back soon enough, and nothing has happened since. Instead, you feel as though you are still vetoing junk food, sniffing at what she orders at restaurants, and making unsubtle remarks about weight. Your tolerance has worn thin, and you're starting to resent how you are positioned as confrontational. It occurs to you that she might be hurting herself by not dieting to get back at you—although it seems difficult to comprehend.

Haven't you pointed out that we live in a world where people judge you by your looks and weight? You've said it a thousand times, all the while wondering how many options she can ruin for herself, including a job, a man, friends who reflect her talents. There is no place in life where a woman's weight won't hinder her chances, you seethe as your daughter reaches for a Mars bar.

Mothers and Weight

As if the fuss about beauty isn't enough for our daughters to contend with, there is conflict surrounding eating patterns and weight as well. As with beauty, mothers are major players in how this works for the daughters, along with the usual culprits:

celebrity women and fashion models who are held up to us daily. Furthermore, there are the expectations within one's social group, which invariably includes someone who is svelte and untroubled about her body image, exuding a confidence and grace that can unnerve many a daughter. Added to the mix is the fact that mothers often battle insecurities around their own weight while having daughters who are in the same boat. According to L. K. George Hsu's *Eating Disorders,* when their mothers and other female relatives are absorbed with dieting, the girls themselves are affected. In this way, the concern with weight is passed on.

Fat Talk

According to a study by Mimi Nichter, adolescent girls' preoccupation with their weight—even if they are not heavy—is called "fat talk." Mothers across the board described their daughters as asking, "Do I look fat in this dress?" Several mothers described their daughters who questioned them as being very thin, the majority of mothers described their daughters as average, and a few remarked that their daughters can't imagine themselves as they really are. In our society, thinness has taken on an undeniable importance: Girls and young women feel it is what attracts men as well as a coterie of "It girl" friends. It is likely that these very friends will not only discuss being fat and feeling fat with one another, but by college will put hours in at the gym yet develop poor eating habits along the way.

The international study commissioned by Dove found that most girls have seen close to 77,500 ads by the time they are twelve years old. InfoNIAC.com reports that of the two thousand girls in the United States and Great Britain who were surveyed for their study, 77 percent thought of themselves as "ugly, fat, or upset" in comparison to the advertisements, and 76 percent have an eating disorder. Christiane Northrup observes in her book *Mother-Daughter Wisdom* that "obesity is as much an eating disorder as bulimia and anorexia," and that "disordered eating" that starts in adolescence "tends to follow women right through adulthood." The National Eating Disorders Association documents that ten million women in the United States are afflicted with an eating disorder and that 80 percent of women are dissatisfied with their appearance.

As Terri Apter points out in her book *You Don't Really Know Me,* mothers can set a poor example regarding weight and thinness, and can "accommodate" a "daughter's destructive habit." Barbara, forty-seven, who works in the catering business and lives in Seattle, describes herself as having influenced her daughters, eighteen and twenty-two, when it comes to weight.

I am always talking about how fat I feel and how I need to go on a diet. I know it's awful for the girls—one daughter is way too worried about her weight and struggles with it. But I've been this way since I was in high school and it's such a part of my life. I do eat lots of fattening things and I love to cook for the family when I have time and I'm not cooking for work. So it hasn't been a healthy environment and I don't know why I can't clean up my act. I go to the gym and then I stop going. I diet and then I eat everything.

It's been terrible for my younger daughter, who worries about what she eats and how much she weighs. I'd say that she has an eating disorder and so do I. Both of us go up and down about ten pounds, on the average, and obsess over it. One of my friends accused me of caring too much about what I eat and how fat I am. I'll talk about how the popcorn had butter on it at the movies, and we'll go to the ice cream stand and I'll want the fattening stuff, not the frozen yogurt. This has really taken its toll on my one daughter. One year she felt too self-conscious to go out and she has body-image problems. I have told her to lose weight on occasion and that she looks fine on other occasions. But I don't think I have any credibility since I'm so crazy about my own weight. My other daughter stays clear, holds on to her sane eating habits, and thinks that we're in bad shape.

Anorexia and Bulimia

As defined by the American Psychiatric Association, anorexia nervosa is the "refusal to maintain weight at or above a minimally normal weight for age and height" and an "intense fear of gaining weight or becoming fat, even though underweight." Bulimia is defined as "recurrent episodes of binge eating" and "a sense of lack of control over eating during the episode." In 2003, the National Alliance for the Mentally Ill reported that more than 90 percent of those afflicted with eating disorders are young women between twelve and twenty-five years old. According to the South Carolina Department of Mental Health, 80 percent of thirteen-year-old girls have attempted to lose weight, one in two hundred women is anorexic, and two to three in one hundred women are bulimic. Their study shows the mortality rate associated with anorexia nervosa as twelve times higher than the death rate of all other causes for females between the ages of fifteen and twenty-four. The Office on Women's Health reports that mature women have eating disorders as well, and according to the National Institute of Mental

Health, 45 percent will be on a diet at some time in their lives.

There is often a strong connection between a mother's issues around eating and weight gain and the daughter's, and the mother's overture to this sensitive topic is a large part of the equation for the daughter. Several other factors also contribute to the outcome:

- How suggestible the daughter is during adolescence regarding body image, as her body is changing
- The daughter's desire to look good for the opposite sex
- The daughter's hope to be popular and socially acceptable
- The daughter's goal to achieve the same appearance as the media suggest she should
- The daughter's poor diet, composed of fast foods and junk foods.

Mothers who are on top of the situation and seek help still report how arduous it is to get a daughter on track. Consider Jordy, forty-six, who lives in Georgia, where she works as a nurse. Although she intervened early on with her daughter, who is now twenty-two, it has been a difficult process.

I knew to get help for my daughter right away, and my husband and I pushed for her to go into treatment. I've tried to be sympathetic and I've tried not to panic during the anorexia that was so frightening. There have been days when I've blamed myself: I thought that I talked about food too much or that I was always on a diet. Other times I see this as her thing, her ailment, and I know she needs treatment. I know she has to stick with the help that I've found for her, and that's half the battle. She'll be okay for a while and then she'll be so preoccupied with this again.

She has missed so much of life, that's how severe this is—school, having friends, a boyfriend—because this takes over. She's been very thin for most of it, too thin, and that's frightening too. She's probably naturally thin, but I'll never know since this has been going on since she was eleven. I see this as something that's now affecting her ability to finish school or to get a job afterward, and I've done so much . . . and I won't give up. I'm plagued by what went wrong all those years ago.

Intolerant Mothers

Similar to mothers who are preoccupied with their daughter's appearance, as discussed in the previous chapter, are those mothers who believe their daughter's weight is reflective of her upbringing. If the mother conveys the message that her daughter doesn't measure up because she isn't thin enough, it only adds to the daughter's battle. Consider Patricia, fifty-six, who lives in a suburb of a Southern city, where she works as an office manager. She has three daughters, who are twenty-six, twenty-eight, and thirty-two.

My middle daughter is very overweight and in my opinion, has done it to herself. Overweight just doesn't cut it and she knows it. She works and lives in a cosmopolitan area where everyone is aiming to be thin. You don't have to be pretty or have a good face, you just have to be thin. She knows this—God knows I've told her over and over—and she doesn't care and she hasn't cared since she was in junior high school. She has what I call self-inflicted fatness and since her sisters are very thin, it's obvious she can go on a diet and stop eating the way that she does. I am thin, too, and I'm sure this is part of the problem.

So when she's eating too much, to me it's a problem. And it's also something she can overcome, if she chooses. She's in her late twenties and should make it better. I'm all over it because I know she can do it and every year that goes by that she doesn't do something is very frustrating to me.

Darla, forty-four, who lives in Detroit and is a political campaign strategist, is greatly concerned by her best friend's approach to her eleven-year-old daughter's eating habits and how this affects Darla's eleven-year-old daughter.

My best friend's daughter is best friends with my daughter, so we spend a lot of time together. This friend is appalled that her daughter isn't built like she is. The friend is petite, probably a size double zero, and obsessed with her body. I think that pregnancy really threw her for a loop because she wasn't her usual self. With her daughter, it's been horrible. This friend basically forbids her daughter from eating any carbs and has her on this rigorous sports schedule. The daughter will sleep over at our home and whatever I make for breakfast, she will eat. Then she is so excited and so happy, but I know I'll hear from her mother by the end of the day. My friend is so strict and she watches her daughter's every move and it's so sad.

All the other mothers in the grade know what's going on and think the daughter is doomed, and the girls are onto it, too. My daughter sees something fishy about the way this friend and her mother interact. What's funny is that the daughter isn't signing on, she isn't paying much attention to her mother. But we all watch and think it's heartbreaking—this girl is just bigger boned than her mother and it won't change no matter how the mother starves her.

Mothers who are aggravated by their daughter's weight, believing that this is a reflection of themselves or a weakness on the daughter's part, are not always keyed in to the possibility that this is a serious matter. A mother who seeks help for her daughter instead, as Jordy did, is on the right path. This also ensures that a mother is there to protect her daughter.

Food as Language

A mother's history with food and body image has tremendous impact upon her daughter. However, for a majority of daughters, a mother's ambiguity over food and the ideal weight remains an unresolved issue. As early as kindergarten the daughters pick up on this, and understand the implications of eating and love, safety and home, juxtaposed with the punishment of dieting and avoidance of sweets and fattening foods. Many mothers are invested in a healthy, balanced diet for their daughters, notwithstanding that they might not subscribe to this goal for themselves. Some mothers are naturally thin, others strive to appear this way and find it hard work. Of the mothers interviewed, 70 percent feel they should disdain food as pleasure and feel quite pressured to be thin and for their daughters to be thin. In listening to this, I thought of Tom Wolfe's novel *The Bonfire of the Vanities,* in which the wives and mothers of pristine young daughters in the upper crust of New York society are described as "social X-rays." The social X-rays are committed to being svelte under any circumstance. If the mothers were victims of the social standard of the 1980s as applied to weight, their innocent grade-school daughters were inescapably in the loop as a birthright.

The Superthin Mother. We've seen this form of mother, one who is so sleek and slender that not only does her daughter not believe she can aspire to this look but other mothers feel the same. Therefore, she's off-putting and can be supercilious about how she presents. These mothers aren't very accepting of a daughter's bad habits, i.e., not eating carefully and not eating merely to survive. They frown upon a daughter who eats for pleasure or who gains weight easily (she's supposed to win this fight by virtue of having a mother who has done so).

The superthin mother ought to be sensitive to how this affects her daughters and be honest about how disciplined she is and what it takes to achieve the desired effect.

The Comfort Food Pusher. While some mothers encourage their daughters to self-soothe through shopping (as noted in Chapter 3), others teach their daughters that comfort food (oatmeal, pasta, rice pudding, ice cream, cookies), will get them through disappointments, including failed romances, college rejections, or job losses. Mothers describe eating these kinds of foods with their daughters as a way to lessen their sorrows and as a mother-daughter venture. However, the remorse for such eating comes with a vengeance—regret and guilt may follow. In this manner, mothers are causing more harm than good and putting into play an eat-and-repent cycle.

This message to the daughter frequently has repercussions, and mothers who subscribe to this crutch should consider the long-term consequences for their daughters.

The Formerly Svelte Mother. A mother who is no longer thin may have her own baggage and some rage for what she's lost, especially if it was hard to come by. Her daughter, whether thin or heavy, suffers her mother's unhappiness and preoccupation with her body image. The mother either continually warns her daughter of how miserable it is to now be heavy and how blissful it was to have been thin *or* she hounds her daughter about her own weight. What happens is the attention paid to both a mother's and a daughter's weight is a constant in their lives.

This mother should consider letting go of her own issues and attempt to be healthy and sound about food and weight, at least for her daughter's sake. It is also effective if she avoids making a big deal of her experience.

The Satisfied Mother. In an ideal situation, the mother who is well balanced in attitude when it comes to weight issues for herself and for her daughter provides a calm, secure environment. Still, a daughter may have her own issues, despite the fact that her mother has none. This daughter may feel less than her mother, either in terms of weight or attitude about food. In such situations, women describe their daughters as resenting how comfortable the mothers are with their bodies and food. This is especially true the more a daughter is caught up in how she appears and her weight.

The satisfied mother, too, would do well to tread lightly with her daughter when it comes to her daughter's weight. Although the mother is in check, this doesn't automatically mean the daughter is in the same place.

Fused Mothers. If the daughter is thin, the mother will be proud and consider herself responsible for this result. If the daughter is heavy, the mother will pressure her daughter because she doesn't want people thinking that she would have such an offspring. Either way, the mother isn't really paying attention to her daughter but to how her daughter's weight and appearance relates to her and how united they are as mother and daughter.

Mothers who confound their daughters' immersion in the world of weight and beauty with their own experience are robbing their daughters of the chance to communicate their feelings. Daughters hope to be understood in this area for who they are, separate from their mothers.

Disciples of Thinness

Not only are daughters persuaded how they should appear, but they are titillated by peers who fall off the wagon. For instance, when Britney Spears gained weight in 2005, the tabloids had a field day, offering up headlines such as "Britney Spears: Weight Gain to 160 Pounds?" on CelebrityDoctor.com. *Star*'s top headline read, "Britney Hits Rock Bottom!" Beyond binge dieting, even childbirth isn't an excuse for celebrities who feel under the gun to keep their figures. The March 2009 issue of *Elle* featured Jessica Alba, who described public expectation to get back in shape after giving birth to Honor, her baby daughter, and how she wore a girdle to facilitate matters.

The idea of an overweight woman finding true love is enough of a joke that a 2001 feature film, *Shallow Hal,* starring Gwyneth Paltrow and Jack Black, was based on this premise. The film challenges the perception that someone who has inner beauty but is overweight isn't a contender for love. Paltrow's character, Rosemary, proves this wrong, which is refreshing because it defies societal proscriptions. The film is also disturbing, however, because it underscores how both women and men are trained to view people.

In the television series *Desperate Housewives*, we observe how a superthin mother, Gabrielle Solis, played by Eva Longoria Parker, treats her two young daughters, Juanita and Celia, who are heavyset and constantly shown eating rich foods. The tension between Juanita, who is only six, and her mother escalates when Gaby, who had gained weight herself and was not in her usual fashionista mode, becomes glamorous again. Mothers who are in the position of being waiflike and stylish while their daughters are not remark that they are damned no matter how this plays out, mother to daughter. Indeed Penelope, forty-nine, who lives in a Southern city and is a mortgage broker, has a twenty-year-old daughter with weight problems.

When my daughter is thin, she's happier. I know it because I'm the same way. So I'll be ten or fifteen pounds overweight and then I'll lose it, but when she gains weight, she's a balloon. No one will date her or marry her if she keeps this up, and I tell her that all the time. Right now she's losing weight, but sometimes she can be thirty pounds more than she should be. She'll accuse me of making her like this, of giving her an eating disorder, of being crazy over my weight and her weight, of putting it on her. But my problem isn't as extreme as hers, which makes her angry, too. It's true that I'm always measuring her portions and policing what she eats—in order to help her.

There's a tendency in our family toward fat, and you have to fight it. I have done all that for her. She's angry and thinks that I'm awful. All I know is that when I speak softly, I'm not heard. This is complicated for her, because she wants to fit in and when

*she was younger, she did. Now, she's too heavy to be treated
properly.*

Consider Vanessa, forty-eight, who lives in a Southern city
where she works in finance and has one daughter, twenty-four,
who is a teacher and has been overweight for the past five years.

*The big deal here is I work hard to be thin and my daughter has
been fat for a long time in a way that borders on an eating disorder. There have been times when I feel responsible for this; I
could have done better so that she wouldn't be so afflicted. I look
at it as one of her vices, and it's my fault, too. My daughter is
sometimes angry about her weight, sometimes not. She is pretty
and smart and aware of how weight can work against you. I feel
very guilty because sometimes it's been such high stress to be
with her—during high school definitely—that I've avoided the
issue, pretending it would go away or that she'd wake up thin.
Maybe that's how this weight issue got so out of control.*

*Today it's a bit different, though she's very heavy, because the
worst years of adolescence are behind us. My daughter has amazing self-confidence—she was a competent child who became a
competent adult. Her self-esteem doesn't seem to be affected by
her weight, and while I'm relieved, I don't see how that can be.*

Societal Mandates

The concern with being thin affects both mothers and daughters across the board, and the attempts for women of all ages to
make it happen can be extreme. In our weight-obsessed society,
young daughters can feel insecure about their weight without

having much recourse. What is key is the way that mothers treat daughters who are overweight, as we have observed in the voices of the mothers above. As it applies to eating disorders, body image, and a preoccupation with weight, the pitfalls are readily in place, including the burden of societal expectations. Mothers, too, contend with these issues as follows:

Equating thin and trim with industrious and driven. Mothers who insinuate that their daughters are lazy because they aren't dieting put their daughters on the defensive. This pervasive judgment applies, ironically, whether the mother herself is weight-conscious or not. Some mothers also second-guess how their daughters ended up overweight without researching any contributing factors or providing healthy alternatives.

Cheryl, forty-nine, who lives in New Hampshire and practices law, has two daughters, twenty-three and twenty-one.

If either daughter gains weight, I say something right away because I don't want it to get out of hand. I won't let them eat cake or junk, and it's been this way since they were small girls. I want them to be athletic and wiry, and not end up having weight issues. I know that on my husband's side it's a problem, and I don't want my girls to be slowed down or upset by this. So why not just avoid it from the start? Maybe I sound tough, but I don't want to dig too far here, I just want my girls to be thin and hardworking.

Exaggerating weight and food intake. Any message a mother gives—serving fattening foods or diet foods, yo-yo dieting, constant talk about her weight—affects her daughter. When a mother is too absorbed with this, the daughter either discards it and rebels, eating what she likes or overtly not caring, or models her mother. Either decision can lead to an eating disorder.

Diana, forty-four, who works in advertising and lives in a small town, has two daughters, eighteen and fifteen, one of whom struggles with her weight.

If my younger daughter isn't looking good because she's put on weight, I carry on and try to get her into the gym and away from junk food. She will start worrying about how she looks and I'll start to worry, too. I was bulimic until I was in my early twenties and I know I have to be careful with the girls. But I also let them know that fat is bad and that all three of us have to work out to look good and not be chunky. I only hope I'm not hurting them with all my rules about eating.

Obsessing over appearing fat. The all-too-familiar "Do I look fat in this dress?" syndrome trickles down to the daughter through her mother's concern for herself or her criticism of her daughter. When she does this to her daughter, she chips away at the daughter's self-esteem. As Marion Woodman explains in her book *Addiction to Perfection,* if the daughter is "bewitched into carrying the mother's anxiety and guilt," only the negative aspects of behavior surface.

Susan, fifty-two, who lives in the Southeast and works in hotel management, has a twenty-year-old daughter who has recently gained weight.

My daughter's weight wasn't an issue until she got to college. Until then I had done a good job and she was in shape. She'd

*stay away from fatty foods and had a positive self-image. I
purposely didn't say much in those days. Once she started to
gain weight and would ask me if I thought she'd gained weight,
I had to be honest. I didn't want to hurt her feelings, but I
wanted her to know she was gaining weight and that it wasn't
healthy for her. I made a fuss about what she ate and pointed
out that she'd been drinking at school. I didn't want her to be
upset, but I had to remind her how unhappy she'd be in the
long run.*

Lying about the problem. There are those mothers who
believe that their eating disorders have kept them thin and that
it can work for their daughters as well. This is rarely discussed,
but in such cases both mother and daughter are bound by a
common lie—that they do not have an eating disorder. In this
case, the mother is too caught up in her own drama to help her
daughter, and instead is leading her down a dangerous path.

Angel, forty-three, who lives in Connecticut and works at a
pharmacy, has a nineteen-year old daughter.

*I tell my daughter not to worry about her weight, but I'm not be-
ing honest because I've got such issues about it. I pretend that
I'm not worried how much I weigh, but I am and my daughter
has learned it from me. I actually got rid of the scale in our house
because I knew she was weighing herself a few times a day the
way I do it. I want to stop being so crazy about this myself and
help my daughter to be normal, but it may be too late. She's been
watching me all these years and when anyone asks if she has an
eating disorder, I say, no, of course not. This isn't something I'm
willing to talk about.*

A mother who is able to accept herself and her daughter for their body types has self-confidence. Dr. Claire Owen recommends that the message from mother to daughter become: "'I am a healthy, attractive person who isn't worried about what size I wear,' rather than being so preoccupied with one's looks in terms of weight."

Fighting Back

With so much information paid to the hazards of eating disorders and the significance of distorted body image for women of all ages, it is no longer a question of mothers being cognizant of the problem—it's inescapable. In addition to studies, the news has covered famous women who have wrestled with this syndrome. An early and shocking story was that of rock 'n' roll singer Karen Carpenter's tragic battle with anorexia. Carpenter died on February 4, 1983, from cardiac arrest that resulted from complications of anorexia nervosa. Actress Jane Fonda has been open about her problems, and the public was well aware of the late Princess Diana's issues, according to CaringOnline.com. The Web site also reports the eating disorders of Britney Spears, Alanis Morissette, Carré Otis, Ashlee Simpson, and Calista Flockhart. Whether it's a question of being in good company or a cautionary tale, mothers and daughters are obviously aware of how common and pervasive the problem is.

If we think this is simply a matter of how women interpret their weight and that with all this knowledge, there would be more understanding, an article that ran in *Marie Claire* in October 2005 proves the contrary. "Gaining Weight Cost Me My Job," by Jennifer Friedlin, shows us how sexist and societal the problem remains. Friedlin tells the tale of a woman named Renee

Gaud, who worked at the Borgata, a hotel and casino in Atlantic City, and was fired when she went from a size 4 to a size 6. Gaud, thirty-five at the time, was told that "Borgata Babes don't go up in dress size" and describes how mortified she was when her supervisor advised her of this. "Even though I've never been fat, like most women, I've always been conscious about my weight," said Gaud. The management informed her that a weight restriction was in effect and that waitresses who gained more than 7 percent of their current weight would be suspended. If they didn't lose it within three months, their job would end. Although Gaud and another waitress filed a complaint with the New Jersey Division on Civil Rights, the idea that such a policy exists at all is chilling. While not all women are placed in this position in their line of work, it's little wonder that a self-consciousness about one's weight exists.

Fortunately, women are fighting back, as described in an article that ran in *The New York Times* on May 31, 2009, "Bingeing on Celebrity Weight Battles," by Jan Hoffman. Hoffman writes, "In the last year, so many celebrities have shared their body battles with us: Carnie Wilson. Kathy Ireland. Valerie Bertinelli. Marie Osmond. Melissa Joan Hart. Up, down, Up, down." Hoffman writes that Kirstie Alley weighed 228 at one point and lost 75 pounds on the Jenny Craig diet—and gained it back, as shown to us in a photograph.

The article also points out that Oprah Winfrey's weight has been newsworthy over the years, and that "health experts say that many famous dieters flaunt weight-loss goals that are unrealistic for most obese women." What's interesting is that Hoffman then reports that a twenty-two-year-old woman, Gabrielle Gregg, who weighs two hundred pounds, is blogging about why she doesn't feel "disgusting," and that several other young women, ages thirty-one and twenty-nine, are beginning to question why they have to feel that their bodies are ugly. And so the debacle over weight, self-perception, and cultural norms continues. For example, Janie, fifty-nine, who is from Pennsylvania, where she works in public relations, and has a twenty-nine-year-old daughter, has been involved with her daughter's weight since she was small.

Because my family has weight problems, I always suggested that my daughter eat modestly, and I tried to provide healthy alternatives at home. However, if she gained weight, I never said anything because I knew how it hurt me when my parents nagged me. Her grandparents often made insensitive comments about her weight, and I knew how this hurt her, so I always told her to ignore those comments. She was an athlete from the age of five and knew she had to keep her weight down to compete, so she ultimately became a self-regulator.

Bari, thirty-nine, who lives on the coast in Massachusetts and works in a spa, has a sixteen-year-old daughter and a five-year-old daughter.

My older daughter was beyond normal, she was so worried about weight for the last three years. And then suddenly she changed and now she's gained weight and doesn't seem to care. I think it's because she's not with a boy and isn't boy crazy. So after my worrying that what she ate wasn't enough for her and trying to serve her the right food and not let her starve, I have a new problem. Now she's ordering French fries and ice cream. She'll drink juices and sodas when we go out together. I have to say to her to be careful of the calories. My big talk with her when she was too thin was about not being too thin and now I have to talk to her about not being too fat. This is as bad as being too

*thin and going hungry. I know she's not out of the woods yet—so
I'm not, either.*

A Sense of Self Tied to Food and Weight

For so many women, there isn't a day that goes by where thought
isn't given to one's weight and food intake. The self-recriminations
are constant: "Tomorrow I'll start my diet." "Today was a bad
day." "My boyfriend is a bad influence." "I felt like eating it." "I
had to have it." Whatever a mother's best intention is, it is challenging for a daughter to defy the reasoning behind her mother's
comments, let alone decipher how it feels to be worried continually about her weight. Most mothers interviewed for this book
said they had discussed food and weight with their daughters by
the time the girls were seven. More than 75 percent of the mothers said they are interested in proper diets and exercise, while
40 percent felt strongly that until their daughters were ten, it
was important to allow them to eat whatever they want. "Why
ruin the birthday party?" remarked the mother of a thirty-one-
year-old daughter who has battled her weight her entire life.
"That's what I told myself and then it was too late—she's
bulimic because she started to gain weight in seventh grade and
then got into trouble with it." The counterargument was made
by another mother, who said, "I always said as little as I could
about what to eat when my girls were small. I didn't want to
make it a big deal, and today it's one area where all three have
an okay attitude."

According to an article that ran in *The New York Times* on
January 8, 2009, by Tara Parker-Pope, "School Popularity Affects Girls' Weights," if a girl doesn't think she's popular, she is
at a greater risk for gaining weight. The study that Parker-Pope

references, published in the *Archives of Pediatrics & Adolescent Medicine,* reported that of almost 4,500 girls between the ages of twelve and eighteen, teens who rated themselves as having a low social standing at school had gained more weight two years later than those who thought more highly of themselves. In fact, those girls who gave themselves a low rating had a 70 percent higher risk of weight gain. Other factors include diet and a mother's weight, which underscores what we have witnessed among the mothers' voices in this book.

The economy is another contributor to weight gain for teenage girls. Tom Jacobs explains this in his article that ran on May 6, 2009, on the Web site of Miller-McCune, "Economic Expansion: Teen Girls Gain Weight During Downturns." Several mothers discussed how they themselves are binge eating because they are nervous about money or have lost their jobs since December 2008. Thus, this becomes a new trigger in the ongoing troubles concerning women and weight, and mothers and daughters can be inextricably connected. "Sure, I'm worried about work, and so is my daughter," begins the mother of a twenty-year-old. "I've taken out a student loan the and my husband lost his job last year. I only work part-time and no one can count on my salary. My daughter moved home to cut costs and commutes to school. The two of us watch TV and eat potato chips or ice cream together. Then we look at *People* magazine and want to cry at how thin everyone is."

Ameliorating Matters

Keep your own preoccupation with weight from spilling into your daughter's life. If you have issues of your own surrounding this, it's important to put them aside and to emphasize that being a certain weight and size is not tantamount to success and happiness.

Guard your daughter against detrimental eating habits. Discourage food as a crutch and a form of self-soothing. Also dissuade rigorous dieting as a penance after "bad" eating and a binge/purge syndrome, which is fundamentally unsafe.

Have conversations regarding the negative effects of media messaging about body image and weight. It is important to point out how destructive this is and how often girls and young women are concerned with how they measure up.

Do not pressure your daughter about her weight. While it's fine to provide healthy foods and to encourage exercise, too much expectation placed on the daughter only exacerbates this touchy topic. It's best to strike a balance.

Take action immediately if your daughter show signs of an eating disorder. If your daughter becomes preoccupied with her weight or has a weight fluctuation and new eating patterns, seek counseling. This applies to daughters of all ages.

Chapter 6

✤

Your Closest Friends Are Your Biggest Rivals

Underestimating Female Friendships

- Do you tell your daughter how important her girlfriends are but fail to set this example yourself?
- Has your daughter observed you be insincere with a female friend?
- Does your daughter know you don't really trust your best friend?
- Have you ever advised your daughter to cancel plans with a girlfriend at the last minute?
- Have you ever encouraged your daughter to "use" a friend?

If any of the above questions apply to you, you are misguiding your daughter when it comes to her female friends.

IT'S SOMEWHAT TROUBLING that none of your three daughters has a best friend, and you suspect it's because you don't care enough about your own friends to have shown them how this could work. Since your eldest daughter is in her first year at a college that is three thousand miles away, you are beginning to think you'd better coach the younger daughters another way. Perhaps warning your daughters against confiding in their girlfriends and reminding them that girls can be backstabbers might not be the only advice to give. Until your first daughter left for college, it was a secure feeling to know that your daughters had one another—they're close in age and you come from a tightly knit family. What you couldn't anticipate, however, is how different each of your daughters is from the other, and how much they each seek out groups of their own.

While your first daughter is the bookworm and is having trouble socially, your middle daughter is gregarious, drawn to a fast crowd, and puts her friends ahead of her schoolwork and family. You wonder how she got like this and advise her to tone down her schedule and steer away from this crowd. Although she refuses to listen, your youngest tells all and is frequently disappointed in her friends—devastated if a plan is canceled. She takes these friendships to heart, and there's often tremendous drama if she isn't included. So you calm her down, distract her—whatever you can do. After all, there are some mothers right in the ring with their girls. Still, you can't shed the sense that these friendships that seem so dire to your daughters are overrated.

The Tangled Web

Female friendships, at every age and stage, are so important yet so intricate—and many times disconcerting. In my research on female friendships, women remarked that being reunited with an old friend was one of their top five experiences, and that they tend to stick with a difficult friend even when they realize the relationship is flawed. There is little question of how much a mother's interpretation of friendship, combined with her own behavior, will affect her daughter.

If a mother is a loyal friend, devoted to these relationships, her daughter understands this can be the case. If a mother is envious, dissatisfied with her own life, and one who complains about her female peers at work as well as her personal friends, her daughter will take this into account. If a mother is dismissive of the idea of close, reliable female friends, her daughter, in seeking out her mother's advice, might realize that her mother is not the best barometer, and will come to her own conclusions.

With so much peer pressure placed upon our daughters today, it is more significant than ever before that mothers lay the groundwork for female friendship and guide their daughters in how to deal with failed relationships as well as how to recognize valuable connections. That said, the mothers who were interviewed on this subject had deep concerns about their daughters' friends, the repercussions of certain relationships, and their own ambivalences.

Kindergarten Onward

As early on as kindergarten our daughters learn the value of a true friend and the energy it takes to find this quality. Enough mothers responded to this chapter with memories of how desirous their daughters were at the age of five or six to fit in and to be included, and how early the socializing kicks in. Categories of friends and typecasting are already in play, and daughters know too well who the popular girl is, the athlete, the brainy one, the wallflower, the beauty, by second or third grade. The food chain is apparent; everyone fills her designated spot. By high school, a young woman's place among friends is defined, with an alpha girl as the leader. According to the *Longman Dictionary of Contemporary English*, the alpha girl is "a teenage girl who is the most important and powerful member of a group of girls who regularly spend time together. Alpha girls are typically confident, attractive, and determined to be successful." Those who follow the alpha girls around are the beta and gamma girls: meeker, milder. Whatever style of friend your daughter is or surrounds herself with, a mother has input on some level yet is powerless to control or stop the cliques, damage, and mean girl behavior simultaneously. Thus from a young age and throughout life a daughter has the lessons of her mother in how she approaches her female friends, and she has the actual challenges—both positive and negative.

Although the world has changed greatly since the mothers I interviewed were in grade school (most mothers report that their daughters had computers by nursery school, cell phones by seventh grade, BlackBerry smartphones by ninth grade, iPhones by senior year), the machinations of female friendship have not changed very much. Consider Claire, thirty-eight, who lives in Washington, D.C., where she does volunteer work. Her understanding of her ten-year-old daughter is that she is extraordinarily shy with her friends, just as Claire was at this age.

My daughter already has self-esteem issues when it comes to her friends. She was recently invited to a birthday party at a Y pool and she wouldn't go because she wouldn't wear a bathing suit. She is self-conscious with all of her friends and it upsets me—it reminds me of how I was. I look back on those days and realize it was a waste—I could have been more popular and

*less tortured if only my mother or my older sisters had realized
what I was feeling. Instead, for years, they'd tell me to pull it
together.*

*The problem here is that I'm probably not much different
now, except that I'm an adult. It took until high school to know
that I fit in and that I could have lots of friends. I've worked at
these relationships and I still do and my daughter sees this. I've
spoken with her about true friends but she knows that I really
want her to belong. Sometimes I wonder if I've been making it
easier or harder for her. I'm torn—I want to make it better and
also for her to learn the skills. But do I know the skills well
enough to teach her?*

While Claire questions whether she can be a role model for
her daughter, Bernadette, sixty-three, who lives in the South
and manages a family-owned hotel, views her role as integral
to her daughters' development. She has four daughters: thirty-
two, thirty-six, thirty-eight, and forty.

*I have stressed what I thought was important with my girls
since they were very little. Their father was an impressive man
in our African-American community and he would have opened
doors for them, but he died. After that, it was up to me and I
knew I had to control the girls' environment and that meant not
only where they were educated, but who their friends were. I
wanted my girls to go to good schools and to meet good people
and to have options. This meant watching very closely who they
befriended. I didn't want anyone to get in the way of their chances
for success. It might not have mattered if we lived in another
area, but it mattered here. Primarily my daughters' friends came
from our church and from their schools. My youngest daughter
was harder to keep on track than the older ones, and I suppose I*

was a bit weary by then. But basically, I had the same approach every time: I watched closely, and if someone wasn't up to par, I let the girls know how and why. My message was that friends make all the difference, and you have to be careful every step of the way. I'd say now that they are adults that it worked, but I was strict and probably didn't pay enough individual attention.

In the interviews above, we recognize mothers who have sought ways to mitigate circumstances with their daughters in order to have impact. While mothers long to safeguard their daughters when it comes to their friendships, teaching life skills is a more practical endeavor.

Cautious Mothers

More than ever before, friendship as the panacea for our ills is shown to us. At the same time, the inherent pitfalls in the relationships become obvious. This mixed message heightens the problem for mothers and their daughters, especially those mothers and daughters who want the same results from their friendships: commitment, compassion, a sense of belonging, and trust. For daughters, the stakes are raised via twenty-first-century slickness, comprising Facebook, text messaging, cell phones, and materialism. In his *New York Times* article "Friends, Until I Delete You," Douglas Quenqua explores the protocol of unfriending via Facebook. "There seem to be several varieties, ranging from the completely impersonal to the utterly vindictive," writes Quenqua, describing being dismissed by a Facebook friend as "a jarring experience, especially considering that the person who dumped you at some point either requested you as a friend or accepted your request. . . ." Notwithstanding this latest vehicle for the dark side of female bonds, Alan Bloom warns in his book *Love and Friendship* that being isolated from our friends and lacking a "profound contact with other human beings" keeps us from true closeness and intimacy.

Since Facebook (http://www.checkfacebook.com) reports to have more than 33 million users under twenty-four, close to 23 million users ages twenty-five to thirty-four, and 27 million users ages thirty-five to fifty-four, we can rest assured that whatever the ages of our daughters, there is a great likelihood that they belong. While daughters hope to be in this loop, there are mothers who worry that Facebook harms their daughters' self-esteem and raises the ante on cruelty among young women. Consider Merry, thirty-five, who lives in Phoenix, where she works as an administrative assistant. She has one fourteen-year-old daughter and has warned her to be wary of her girlfriends.

I see my daughter as very influenced by the media and hip-hop and Beyoncé. She's been through enough with her friends to want more guy friends than girlfriends. I have taught her to not trust her girlfriends, but the truth is, she's learned on her own what it's like. Already, it's the same old story: At first she's with a group and everyone is e-mailing one another like crazy, they're all on Facebook, and then it turns ugly. So my way of showing her what works is doing things with my sisters and my mother and not with my friends. She knows this is my support system and that I don't rely on women outside of family. My message is loud and clear—friendships can go sour.

Similarly, Dara, fifty-nine, who lives in Los Angeles, where she works part-time as a mediator, views having a clan of friends as an unrewarding experience. She has passed this on to her two daughters, thirty and twenty-four, who purposely avoid cliques.

I don't know how things got so out of hand with my older daughter and her friends, but it was a reminder of what it was like for me, years ago. I made all these efforts with my friends and it was constant disappointment. I wanted to be close with women, but sometimes it was too tense and not very comfortable. I was hoping this daughter would have an easier time if I was easy on her when it came to her social life. But it feels like it's my fault in some way that she's had issues—maybe I didn't teach her or my example proves reliable friends are rare. So she has a few, but she doesn't have one group and she doesn't seek out friends like some women her age do.

My other daughter is also picky and not looking to run with a certain group. Both girls are very close with me, but we also have our own lives. And I see that both girls are close with a handful of friends—they expect a lot from them. Sometimes I hear stories about how a friend did something wrong, and I worry that the girls don't have enough selection for this to happen. Then I say to myself, we should just stick to whomever we can—some kind of group—and have less hope.

Often the mother has shown her daughter her own vulnerability when it comes to her friends and her desire to belong, and the daughters take this to heart. "Daughters are not always equipped for the ups and downs with their girlfriends because their mothers wrestle with their own friendships and haven't been able to sort it out," comments Dr. Ronnie Burak.

Our Accelerated World of Friendship

In a culture where *The New York Times* runs a front page article, "For Teenagers, Hello Means 'How About a Hug?'" by Sarah Kershaw, we know that the ramifications and innuendos of relationships loom large for our children. Kershaw describes "girls embracing girls, girls embracing boys, boys embracing each other—the hug has become the favorite social greeting when teenagers meet or part these days." According to sociologists, Kershaw reports, the hug is about young people being "less cynical and individualistic and more loyal to the group."

When I mentioned the trend to mothers interviewed for this chapter, several commented that their daughters are open and intimate with their friends in ways they themselves had never been. "I'm sort of stiff with my closest friends," one mother told me. "And my daughter is so affectionate. Everyone seems to be her closest buddy." Another mother remarks, "I wouldn't have the guts to be as out there as my daughter and take the chances she does with her friends. But she seems to get more out of the relationships than I ever did." A third mother views it in another light: "My daughter doesn't want to take responsibility for her friendships and she doesn't want to offend anyone. That's how she sticks with them, by being sort of superficial." Mothers describe their daughters as choosing one of the types of friends cited below or being one of these types themselves:

Controlling Friends. Sometimes it's easier for daughters to choose friends who manipulate situations and take charge. This usually happens if the mother is controlling and runs the show, and it's comfortable because it's familiar. Lisee, fifty-four, with two daughters, twenty-three and twenty-seven, welcomes her daughters' friends who call the shots.

I've pushed for my daughters to be popular. One gets noticed first, and her friends gravitate to her. My other daughter is also popular but more on the quiet side. Both like their friends to organize things and to have strong opinions—which is sort of what I'm like as a mother.

The It Girl. When the daughters are under the age of twelve, this type of friend is more accessible, since she's just gearing up for her role. Daughters find that this friend provides immediate social acceptance, which mothers welcome. The "It girl" can be kind or merciless, and even ambitious mothers flinch when she's ruthless or overshadows her daughter. Mothers both encourage and discourage their daughters from the It girl. Indeed, Ronnie, forty-seven, with one twenty-two-year-old daughter, steers her toward the It girl.

I wanted my daughter to be outstanding and she turned out to be offbeat. I begged her to have friends who were in the mainstream. That way, at least she'd survive socially. But sometimes it's backfired and made my daughter feel self-conscious. I wish she could hang on with the popular girl, for her own sake.

The Gofer. A mother whose daughter is shy and eager to please will welcome anyone who befriends her daughter. Mothers with It girls or stronger daughters than a "gofer" are often perplexed that their daughter has such a retiring friend. If the mother is a gofer or was a gofer, she prays for her daughter to find her own voice.

Deborah, forty-four, hopes that her nineteen- and twenty-one-year-old daughters will shine eventually.

My girls were raised to be good girls and they've been very careful with their friends. They've always taken the backseat and I haven't said much. They've done well in school and have tried to please their friends. I'm waiting for this phase to finish, for them to be more alive.

The Prom Queen. The emphasis placed on beauty (as evidenced in Chapter 4), cannot be disputed, and as we have seen, mothers go to great lengths to capitalize on their daughters' appearances. Beauty mixed with popularity still renders the "prom queen," a highly coveted position. Not only do mothers want their daughters to achieve this, but they also want them to be friends with the contenders, the inner sanctum. Dora, fifty-one, with three daughters, eighteen, twenty-two, and twenty-five, has pushed for this recognition with each daughter.

I was the prom queen and it was a great tribute, so my girls know I believe in it. Two were runner-up and one won. It's not only winning the crown but being this kind of girl. They are friendly and pleasant to everyone—not too friendly, so that your top secrets become gossip—just friendly enough.

The Leader. The mother-daughter bond is such that a mother who is a leader among her female friends has conditioned her daughter for the same destiny. While there are also daughters as leaders who have gofer mothers, more than 65 percent of the mothers who are leaders have daughters who become leaders.

Laurie, thirty-nine, who has a fourteen-year-old daughter, describes her as "leading the pack," and would be unhappy if her daughter didn't sustain this role among her friends.

My daughter has been groomed to succeed with friends, in school, and at her volunteer job, because that's how I am. I have seen her potential and I've pushed her since I know the perks. Her friends depend on her and she comes through—she knows what to do. She's watched me for years and she knows how to make it work.

In any of the above descriptions, mothers are behind the scenes. Dr. Barton Goldsmith recommends that the mother emphasize balance in these relationships and not put her interests at the center. "If the mother is overly enthused about her daughter's friends for whatever reasons, and attributes to them a maturity these young women don't have, it's tough on the daughter. She won't be able to figure a way out of the emotional problems of friendship, and her mother isn't helpful if she has her own motives."

Social Games/Social Climbing

As if the fast-paced situations described above aren't enough, there are those mothers who regard their daughters' friends as serving a social purpose. In a culture where gaggles of females have more power than a pair of friends, the glue of these groups is frequently a common interest. If it appears expedient, some mothers will encourage their daughters to develop a specific interest or a sport "du jour." A mother who is invested in social networking will encourage this, as if her daughter is her only hope. The danger here is that the mother might be blind to her daughter's desires and put her own ambitions first.

Mothers as Opportunists

Although a mother knows instinctively who is the wrong friend for her daughter, there can be a conflict of interest that causes a mother to promote a relationship nonetheless and put her own interests ahead of her daughter's. This transpires if the mother believes that this friend can somehow be useful to her daughter, and deliberately overlooks the negatives. In this scenario, the daughter's circle of friends represents what the mother always wanted for herself and was not able to achieve. Ironically, the daughter may reject her mother's intentions, partly as an act of defiance, partly because keeping up can be exhausting and she *isn't* an opportunist. When pushed to this extent, the mother's need confuses the issue and the purity of female friendship may elude the daughter.

Consider Stella, forty-three, who lives in a Midwestern city, where she works in the restaurant business and is raising two daughters, nineteen and sixteen.

I was always aware of what girls and their families would be good for my girls. I knew the private school I wanted for them and pushed through connections to get them in. When one daughter couldn't cut it academically, I made sure that my younger daughter did okay. I got her tutored early on so she could stay. I thought this school offered her a better life and this was a better place. If she had also disappointed me, I'm not sure what I would have done—I never had the chances she has. But luckily, she came through and has managed to stay in this school with these friends. The only thing I find is that she doesn't care about it the way that I do. I have to talk her into going to the parties on weekends and being involved with after-school activities that will help her to stay in the loop.

Daughters Who Rebel

Because her mother had such power over her own friends for her entire life, Siddalee Walker, the protagonist of Rebecca Wells's novel *Divine Secrets of the Ya-Ya Sisterhood*, resists the experience. However, once Sidda seeks her diva mother out, her mother sends her the scrapbook of her past and the secrets unfold. The reader imagines the Ya-Ya Sisterhood as clannish, daring, and devoted. But what is striking is how Sidda chooses *not* to repeat the intensity of her mother's place with these women during the Depression in Louisiana. Rather, Sidda forges a career for herself and opts for a more solitary existence. Consider Bethany, thirty-eight, a stay-at-home mother living in a small town in Ohio with her two daughters, thirteen and eleven. Bethany is infuriated by her daughters' refusal to be with friends who suit her.

My daughters are very independent when it comes to their friends. I'm raising them in the same place that I grew up and I know where they should be in terms of their friends. And they should get started now, like I did, so that it lasts through high school. But already they don't listen to me and I'm at my wits' end. Sometimes I'm forced to spell this out for them—the advantages of it all with the right friends. And as different as the girls are from each other, they're the same about this. They're very independent and they like who they like. It upsets me to see them giving up these chances to have a better social life.

Mothers who venture into their daughters' social lives are not considering what is healthy for the daughter and would do well to question their motivations. A daughter's search for friends and society may differ from what a mother hopes for, but recognizing what works and satisfies the daughter is at the heart of the matter.

Buddying It Up: Mothers and Daughters as BFFs.

According to a survey by Kelton Research, 71 percent of women between the ages of twenty-one and fifty-four believe their mothers to be "one of their best friends." On the reality television series *The Real Housewives of New Jersey,* Danielle, forty-seven, one of the four housewives, remarks that her two daughters, ages twelve and sixteen, are her "best friends." Danielle describes her daughters as her "girlfriends" and only hopes that their lives will be better than what she's had. But can it be that the mother suffices for her daughter as her best friend rather than a mentor? Indeed, Ashley, forty-two, who lives in Maryland, where she works as an administrator, believes that she and her sixteen-year-old daughter are bonded in a way that is successful and views their "best friendship" as viable.

My daughter and I are so close. She would tell me if anything is wrong and we confide in one another. My daughter watched me go through an ugly divorce and how I cling to my job. We take care of each other and we understand each other. I also think that a few of her friends have betrayed her and that makes our closeness more important. If she could count on her friends, maybe she wouldn't count on me as much. And I've had this stuff with my friends, too, so I know how it is for her and we talk about it. I would say that my daughter is my best friend. I'm already worried about the day she leaves for college. I wish I could go with her. At the same time, I know there's room for the right girlfriends, and that won't change how close we are.

Another interviewee who feels as connected to her daughter is Naomi, fifty-three, who lives in northern California and practices medicine. She and her daughter, twenty-seven, who recently married, are now separated by physical distance.

I am so lonely without my daughter and there is no one who can make it okay. I look back and see how maybe it wasn't a good idea to lean on her all these years and for her to lean on me. It got us through the bad times, but I doubt it helped my social life or hers. I probably should have encouraged her to have more friends her age and I should have had more friends. Then I wouldn't have pushed her to be my pal and it would be easier today. She's married to a great guy and this helps her, but where does it leave me?

While Ashley and Naomi are convinced of the strength and legitimacy of their best friendship with their daughters, it's important to note that this is frequently about a void in the mother's life. Not only does this hamper the daughter, but as circumstances change for either mother or daughter, the "best friendship" might be fractured, while the mother-daughter connection, if based on the mother's supremacy, would not be. Beyond that, the idea of a mother and daughter bond preempting age-appropriate bonds—for both mother and daughter—is unsuitable. Consider Liza, forty-seven, who lives in the Northwest and is a clothing designer. She has a fifteen-year-old daughter.

I asked too much of my daughter at times and I'm sorry now. I was going through a rough patch and I told her too much. She began to feel responsible for me and it sort of robbed her of her childhood. For a long time—about four years—I let this happen and I led the way. And then one day I saw how torn she was about being with me, and keeping me company and not getting to go out with her friends. She's older now and it doesn't matter what my life is about—she's entitled to hers. I had to let go and I knew I shouldn't have ever started this business of her being my best friend. Her best friend, nice or not at times, should be someone in her class. So now I know, and it's better for both of us. I joined a gym and I'm taking Spanish classes to meet people.

When the mothers and daughters are enmeshed, and mothers defend their position of best friends forever with their own daughters, the mother-daughter bond is in jeopardy, despite the fact that it might "feel right" for both parties. As therapist Brenda Szulman remarks, a mother-daughter relationship should be hierarchal. "If the mother's ego is intact, she focuses on the daughter with the right amount of separateness. If the mother pushes to be closer than this, it blurs the picture and keeps both mother and daughter from seeking outside relationships that are age appropriate."

Keeping Our Daughters Safe

What mother doesn't know the duplicity of female friendship, and hasn't unresolved issues of her own? Because female friendship is fraught with betrayal, mothers want to screen their daughters from the start. As Carol Gilligan and Lyn Mikel

Brown note in their book, *Meeting at the Crossroads,* "The slip-
periness of words and the treachery of relationships which ten-
and eleven-year-old girls are acutely aware of have become
solidified and normalized by twelve and thirteen." What follows
is self-consciousness and caution, an inability for these girls to
express themselves because, as the authors explain, they are
protecting themselves "by removing their deepest feelings and
thoughts from public scrutiny."

As daughters move through adolescence into adulthood,
they are trying to survive the machinations of female friends
while simultaneously attempting to understand the complicated bond with their mothers. Trust looms as a large issue if
the mother doesn't exhibit trust herself with her daughter or
if the mother doesn't believe that she can trust her own friends.
Hitherto, the daughter has looked to her mother for safety in an
unsafe world; by junior high school, the daughter leaps into the
world of much more vulnerable relationships with her female
peers. Mothers of daughters who are young, adolescent, or
adult may end up standing by, watching their daughters floun-
der in the all too familiar debacles with their friends, despite
the mother's knowledge and experience. Most mothers describe
themselves as rendered powerless when a daughter is hurt by
her peers. Consider Natalie, forty-four, who works in fashion,
lives in New York, and has an eighteen-year-old daughter.

*My daughter is struggling with her friends and I feel like I've
seen it all. Everything that happens to her has happened to
me, but I know, after all these years, to keep quiet or I seem
negative. I want to fight for her, and I can't. She says very little
and suffers. I sometimes wonder about that and how it's changed
since junior high for her and the truth is, it hasn't changed, it's
just worse. I know to stay away from my friends if they're using*

me or to avoid those who don't come through. Sure, my daughter could learn from me and I try to talk to her about it. I've suggested having fewer friends, a handful of friends who are for real—over and over again I say this. But she always wants this whole group and they aren't very nice and don't have any values at all.

In contrast to Natalie is Maura, fifty-two, who lives in northern California and describes herself as a less-than-perfect friend and views her daughter, twenty-three, as having learned from her, bad habits and all.

I pretend to be sincere sometimes, in order to get what I want with my friends. I can be very warm or I can distance myself. I'll be in touch and then pull away and my daughter has these same traits. I have called her on it, but what can I say? It's worked for me and if she thinks I'm phony or out for myself, she also sees the positive side. I'd rather be the friend who inflicts some pain and has some muscle than be the one who is falling apart because her friends are doing awful things. What happens to her is that there's something planned and then a problem and the friends do some nasty stuff—over a boy or a party, a roommate. . . . My daughter knows to look caring, to look good and then do what's best for her. There are different friends for different times, and that's what I've always said. Going for what you need isn't all bad. I tell myself that at least my daughter and I aren't the ones who are crumbling—but it feels slightly nasty to be in our shoes, too.

Mothers have confided that a daughter's pain over her female friends is extremely disturbing to them. Debbie Mandel, author of *Addicted to Stress,* views a mother's involvement with her daughter's social life as a stressor. "The mother today is very close to her daughter, and this intimate level includes shared details about unfortunate friendships. To be responsible for another person's happiness—in this case, one's daughter's happiness—is anxiety provoking."

A Mother's Message

Encourage self-esteem. If your daughter feels good about herself, she will attract appropriate friends and be the right kind of friend in return. It isn't about "fitting in" but about having confidence and knowing yourself.

Discourage clannishness. While it might be appealing initially to see one's daughter a part of the "in" crowd, in the end, it's giving tacit approval to being unfriendly or unkind to "outsiders." Furthermore, a daughter who values popularity or is a social climber has less chance of being empathetic and developing authentic friendships.

Teach responsibility in friendships. If we have taught our daughters to make excuses (as discussed in Chapter 1), they might not know how to be a dependable friend or how to be supportive to a friend in need.

Do not expect your daughter to be your best friend. Being best friends with your daughter can stymie your daughter from reaching out to females her age and confuses issues in mother-daughter relationships. A mother is a teacher, a protector, and a role model, and for this to have an effect, a hierarchy should be in place.

Guard against female rivalry. If the mother herself is competitive with her friends, this is a model for the daughter. If a mother feels positive about herself and isn't locked in a rivalry with her friends and coworkers, this, too, is a model for the daughters.

Encourage successful female bonds. Advise your daughter to cultivate healthy friendship, and share your own strengths and weaknesses and experiences in this arena with her.

Chapter 7

❋

I Don't Think He's Good Enough for You

Sex and Love: Approaches to Romance

- Did you raise your daughter to expect a knight in shining armor?
- Have you been cynical when talking about romantic love with your daughter?
- Are you the one who taught her about sex?
- Does your daughter think of you as sexless and clueless?
- Has your daughter watched you slug it out in an unhappy romance?
- Do you encourage your daughter to marry well rather than for true love?

If you answered yes to any of the above, you've given your daughter mixed messages about romance and sex.

YOU CONSIDER YOURSELF fortunate that your marriage is still intact, but the truth is romance isn't at the heart of it anymore. So while your romantic life is diminished, your eighteen-year-old daughter's romantic life is flourishing. You have watched her with her boyfriend these past six months, and love is in the air—and so is your relief that she's not in junior high anymore, going out in groups and doing all sorts of things with boys she described as "just friends." Now that she is a bit more mature and has moved into a steady relationship, she confides in you on occasion. When she does, you are very matter-of-fact and conscientious: You arranged for her to visit a doctor and to get birth control, and you signed her up for the HPV vaccine. But when it comes to talking about sex, a thorny subject, despite how open you are about most topics, you are uneasy. Sometimes you wish you were a gay divorcée, like some of your cool single friends who have active sex lives and no commitment to any one man. They seem so carefree and have conversations with their daughters that you can't imagine having, trading dating secrets. Instead you are a "good girl" who lost her sexual and romantic self years ago when your children were toddlers. Your daughter's budding romantic life reminds you that you are stale and haven't all the answers. To top it off, you remember what a true romantic you used to be.

The Lure of Romantic Love

Romantic love is elusive for the best of us and uplifting when it goes as expected. It's little wonder that women across the country are eager to read articles about First Lady Michelle Obama's relationship with her husband and how he describes time set aside for her on a daily basis as "Michelle time." In a June 7, 2009, *New York Times* article by Jan Hoffman, "If They Can

Find Time for Date Night . . . ," Hoffman details the Obamas' visit to New York City for dinner and a Broadway show as a promise that the president "fulfilled"—and one that evokes "sounds of romance envy" from women in long-standing marriages with children. Hoffman reports that on *The Daily Show,* Jon Stewart "screeched, 'How do you compete with that?'" and "warned Mr. Obama, 'Take it down a notch, dude!'"

Women of all ages yearn for this connection to their partners and envision it as a panacea for their troubles. As the world grows more complicated, romantic love is simultaneously idealized and narrowed in scope, offering safeness, assuaging pain, and assuring happiness ever after. In her book *Why We Love: The Nature and Chemistry of Romantic Love,* anthropologist Helen Fisher, who performed brain scans on people who were falling in love, writes that the behavioral aspect of romantic love is looped into our systems. When we add this to how we've been indoctrinated, it's no wonder romantic love is alluring for females of all ages. Daughters, whether in grade school, high school, college, or beyond, were raised on fairy tales and are aware of celebrity liaisons on an ongoing basis. On June 15, 2009, *OK! Magazine* highlighted the possible love affair of Robert Pattinson and Kristen Stewart, stars of *Twilight* and on-screen lovers. According to the lead article by Richard Jerome and Carole Glines, "Inside Robert Pattinson and Kristen Stewart's *Twilight* Love Story," despite Kristen's five-year relationship with actor Michael Angarano, she and Pattinson share a mutual attraction. What makes it all the more titillating is the fact that this is a romantic triangle that begs the time-honored question of commitment versus runaway longing.

Mothers and daughters subscribe to the *Romeo and Juliet* motif, where the heart battles adversity and love, and love, tragic as it is, triumphs. By the time women reach motherhood, they've not only witnessed film stars go down this path (Angelina Jolie and Brad Pitt, Meg Ryan's encounter with Russell Crowe while she was married to Dennis Quaid, the triangle of Heather Locklear, Denise Richards, and Richie Sambora), but they have also found themselves in some complicated romantic situations—having chosen unfortunate mates, had their hearts broken, or unexpectedly fallen in and out of love.

Eighty-eight percent of American women between the ages of twenty and twenty-nine believe that they will meet their soul mate, according to data on www.drphil.com. Therefore, the trajectory of wife to mother is fairly predictable, and yet the belief in true love winning the day is on all our radar screens. Almost every married mother interviewed lamented the days of passion with her partner, and many commented that motherhood excluded a woman from her sexual self. Divorced mothers, or widowed mothers, in contrast, who were actively dating, placed a premium on finding a satisfying relationship, including sex and romance. As Jann, forty-eight, who works as an administrator and lives in the Southwest with a seventeen-year-old daughter, notes:

My daughter's seen it all through me these past four years—a happy marriage that turned bad, an ugly divorce, a nice boyfriend, a mean boyfriend . . . a hot boyfriend. She knows I'm looking for the real thing. She's known about sex since she was little and that it was part of my relationships. . . . I think she felt safest about it when I was married and she was little and didn't have to face this about me or go out and have a sex life of her own. I sometimes doubt that anything I did has given her the right idea. When you have a kid with someone, you can give up the sex and love part, for a while anyway. When you don't share a kid, you want all the goods. Either way, I wasn't up for

giving her all the info and, I'm sorry to say, she watched and
spied on me and learned that way.

Cautionary Mothers

Throughout literature, theater, and film, we're shown the
myriad ways that mothers address the tangled web of romance
in their own lives and how this is the jumping-off point for
daughters. In the Broadway musical *Mamma Mia!*, a young bride
seeks out the man who fathered her by inviting her mother's
previous boyfriends to the wedding on an island in Greece.
Having been raised solely by her mother, the daughter is on a
quest for her true father. Although her desire is understandable, it also contrives an awkward situation, one that casts
doubt on what romantic love means to her mother. In Larry
McMurtry's novel *Terms of Endearment*, Aurora, a widow, raises
her only child, a daughter, in the 1960s without a father figure
in her life (as in *Mamma Mia!*). When her daughter marries a
man whom Aurora finds too ordinary, she is disappointed and
concerned. Yet without any model, what kind of man does the
daughter choose?

Another aspect of motherhood and the lessons of love are
shown to us in the 1978 feature film *Pretty Baby*, starring
Susan Sarandon as Hattie, the mother of twelve-year-old Violet,
played by Brooke Shields. The story takes place in 1917, at a
brothel in New Orleans, at a time when prostitution was no longer legalized. Violet has her sights set on a photographer, Ernest
J. Bellocq, played by Keith Carradine, and hopes to marry him.
But what she knows about love and sex is questionable, having
been raised in the home of Madame Nell with a mother who
worked there.

A mother's high hopes for her daughter become apparent in the romantic drama *The Light in the Piazza.* Margaret Johnson takes her beautiful daughter, Clara, to Italy, where Clara falls in love with Fabrizio, a young native from a fine Italian family. In spite of Clara's problem—she is mildly retarded as the result of a head injury—the mother has always wanted her to lead a normal life and has fiercely fought her husband's suggestion to have her institutionalized. When Fabrizio asks Clara to marry him, Margaret wants her daughter to have this chance at romantic love. Yet she's torn between her own dreams for her daughter and the reality of what Clara can handle when it comes to marriage and motherhood.

The Right Message for Daughters

Inevitably, the mother is invoked in her daughter's choices and decisions. Still, many mothers have remarked that their best intentions have fallen by the wayside. Part of the issue is that dating today has another connotation and style than was common as recently as fifteen or ten years ago. In her study "Parents' Management of Adolescents' Romantic Relationships Through Dating Rules," Stephanie Madsen found that parents of girls ages seventeen to nineteen tend to be more strict when it comes to curfew and sexual activity when daughters begin to date if the parents are in relationships with spouses or partners. A salient reason that parents set rules is because this protects the teenagers when it comes to risky sexual behavior.

The best intentions, however, can go awry, and not all mothers, as we know, are in happy unions when their daughters begin to date or fall in love. One widowed mother to two teenage daughters admitted to mixed feelings when her older daughter began to date. "I'm so glad that this boy returns her affection, but I don't know how to make her listen or what to say about being with the right person. I have no basis, no real knowledge. I'm alone, without anyone, and they're out there." For Brenda, fifty, who lives in North Carolina and works in marketing, a rich love life has never been part of the picture. She has two daughters, ages twenty-five and twenty-two.

Sure, I've stayed married to their father and together we raised our girls. But when it comes to yearning for a man, they've never seen it. And they know, they realize, it's not how I feel about him—he's my teammate but not my romantic partner. My older daughter is madly in love and hopes to always be with this young man. It's strange, as a mother, to know your daughter has something you never had. From me they get a poor view of men and believe men are inept. How can they want guys who have foibles? I taught them not to look for crazy love, and my younger daughter says she's already kissed plenty of frogs. She describes men who are babies and have to be pampered. . . . Still, she'll bring home a guy, praying he is the person she hopes he is.

A mother's love life has impact on the daughter and the selection she will make. Although enough mothers interviewed felt that their daughters view them as washed up when it comes to romance, others believe that their initiatives have been obvious to their daughters, and promising. As one single mother explains her stance, "If I didn't care about romance, my daughter would think it's over for women over forty-five and that all I'm supposed to do is care for her. I adore my daughter, but this matters, too." A married mother observes, "My daughter knows that this marriage is about family and stability. When she pictures me when I was young and in love, she knows it's from another time." The variations on the theme of romantic love for mothers, and how the daughters absorb the outcome, fall into several categories:

Loveless Matches. The common wisdom is that marriages and long-standing monogamous relationships lose their romantic luster. If the daughters have mothers who are disappointed when it comes to romance, it either discourages the daughters or makes them proactive and compelled to get it right in their own lives.

The Single/Dating Mother. The daughters sense their mothers' hope to meet someone and extract how meaningful it must be to have a partner. Half of my interviewees feel that their daughters respect their goal for a full life, including a love interest, but sense that the daughters, especially those in grade school or high school, dislike that their mother's romantic life is a part of their lives.

The Bitter Divorced Mother. When the daughter is drawn into the drama of her parents' divorce, this hardship can alter the daughter's view of a happy, successful romantic union. Yet the daughter's determination to succeed frequently surfaces. The Center for Disease Control and Prevention reports that the divorce rate in America is 3.5 per 1,000 of the population and the marriage rate is 7.1 per 1,000 of the population. This means that approximately 50 percent of marriages end in divorce.

Committed Daughters/Single Mothers. When a single mother observes her daughter in a happy love relationship, it can stir up envy and a sense that opportunity and time have passed the mother by. This can make the daughter feel guilty, as if she's abandoned her mother for her own romantic life. If the mother meets someone and her attitude changes, the daughter is relieved.

Single Mothers/Single Daughters. If mothers and daughters count on each other to fill the emptiness when neither is in a romantic relationship, it obligates both parties. This also churns up resentment when either mother or daughter meets someone and begins to date. Close to 25 percent of mothers and daughters share their dating woes. Twenty-five percent of mothers reported that their daughters view them as too sexy and out there—furthermore, it isn't comfortable for the daughters.

Traditional Romances. Sixty percent of daughters have followed in their mothers' footsteps when their mothers are in satisfying relationships or marriages. The other 40 percent report that their daughters are too sheltered and lack the savvy to discern the best partner and unhealthy patterns. Of mothers who are victims of a broken heart (husband asking for divorce, a long-standing boyfriend who leaves), 70 percent of their daughters have endured unhappiness with boyfriends and the mothers feel they are to blame on some level.

The Language of Sex

When *Sex and the Single Girl,* written by Helen Gurley Brown, was published in 1962, it was a sensational idea that "nice girls" were enjoying sex before they were married, including trysts with married men. During this era, such escapades were banned on the surface, while motherhood filled a prescribed role. By the mid to late sixties, the second wave of feminism and the sexual revolution would change all this. Not only would the world of female sexuality be turned on its head when the birth control pill was launched in 1960, but both married women and single women would be liberated. Married women would be able to plan their families, and single women (eventually, since male gynecologists were reluctant to prescribe the pill to unmarried women at first) would be able to explore sex without the risk of pregnancy and the constraints of marriage.

If we fast-forward to 2010, birth control is certainly used, but the puritanical aspect of our society still teaches daughters that sex is sacred, the highest expression of love. At the same time, much of daily life is sexualized, even parts that have little to do with romance. This confuses the issue for adolescent girls as sex as experiment, sex as sport, or sex as a social tool clouds the picture. So while the mothers tell their daughters that sex is about romantic love, these young women are often having sex without this key component. To complicate matters, approximately half of the population of mothers today are married and half are single, therefore the daughter's interpretation depends greatly on what her mother's experience is.

A study by Jocelyne Thériault at the University of Quebec found that the mother-daughter bond had a profound effect on the daughter's ability to be sexual and not sexual in a romantic relationship. Thériault reports that those daughters who were independent and able to be assertive were less fearful of both sexual intimacy and nonsexual intimacy than those daughters who were less decisive. Darcie, sixty-five, recalls how it was to be young and single in the mid-1960s and reflects on her influence upon her thirty-two-year-old daughter:

My mother just wanted me to marry in case I wasn't a virgin and she pressured me. I wanted to have sex and then decide if I loved someone. In the end, I got married early because I was the good girl and didn't have the guts to stay single and have some freedom. So I got to be mother, wife, and teacher, all the normal stuff, and anything sexy was pushed away. I told my daughter to try out at least a few boyfriends before she settled down. She listened to me because she saw that I'd been trapped, and what I said made sense—as much as what her friends were doing. At thirty-two she's had sexual experiences, true love, and then married the last guy. They have a child and she seems content, more so because she never gave anything up to get this package, like I did.

Mothers are able to discuss the pluses and minuses of romance and sex today in ways that were taboo in the recent past. This puts the daughters at an advantage when it comes to their state of awareness, but can also dampen their confidence. "It's true that mothers are more permissive with their daughters and less conservative today," remarks Dr. Ronnie Burak. "But there's also a situation where the mother's love life is an open book, for better or for worse, for the daughter."

Mothers on Sex

The Feminine Mystique, by Betty Friedan, published in 1963, spilled the beans on how "perfect" wives and mothers across America really felt. These women, sequestered in suburban America, had begun to identify "the problem that had no name"—the inertia of their lives, as they existed to please their husbands in sexless, uninspired marriages. These marriages were unsatisfying at best, and at worst had dark secrets of alcoholism, abuse, and emotional neglect. But the women stayed. Few had the means to make their own money, since only a handful of women worked, and the world beyond the home was virtually unknown. Their daughters, a population of whom are now mothers in this study, would not necessarily tolerate their mother's life. A young daughter who is emblematic of these times is the ten-year-old character Sally Draper, played by Kiernan Shipka, in the AMC television series *Mad Men*. In the show's third season the year is 1963, a time when emotions weren't on the table, and Sally quietly absorbs the misery and unrest of her bored, beautiful mother, Betty Draper, played by January Jones.

Although there were no guarantees that the daughters of this generation of mothers would get it right, they were motivated to try. If it didn't work out romantically for the women raised in the sixties, at least they had the option of divorce and a second chance at romantic love—something their own mothers didn't entertain as a possibility.

Breaking Free

Consider Leslie, forty-seven, who lives in a small town in the South, where she works as an office manager, and has two daughters, twenty-two and twenty-four.

Based on my marriage and divorce, my daughters have seen a lot. I think back to the way I was raised and any misery with a husband was kept a secret. I suppose that's why I waited to divorce their father. I did what I thought I should and tried to keep the family together, but the girls knew what I was doing and I'm not sure it was the best thing. I'd say that the girls learned that you can try to stick it out but you can also leave anytime. They learned it's easy to be fooled when you're in love, though there are signs of trouble. It's hard to listen to your brain when your heart is giving mixed signals. They've seen all along, because of their father and me, that when you're in love, you're capable of making mistakes.

One of my daughters understands what I've tried to teach them but the other was with a few losers, trying to fix things, and I steered her away from that early on. Now she's purposely not dating anyone and trying to be on the right track. I always worry and hope that history won't repeat itself. I am not quiet if I'm worried about either daughter's love life after what's happened to me.

Control in Relationships

For the women who followed the boomer daughters and came of age in the seventies and eighties, the idea of a love relationship among equals encompassing sex, romance, and companionship was not only the hope but the anticipation. Surprising enough, their daughters between the ages of fifteen and thirty want this *and* compliant partners, which means that the daughters have more control. In part this is the result of how disappointed their mothers were when their fathers did *not* meet them halfway. In response, daughters might reject their mothers' idealism and instead be strident about what they expect from their mates. For instance, Julianne, forty-four, who lives in the Northeast and works in fashion, is both repelled and entranced by her sixteen-year-old daughter's relationship with her boyfriend.

I watch my daughter and think about my own romantic life and my mother's. My mother hadn't much connection to my dad and took care of the kids and basically read books or played cards—I doubt she ever had sex. I knew I didn't want that. My deal with my husband was that we'd share in everything, we'd be friends and lovers, and we'd be honest about our feelings. I always hoped that my daughter appreciated how I didn't want to lose myself to being a mother and wife. I thought I taught her that you can be in love with someone without giving anything up, including work, including parts of yourself. That's why I'm so surprised and worried at how controlling she is with her boyfriend and how she carries on in their relationship. They are only juniors in high school, but already she's a shrew. If her boyfriend has plans with his friends on a Friday night, she rants until he cancels and does what she wants and spends time with her. I've told her this isn't a good idea and that it will ruin everything, but she won't listen and she sort of likes it. What worries me is how she's not working on herself because she's so busy being in charge of their relationship.

There are mothers, as well as daughters, who want control in their romantic relationships and exhibit how this works for their daughters. For instance, in contrast to Julianne is Patsy, thirty-five, who lives in a Southern city, where she works in business management, and has two daughters, eight and seven. Patsy's deliberate plan for her marriage has already been impressed upon her daughters.

My daughters already know that my marriage is sort of a one-way street. I call the shots with the girls, with money, with how we live, where we go on vacation. I have more say, and my husband is fine with it. He thinks I'm smart and is probably a bit afraid to anger me. So while I'm aware that not all husbands are like this, I want my girls to find those who are. It's the only way to get what you want—by having more power. I know that my older sister and some of the women at the office believe in marriages where the partners are equal, but that wouldn't work for me. My mother has warned me that my husband will tire of this and says I'm too bossy, but I'm fairly sure that's not true. He's happy to have his life in order, his home in order, his girls in order and to basically say yes. When my older daughter asked me what it's like to be married, I told her it's about being with someone who will do anything to please you and keeping it that way.

Mothers as Seducers

There are few places where the dark side of motherhood manifests quite like a mother who seduces her daughter's love interest or who is interested in the same age male as her daughter. A taboo subject when it comes to love and sex in the twentieth and twenty-first centuries is that of mothers competing with their daughters by lusting after their young boyfriends. The most famous among these tales is shown to us in the 1967 film *The Graduate,* starring Anne Bancroft as Mrs. Robinson, the married mother of Katharine Ross's character, Elaine, who both like Benjamin, Dustin Hoffman's character. While Mrs. Robinson is one of the greatest mothers as seductress of all time, what we take away is knowledge of the slippery slope of inappropriate longing that can brew in the heart of the hapless housewife. Notwithstanding that the daughter wins Benjamin's heart in the end, one can only imagine the havoc this wreaks on the mother-daughter bond.

Single mothers have their own brand of seduction that can overlap with their daughter's love interest. We see this in *Mermaids,* the 1990 film featuring Cher as Rachel Flax, Winona Ryder as Charlotte, her sixteen-year-old daughter, and Christina Ricci as Kate, the little sister. When Rachel moves the family to a small East Coast town, Charlotte develops a hopeless crush on the handsome local church bell ringer, who is ten years her senior. Despite the fact that Rachel has had plenty of sexual experiences and now has an age-appropriate love interest, Lou, played by Bob Hoskins, she begins to flirt with and seduce Joe, knowing how her daughter feels.

In the 2001 feature film *Life as a House,* Mary Steenburgen's character, Colleen Beck, sleeps with her teenage daughter's boyfriend, putting a wedge between herself and her daughter, Alyssa, played by Jena Malone. While thankfully, real-life competition and boundary blurring between mother and daughter doesn't always escalate to this level, there are those mothers who view their daughters' nubile boyfriends as quite appealing. Part of the attraction is tied in to the mother's ego and loss of youth, juxtaposed with her daughter's ascension. Another explanation is that the mother is simply attracted to younger men, regardless of how it affects her daughter. Consider Jacqueline, fifty, who lives in a Midwestern suburb and runs her husband's business. Both she and her nineteen-year-old daughter found the same young associate at the office alluring.

I don't think I've ever done anything as destructive as had a crush on the same guy as my daughter. I was ready to seduce him when I saw that my daughter liked him, too. In a way she saved my marriage and she also saved me from making a fool of myself. Who knows where it would have gone? And while it felt irresistible, I doubt I'd have been happy with myself once I did something more than flirt. I did flirt until my daughter came home from vacation and accepted a date with him. That's when I stopped and thought about my age and about how close my daughter and I are. Maybe I'm getting older and that's all that it was about, and maybe if my daughter hadn't been in the picture I'd have gone through with it.

If a mother, whether married or single, feels denied a happy sex life or becomes cynical about it, she might not provide the best advice. In contrast, a daughter who learns from her mother that a satisfying love relationship includes healthy sex is well advised.

Awkward Moments: Sex Talks

Ironically, it isn't only forbidden sex as described in Jacqueline's case that's a complicated topic, obviously, but honest conversations about sex and the consequences. I was surprised to hear how many mothers felt uncomfortable having a direct conversation about sex with their daughters. This applies to daughters in seventh grade and to daughters who are married with children of their own. As Amy Bloom writes in her article "The 'Eew' Factor" in *O Magazine,* "They're teenagers; it's all about them all the time, and every time you bring up your own feelings and your own experience of sexuality, it's like a thick curtain falls in front of their eyes and ears." Bloom does, however, recommend "straight talk" with our daughters, including speaking about oral sex and "hooking up," and emphasizes that the "best sex comes with love," while the "worst sex . . . comes with coercion, shame, and fear."

According to Aimee Lee Ball's interview with sex therapist Laura Berman in *O Magazine,* "Everyone's Doing *What*?," "sexting" is the new high-tech method for 22 percent of girls, who send nude or seminude pictures of themselves to boys on their cell phones. Dr. Berman also recommends mothers talk with their teenage daughters about boys and sex, the risks inherent in dangerous behavior, pregnancy, STDs, rapists, and pedophiles. Indeed, Arlene, forty-three, who lives in a Northeastern city and teaches grade school, believes that her seventeen-year-old daughter needed birth control by the time she turned thirteen.

What was I going to do? Pretend that my daughter wasn't having sex? She came to me and described these graphic sessions with boys whom she didn't particularly like but would give oral sex to in junior high. And she certainly wasn't alone—all of her friends did it, too. That's when I decided to take her to a gyno and get her some birth control, in case it became more than that. I also wanted her to be careful about STDs and I'm considering having her get the HPV shots. I feel I have to be very on top of this or it will ruin her love life one day. Meanwhile, I'm always talking about finding the boy of your dreams. She isn't thinking that way at all yet. I don't want her scarred or traumatized before she meets some nice boy. I'm doing all this to protect her as best I can and to educate her, if she'll pay attention.

Violence Against Females

Whether your daughter is fortunate enough to be sheltered from emotional or physical scenes of domestic violence or not, it is a grave issue for women in America. According to research conducted by the Family Violence Prevention Fund, one in every three women across the globe has been sexually, physically, or emotionally abused. When a mother has been in an abusive relationship, this colors the daughter's view of how her own relationships will play out. Callie, forty, who lives in upstate New York, where she works as a nurse, has three daughters, twenty, twelve, and ten.

We don't talk much about anyone's love life or what's ahead be-
cause I've been through too much. I'm divorced from their father,
which was something I had to do. I was married very young and
that's one thing I would discourage my girls from. My big mes-
sage is that they should never allow anyone to mistreat them and
that I'm living proof of what can go wrong. I barely survived
what he did to me, and it's only because I was educated that I
could get a job and get back on my feet. It isn't that I don't want
my girls to be happily in love, but that they have to be indepen-
dent women and never allow anyone to mistreat them. I know my
twenty-year-old likes someone and I want it to work out, for him
to be respectful and kind to her and to love her. If my girls don't
know to do this, then they haven't been listening to me.

Decompartmentalized Sex: Oral Sex

When *Good Morning America* produced a segment on May 28,
2009, about how prevalent oral sex is for teenage and preteen
girls, it was cautionary, based on an interview conducted with
filmmaker Sharlene Azam regarding her documentary on the
topic. Azam portrays teenage girls using oral sex in exchange
for money and homework or to facilitate a relationship, with
teenage girls explaining that oral sex is "no big deal." The National Center for Health Statistics reported in 2005 that more
than 50 percent of girls ages fifteen to nineteen have had oral
sex; for eighteen- and nineteen-year-olds, the stats jump to 70
percent. Because oral sex is often called decompartmentalized
sex, young girls do not view this as true intimacy but as part of
a rite of passage. Indeed, Joni, forty, who lives in Oklahoma,
where she works in a library, is concerned about oral sex, STDs,
and AIDS—and her twelve-year-old daughter.

I look at sex as if it's a potential danger and that my daughter has to understand it. It's one thing to be in the moment, but to know what misery is ahead if you are unprotected is the real problem. So I'm pulling myself together and telling her how sick you can get if you have unprotected sex, and I'm also telling her that sex without love means nothing. I wish I didn't have to harp on this, but it wouldn't be fair to her. So I keep hoping that if I drill this into her early on, she'll make the right decisions. I'm not frightening her on purpose, but I'm trying to have a daughter who stays out of trouble and makes some smart decisions. Meanwhile, for all I know, she does half of what I'm warning her against—she's very mature and popular and pretty, too. I worry most about the oral sex because she thinks it's like a kiss.

Warning Against Date Rape

According to the Sexual Assault and Relationship Abuse Prevention and Support Web site, 80 to 85 percent of women who were raped knew who had assaulted them, and one out of eight women will be raped while they are college students. Author Joyce Carol Oates addresses how difficult it is for families to face the repercussions of date rape in her novel *We Were the Mulvaneys*. Oates's story takes place in 1976 in upstate New York, where the Mulvaney family is well regarded and proud. When the daughter, innocent and lovely Marianne, is raped by a classmate the night of the prom, the entire family unravels. The father insists that his daughter be sent away to live with a relative, and while the mother complies, it is the end of her happiness and security. One can't help wishing that the mother had been able to shield her daughter from this cataclysmic incident and wonders why she didn't stand up to her husband when Marianne is banished. The tale points out how much we owe our daughters information and, if they are wronged, the importance of instilling self-esteem and support. Without this, a daughter will be reluctant to speak up without shame. Kitty, forty-two, who lives in Ohio, where she manages a store, has one daughter, who is seventeen.

My advice is that my daughter not be so trusting of everyone, especially the guys. She has a guy friend who would like to have sex and I tell her no, to wait. There have been times when he's practically forcing this and it's not right. She's come close and she feels pushed by him. . . . This is when I get nervous and have no control—I'm not in the room. I say it has to be special and that she isn't there yet, hasn't met anyone like that. I know it's hard to resist, when her friends are caught up in this, and that I'm old-fashioned. But I have been hurt and I was naïve. I don't want my daughter to go through that. She's already been crushed by a boy and I had to watch this. If she had sex with him just because he insisted, it would have been worse—she would have been more upset than she already was. She's too young to have sex and think it's love, no matter what I did or why I did it, no matter what her friends do or girls do today.

Ill-prepared Daughters/Ill-prepared Mothers: Teenage Pregnancies

Although we live in a world where mothers are hopefully open with their daughters about sex and pregnancy, it's nonetheless possible for a daughter to end up with a problem. The National Campaign to Prevent Teen and Unplanned Pregnancy reveals that eighty-four per thousand teens become pregnant in the United States despite access to birth control and sex-education classes. As reported by wowt.com in "Teen Charged for Putting Stillborn Baby in Trash," a seventeen-year-old girl from York, Nebraska, was charged with "unlawful disposal of human remains" after her stillborn baby was found in the trash. Her action is a Class IV felony charge that carries a maximum sentence of a five-year prison term and a $10,000 fine. We have to wonder where the mother was in this incident, from teen pregnancy to the sad ending, particularly in the twenty-first century. Not only is there a premium placed on mother-daughter communication, but sex education classes, Planned Parenthood, and social welfare systems are readily available. This is in contrast to Lola's experience. Having grown up in a small town in the Midwest, where she works as an administrator, Lola, forty-five, has two daughters, twenty-eight and twenty-one.

I had my first child when I was a senior in high school and it worked out but has always haunted me that life could have been another story if I hadn't gotten pregnant. I raised my girls to know they have choices, that they shouldn't have unprotected sex and that sex is only for if you love someone. I told them I might have been young, but I loved their father and that part worked out. But why get yourself into trouble when all you need is a conversation with your mother and birth control? Raising my girls, I've been very aware of date rape, STDs, anything that can go wrong because I was so young and not prepared for life. Today girls can be told everything by their mothers, on the Internet, by friends. Mostly it's up to the mother, though. If I did anything right, it's talk to my girls and tell them everything at home, so they know what it's all about, what can happen.

Ignorance Is Not Bliss

According to the Center for Adolescent Health and Development, if a mother is against her daughter having sex and communicates this, the daughter will be less likely to do so at an early age. The Kaiser Family Foundation's report "U.S. Teen Sexual Activity" also states that 17.4 is the median age for first intercourse for girls, while 49 percent of females between the ages of fifteen and nineteen have given oral sex.

Despite the statistics above, 50 percent of my interviewees said they had not spoken openly about early sexual encounters, date rape, sexually transmitted diseases, or teenage pregnancies with their daughters. Instead, they have raised their daughters on the panacea of romantic love, fairy tales (the most popular being "Cinderella"), without warning them of the real threats posed to a young woman's health from the time that her sexual and love lives take off. These mothers worry about their daughters being defenseless when it comes to sex and romantic relationships yet feel that the topic was uncomfortable enough to avoid. Many hoped that their girls would be educated in health class or through their friends. Adele, forty-eight, who works in advertising and lives in Massachusetts, has two daughters, eighteen and twenty-four.

I'm a hopeless romantic and my girls know it's the only way to be. It's also a letdown and unnerving. I've never had the romantic life I imagined I'd have, and sex for me has been more about the atmosphere and a moment. The perfect setting works better for me than the act itself. My daughters get what I mean by romance, but I have never said much about sex. It's like sex is a subject we skip and romance is worth talking about. My girls go

into relationships looking for love, thanks to me, and maybe not
focused on the sex. At least that's how I think they look at their
love lives. I feel responsible and guilty at the same time, but I
can't be anyone but who I am. I wish I knew important ways to
tell them what to do, it would be better all around. If they want
the facts, they'll have to ask someone else—maybe a friend's
older sister or someone else's mother.

It is irresponsible of the mother, regardless of her personal
style and take on sex and love, not to communicate the posi-
tives and negatives of being sexually active to her daughter.
This includes getting her to a physician and informing her of
all that can occur. This can be challenging if the daughter
is defiant or secretive, swayed by her peers or influenced
by media imagery of sexualized young women and romantic
liaisons.

Money and Love

What mother hasn't advocated her daughter's attachment to a
successful man, or someone from a "good family" with the
"right credentials"? Yet some mothers can take this too far, encouraging their daughters to search for "the deal," rather than
true love. For those mothers who have indulged their daughters
materially, it stands to reason that their daughters will consider the perks of marrying for money but hope that love will
exist, too. The classic novel *Pride and Prejudice* by Jane Austen
details how heightened this outlook can be when one's entire
social life and aspirations are tied in to making the correct
match. This nineteenth-century tale of the three poor but

charismatic Bennet sisters and their mother's scheme to marry them off also addresses the romantic side of matrimonial manipulations. When Elizabeth Bennet first meets Mr. Darcy, she finds him insufferably proud and listens to the gossip about him. It is only once she really knows him that love falls into place, and, fortunately, he's one of the wealthiest eligible men to boot. No wonder this book has been a hit for nearly two hundred years, and adapted for feature film as well, including a version that stars Keira Knightley as Elizabeth Bennet and Matthew Macfadyen as Mr. Darcy. Mothers today frequently share the view of Mrs. Bennet. For example, Jane, fifty-nine, who owns a luncheonette and lives in northern Florida, feels that she herself didn't have enough opportunity and that her daughter, thirty-four, should have a moneyed life.

My daughter married the first guy, someone she had dated in high school. They went to the same college and then they were married. I wanted her to have more experience because I was so young when I married her father and I knew nothing, I knew no one. My mother told me nothing except to marry someone who was our religion who was going to make a good living. She said nothing about sex or love, and I wanted my daughter to know this was part of it. I admit, I never taught her about love because I don't believe in romantic love and I saw nothing in my own childhood to make me think it existed. But I told her plenty about money and what it's like to not have it. I told her that it's great to love someone but make sure he has deep pockets, too. I made the point that money buys happiness, no matter what anyone says. I've reminded her that she likes nice things and a nice lifestyle and that it's easier to work on a marriage than to count on a job to get all that.

There are those mothers who advocate a daughter finding a partner who is successful, and many times this is their story as well—or, having suffered financially, it's the story they wish was theirs. Other mothers will veer away from this style and hold true love in highest esteem, without any financial or social requirements.

What We Teach Our Daughters

I remember being struck from the start of the HBO series *Sex and the City* by the fact that none of the four principal characters has a mother in the picture. I wondered if this affected each character's sexual and romantic proclivity: sex as a game (think Samantha, and Miranda on occasion), sex for love (think Carrie), and for marriage (think Charlotte). The diverse styles of the four friends were punctuated in the feature film of the same name, in 2008, when Carrie Bradshaw's wedding falls apart on the actual wedding day and it is her three best friends who nurse her through this trauma; there is no mother on the scene.

When it comes to a successful or a failed romance, a wedding, a divorce, or a remarriage, a mother's presence is of great value to her daughter. Although some mothers in this chapter question their own practices, others keenly discern the ups and downs of romance and triumph over adversity. Ultimately our daughters make their own decisions when it comes to their sex and love lives, yet mothers who stress respect and honesty in these relationships are providing their daughters with the essential tools.

Highlighting Healthy Relationships

Do have conversations with your daughter during her early adolescence regarding pregnancy, STDs, and AIDS, and provide information. Be available on an ongoing basis concerning these issues and be vigilant about your daughters' whereabouts at this stage.

Do not hesitate to voice any real concerns about the person your daughter is dating. Try to see the relationship through your daughter's eyes. Is she happy with this person or simply afraid to be without a romantic partner? Is there something egregious about him, or is he acceptable? If you have any hesitation, let your daughter know.

Discourage your daughter from controlling the relationship. If your daughter has a tendency to be controlling, advise her that this can harm the relationship. If you have been a model for this in your long-standing relationship or marriage, it's a good time to reevaluate the pros and cons.

Teach your daughter not to lie in love or about her feelings. If your daughter has an agenda, be it a rebound relationship or a search for a mate with money, or if she feels pressured to be engaged or start a family, discuss whether this relationship is right for her. Advise her that she has time to find the real thing.

Do not allow your own past or a bitter divorce to color your advice. Being objective will help your daughter and earn her trust in your advice. Besides, your modeling won't always hold up, and your daughter's risk/reward ratio is her own.

Keep the lines of communication open if your daughter has a broken heart. Be subtle when suggesting that she start dating again. And remember that she and her ex might get back together, so your support has to be for her choice—don't say too much that is negative.

Chapter 8

❋

Let Me Help—
You Can't Handle It All

Minimizing Self-Esteem, Independence, and Personal Authority

- Have you taught your daughter to make her own decisions?
- Do you see her maturing with the years and becoming more certain of herself?
- Do you feel that you and your daughter are stable when it comes to closeness and independence?
- Does your daughter engage in healthy acts or in destructive ones?
- Have you encouraged your daughter to be an independent thinker?
- Do you foster your daughter's individuality?

Or is it more complicated than that, and do you find yourself holding your daughter back in some manner?

MOST OF THE TIME you feel as if you can't win. If you praise your daughters, ages nine and eleven, saying they are beautiful and brilliant, they could become full of themselves. But you have to say something, because everyone does, and how can they believe in themselves if you aren't commenting on their art project or book report or gymnastics feat? Perhaps if you praise them for something they've done, it's more of a reward than empty praise, which you've read is inappropriate and misleading. Surely you have to do something, especially when you think of your own mother, who was strict and demanding without offering any support or encouragement. It took you years to get over this—if you ever did. No wonder you want to make up for it.

You are trying to figure this out, especially since you've watched your sister, whose teenage daughters are terrors—they have body piercings and one has a tattoo, as do their friends. Worse, your nieces have no self-esteem and put your sister through the ringer. These were sweet young girls just five years ago. You watch your sister and worry sick that you're next. Already it's dicey: One day your daughters deserve to be complimented and the next day you're finding fault with them. Then you read about how daughters fall into bad patterns . . . and you begin to question your instincts. However, you never lose sight of the goal—for your daughters to have enough confidence and sense to stand on their own as they grow older.

The Female Path to Self-Esteem

In listening to the voices of the mothers for this study, it becomes apparent that the majority wrangle with self-esteem issues, just as their daughters do. Not only do many of their daughters suffer from low self-esteem, but also the daughters' issues are often tied in to the mothers' self-perception and what they project.

In his book *The Six Pillars of Self-Esteem,* Nathaniel Branden informs us that mothers send a different message than do fathers and have a separate outlook. Daughters need to feel "visible," and this means a parent responds by giving "appropriate feedback." If this doesn't occur, Brandon advises, children will feel alienated and unsafe, invisible to themselves. Another pioneer in self-esteem research, Abraham Maslow writes in his book *Toward a Psychology of Being* of a "hierarchy of needs." The first three "needs" are all familiar to mothers: biological needs, such as food, water, and air; safety; and love and belonging. The fourth need is self-esteem, which Maslow believes can be established only after the first three needs are addressed properly. He defines the need for self-esteem as twofold, coming both from other people and from how we see ourselves.

The popular contention is that girls' self-esteem is lower than boys' by the time they approach junior high school. In *Reviving Ophelia,* Mary Pipher writes, "Girls are more likely than boys to say they are not smart enough for their dream careers. They emerge from adolescence with a diminished sense of their worth as individuals." With mothers alerted to the problem, there is an understandable push to build self-esteem in our daughters, and to propel them toward success. Analise, forty-one, who works in a spa and lives in Florida, explains her way of dealing with her fourteen-year-old daughter:

I simply tell her everything she does is great, including when it isn't. I tell her she's a genius and a star. And still she feels awful about herself. But I have to do this because I'm getting divorced. I feel guilty and I feel like a loser. I don't want my daughter to ever feel like this and as I recall, my mother never told me I was great. I actually don't know what she thinks. But I have an obligation to keep my daughter on track, especially during this period, so I say only positive things. All the time, because I don't want her beaten down—by friends, by boys, by my divorce. I wish it would work.

Other mothers make a conscious decision to build self-esteem and at the same time to keep a reality check. Consider Dorothy, fifty, who lives in Atlanta and is a businesswoman. She has three daughters, twenty-seven, twenty-five, and twenty-two.

For me, it was always about having daughters who could go out into the world and make it. That doesn't mean we don't talk almost daily or that we don't get together as much as we can or that I've abandoned them. But it does mean that if I'm not around, they'll get the same thing done or make the same decisions and feel good about it. This has worked for my younger two girls, but my oldest daughter, who is twenty-seven, has had problems with her work, her weight, her love life, and she's a wreck. I've been there for her and have tried to be supportive, but ultimately, it's her life and I've given her the tools, now it's up to her. I won't have her falling apart and acting infantile, I simply can't handle it. There has to be a point where these girls are on their own and I'm not cleaning up their mess anymore because they don't have the confidence to do it. She's called me coldhearted and critical, but frankly, I'm just worn-out and feel like a broken record.

Unfortunately, self-esteem can be impaired easily in the daughters' lives, and requires effort to rebuild. Therapist Brenda Szulman remarks, "The problem is if the daughter doesn't see her mother as strong, and the father is too powerful, or the mother hasn't gotten her life together and isn't an authority figure. Then the daughter thinks that her mother isn't standing up for herself and isn't shielding her daughter."

Self-Destructive Behavior

Part of the problem occurs during the teen years when the daughter is very tender and has not fully developed as a person. Most mothers find it trying and occasionally impossible to reason with their daughters between the ages of thirteen and seventeen. Whether or not a mother coerces her daughter about school, weight, or friends, there is the culture of peers, boys, and media, as we repeatedly see, wielding influence. A daughter may be so caught up in this that her mother's wisdom falls on deaf ears. Alternately, the mothers are reluctant to impose, fearful of upsetting their daughters or disapproving of their lives and priorities. It becomes more complex when the mother isn't credible based on her own life choices.

Devastating Methods

As we have seen repeatedly throughout this study, our daughters are bogged down by societal pressures; young women are objectified and judged by their looks, weight, and achievement. With these expectations overwhelming daughters, destructive behaviors have become more common. Stephen Hinshaw and Rachel Kranz's book, *The Triple Bind: Saving Our Teenage Girls from Today's Pressures,* explains why teenage girls are in jeopardy due to depression, eating disorders, and self-mutilation (cutting, biting, and burning). Hinshaw reports that from 2003 to 2004, the national suicide rate for girls aged ten to fourteen rose by 76 percent; for girls between the ages of fifteen and nineteen, the rate rose 32 percent.

Jocelyn, forty-eight, who works in manufacturing and lives in a Midwestern city, has had these issues with her twenty-year-old daughter since she was in junior high school.

My daughter was anorexic first, when she was thirteen until today, and then a cutter the next year, but finally we got some help and that stopped. On top of it, she had all these issues with her friends, who could be nasty to her, or worse, she'd join them in being mean to someone else. It was awful for her, and I made it worse because I wanted her to be okay. I wanted to have a boyfriend and go out some and I couldn't because she was a problem. So I gave up my social life for her but I wasn't happy about it, and I worked long hours, too. She knew it and that made it all worse. She never thought of me as loyal to her or about how I felt—what I wanted and couldn't have, and it was depressing for both of us. We were just angry. I was angry about being divorced with a daughter who had too many problems, and she saw me as someone who couldn't get her act together. This went on for years, and then she left for college. But it's never really been worked out—on holidays or when she comes home in the summer, it's the same. I'm always checking that she isn't doing something wrong—starving or cutting herself.

Female Bullying

The way that young girls treat one another, called alternative aggression by Rachel Simmons, author of *Odd Girl Out,* is familiar to both mothers and daughters. This form of bullying is the result of young girls not being allowed to express themselves. Thus, if they are jealous or rivalrous, it manifests in victimization and cruel treatment. Simmons believes that this diminishes the victim's self-esteem. Rosalind Wiseman, author of *Queen Bees and Wannabes,* shows us how far a "mean girl" will go and the covert behavior of aggressive teenage girls. For example, Kathy, forty-four, who works as a clinician and lives in Maine, has little control over her thirteen-year-old daughter.

My daughter is sneaky on a bad day and fine on a good day. Her enemies keep her very preoccupied, and I know she's the ring-leader with the other girls. Whatever goes on in eighth grade, she's the one who starts it all. I doubt she does any of her home-work, so she must make someone else give her the answers—or else she'd be failing. I imagine that she's writing awful e-mails about other girls at night when she should be doing her home-work. I have tried to cut back on Internet time, on bedtime, but no matter what I say, she isn't listening and thinks I'm a loser. She's out for blood and she's undaunted. I stay awake at night, wondering how my husband and I ended up with this daughter, since we're both good people, since we both care for others in our line of work. Maybe I didn't raise her with a strong enough hand, maybe I didn't talk to her enough about respecting others.

Female Violence

According to the office of Juvenile Justice and Delinquency Prevention's May 2008 study, "Violence by Teenage Girls: Trends and Context," there has been a 24 percent increase in the num-ber of girls arrested between 1996 and 2005, and mothers are at the receiving end of their daughters' lashing out. An article on the CBS Web site, "Girls Getting Increasingly Violent," by Bootie

Cosgrove-Mather, notes, "Around the country, school police and teachers are seeing a growing tendency for girls to settle disputes with their fists. . . . Nationally, violence among teenage boys—as measured by arrest statistics and surveys—outstrips violence among teenage girls four to one, according to the Justice Department." Cosgrove-Mather reports that this trend is a reflection of girls growing up in a more violent society, and notes that breakdowns in community that have caused the rise in violence for boys are affecting girls, too.

While the majority of mothers interviewed for this project felt that their daughters were exposed to films and television that endorsed violence, they also believed it wasn't a part of their personal lives. Several mothers admitted that their daughters were capable of being violent toward them, a sister, or a friend, and several mothers regretted that they themselves had a "violent streak" that influenced their daughters.

Consider Lindsay, fifty-five, who works for a corporation and lives in a Southern city. She and her two daughters, twenty-five and twenty-seven, have engaged in violent acts toward one another.

I am not a saint, and there have been moments in this family, with my husband and the girls, that I'm not proud of. There's been shouting and it's escalated and there's been punching and carrying on. My girls learned this at home when they were small but wouldn't have ever taken it public, either by acting this way or by talking about it. Now that they're older, I see that my first daughter wants a very quiet life with this mousy man, and it's probably to avoid our family history. My other daughter goes at it with her husband, and it's because it's what she knows. She's been like this outside our family, too, with her friends in high school. It worries me that this is what is familiar. Her husband is exactly the same. They act like street people, and I suppose it's my fault.

In the scenes that deal with self-destructive behavior, each mother takes a portion of blame for what has occurred, but none has the fortitude or determination to stop it. It is the mother's responsibility to keep her daughter in a wholesome environment and to step up when dangerous activities take place. This can require working on herself and her own habits and tendencies, as well as her daughter's.

A Mother's Influence

If a mother is not pressuring her daughter, the culture is demanding a great deal of teenage girls and young women. Unfortunately, these teenage girls cannot always judge what's best for them, and a mother is expected to intervene. If a mother is not equipped to prepare, warn, and defend her daughter, all eyes fall on her as a failure. Meanwhile, time and again, there's a daughter who, regardless of her mother's efforts from junior high school through her college years and beyond, is suffering from low self-esteem and a lack of direction. The following scenarios describe the mother-daughter connection and self-esteem.

Narcissistic/Ego-Driven Mothers. If a mother hasn't enough self-esteem and views her daughter as a way to gain it—a second chance, and a reflection of herself—then she puts the screws to her daughter for these reasons. Or if the mother is vain, the daughter feels she has to have "the life" for her mother. Vivien, forty-six, counts on her eighteen-year-old daughter to uphold her style.

My daughter wears the right clothes and has the right friends and goes to the right school. She has every chance to feel good about herself, but she also knows that I'm always in the picture—we sort of share her success. She has to do well for herself, but she also knows she can't fail me.

High Expectations/Mothers to Daughters. When a mother expects too much of her daughter in terms of academics, looks, social life, or relationships, she creates anxiety for her daughter and makes her worry that she could easily fail. Jolie, fifty-six, mother to a twenty-nine-year-old daughter, embodies this scenario.

I can't imagine my daughter as a nonworking mother because she has put so many years into her education, working to climb up the corporate ladder. I would like to see her have a family and be well-placed in her career, not only in earning power but in status and national reputation.

High Expectations/Daughters to Mothers. If a daughter feels entitled, and expects that her mother will duke it out for her in terms of academics, looks, or social life, she may become anxious when she is left to her own devices. Felicity, forty-three, whose fourteen-year-old daughter depends on her, has found this to be the case.

Not only have I made it so easy for my daughter since she was a toddler, but she thinks it's all coming to her since she's started high school. She keeps thinking I can work magic, and I see that she doesn't have any of her own ideas. She has to get out there and make things happen, but I'm also wondering what I can do.

Never Right/Never Enough. When a mother is overly censorious, perhaps due to her own unhappiness, her daughter feels insecure. Some daughters spend their time trying to please a mother who can't be satisfied, to the point that the daughter begins to doubt herself. The mother may also be a tough grader in general, and it extends to the daughter. Gabby, thirty-nine, mother to an eleven-year-old daughter, believes in rules.

I'm strict with my daughter because I was raised this way —still, my mom wasn't as strict as I am. My daughter isn't showered with gifts and clothes between seasons, and I don't praise her all the time, because I don't believe in it. Thinking you're the greatest isn't going to get you anywhere. My daughter can always improve her schoolwork and her friends—she's only in sixth grade.

Weak Mothers/Vulnerable Daughters. If a mother isn't steady in her own life but instead operates from fear, it's more difficult for her daughter to steer her own course. Although this situation usually doesn't come about by choice, a mother who is stuck herself affects her daughter's development. Cara, thirty-eight, mother to four daughters, nineteen, seventeen, fourteen, and twelve, believes this happened to her.

I was abused in my marriage, which my girls saw, and I kept trying to make it better. But really I was just taking it sitting down. My girls watched and now they have nothing to say and are so quiet and so afraid. I've let them down, but what's worse is that I can't get back on track to show them how to do it. Recently I left their father, but we're all scarred. So they think about me being treated horribly and I can't be one of those strong moms that everyone needs.

Negative Self-Image: Daughters who are not perceived positively by their mothers have difficulty forming a positive self-image. Since daughters are influenced by their mother's view, anything negative can churn up self-loathing. Elina, forty-six, has serious conversations with her sixteen-year-old daughter:

My daughter has to lose weight and we both know it. If she looked better, she'd feel better, and this has been going on for years. I worry that it won't ever get better and it's no favor for me to say she doesn't look fat in a dress. I'm not very understanding because I don't think it helps matters and she has a poor sense of herself.

Flip-Flopping Mothers. Mixed messages come from society, peers, and the media, but when a mother changes her tune, her daughter's trust is diminished. Although mothers who do this defend their change of heart, it can be destabilizing. Doris, fifty-seven, has two daughters, thirty and twenty-six. The older one is getting divorced.

I know that my daughter wonders why I was adamant that she marry someone of our religion the first time and didn't care about it for her second marriage. I wanted to see her happy, but now that she's anything but happy, I do blame it on the fact that he's from another background. My daughter says she doesn't know what I really mean anymore, and she can't rely on my opinion.

Not hearing a daughter's request and putting our own designs ahead of a daughter's can lead to trouble. As Dr. Claire

Owen observes, there is too much emphasis on how a daughter is "supposed to be." "Self-esteem is about allowing daughters to be who they are, not telling them who they have to be. If one sticks with this plan, a daughter will flourish."

The Latest in Self-Esteem

While Nathaniel Branden's research, referenced earlier in this chapter, encourages mothers to give children "love, apprecia- tion, empathy, acceptance, and respect," the past few years have yielded new studies on self-esteem. Building self-esteem is now defined as empty praise if it isn't designated appropri- ately. This means that lauding a daughter to the hilt and try- ing desperately to make her feel okay about herself can actually backfire. A book by Carol S. Dweck, *Mindset: The New Psy chology of Success*, illustrates how making excuses for a child who has failed rather than facing the failure keeps her from having any flexibility. According to an article in *Science Daily,* "Parents' Expectations, Styles Can Harm College Students' Self-esteem," a study conducted by Kimberly Renk found that parenting styles have tremendous impact upon how students adjust when they get to college. It is a parent who is warm, demo- cratic, and has a "demanding nature" who most helps a student to feel good about herself.

The operative stance today is to avoid hollow approval and en- courage daughters only for what they've done right—and to dis- sect what they've done wrong. Recent research indicates that anything else keeps young people from developing basic work hab- its and the fortitude necessary to do well in life. In a chapter titled "The Self" in *The Handbook of Social Psychology,* Roy Baumeis- ter declared that the significance of self-esteem is exaggerated.

But this new take on self-esteem doesn't change how females lose confidence in their abilities. Consider Lori, forty-seven, who lives in the Southwest and works part-time in an office, and has a twenty-one-year-old daughter.

It's funny how I meant to teach my daughter to be a good citizen and instead she's always been bossy, a sort of conceited daughter. I don't know how it happened that she's just so sure that everything is coming to her. I feel like I work for her and still I let this happen. Most of my friends aren't much better when it comes to their girls. If I think about it, when she was in grade school, I'd jump to please her, if she cried, if a playdate was canceled, if she couldn't find the right boots at the mall. I told her it was never her fault, and that it was everyone else's fault. It's because she would upset me, then I'd try to fix it. I was always there—I felt I was responsible for her and made her think she was perfect.

Now that she's graduating college, I can't imagine her working for someone, having to answer to someone, going out into a world where she doesn't have final say. I don't think she can adapt. I know I didn't do the right thing, I know my daughter is in for a rude awakening and I built her up in ridiculous ways.

Carla's experience is a great contrast to Lori's take on placating her daughter and building her self-esteem. At fifty-nine, Carla lives on Long Island, where she works in music sales and has a twenty-seven-year-old daughter.

I thought I gave my daughter self-esteem, but she says I was too tough on her, and I probably was. I expected her to do well in school, to take care of herself, to look good, and assume some responsibility for herself. I was a single mother, and I have three sons, too. My sons are older and they were self-sufficient, I wasn't ever worried about them like I was about my daughter. There was probably too much pressure on her. I was spoiling her because she had no father and I felt bad about it, and I was also pushing her because I wanted her to be someone.

I wasn't going to tell her she was great when she wasn't—that wasn't my plan. I told her what was important in life. She wanted to find out for herself and she wasn't about to listen to me either way— if I said she was doing well or if I said she could do better. It didn't seem to matter when she was younger, especially a teenager. I look back on how I raised my daughter and I wonder if I was fair, if I didn't expect too much. I thought I was supporting her emotionally, but probably I was pushing her and not allowing her to feel good no matter what.

The jury is still out on telling our daughters how special they are to build their self-esteem versus attributing praise only when it's earned. Most mothers lean toward boosting self-esteem and extolling their daughters indiscriminately rather than being harsh or judgmental. Psychologist Seth Shulman remarks, "A mother will try to prepare her daughter for life with the best intentions, including complimenting her on a large and small scale. But the result might not be that her daughter is better engaged or more mature as a result."

Underestimating Independence

It isn't only a daughter's self-esteem that is precarious and in flux but also how a mother helps her daughter develop independence. This developmental task, according to every mother with whom I've spoken, is linked to the daughter's self-esteem, and heightened by peer pressure and a daughter's need to break free while simultaneously remaining safely attached to her mother (who, naturally, has her own issues). As mothers, we are expected to foster independence, and in the abstract, this makes perfect sense. But the complexities of real life have a way of skewing how a mother deals with letting her daughter go out into the world. Another factor is who the mother is in the equation. Is she someone who has a sense of self and a full life, including a career, a love interest, friends, and family? Or does the mother rely on her daughter to fill the emptiness and isn't quite ready— despite the fact that her daughter might be—to let go? Does the mother know, at least intellectually, that it's time for her daughter to forge ahead?

The Mother Lode. This mother overshadows her daughter and influences her without considering her daughter's individual needs. In Janet Fitch's novel *White Oleander,* a mother is self-involved in a way that keeps her daughter from any independence. It's as if Astrid, the daughter, has a life that merely revolves around Ingrid, her mother. Ingrid, both stunning and talented, is a poet who seduces others, including her own daughter, into thinking she's magical. When Ingrid is sent to jail for poisoning her former lover, Astrid is left alone to develop her own sense of self, juxtaposed with her mother's inflated ego. This reminds us that the best situation is when the mother can respect her daughter's requirements and still preserve her own interests. Consider Jayna, fifty-two, who has a twenty-seven-year-old daughter.

I have tried to be an engaged mother without devoting my whole life to mothering a daughter. I worked very long hours in an emergency room when my daughter was young, and I wasn't very

*involved in her life. When she started to feel left out, around age
eight, I rearranged my career, went into another business, and
was available after school and on weekends.*

Codependent Mothers and Daughters. Sometimes the
more a mother needs her daughter, the less likely she is to be
there for her daughter, instead expecting her daughter will
be there for her. Leaning on a daughter rather than supporting
her creates tension in the relationship and hampers the daughter. The daughter's independence is stymied because she feels
so responsible for her mother that she forfeits her own personal
growth. In the novel *Like Water for Chocolate* by Laura Esquivel, the youngest of three Mexican daughters, Tita, suffers
when the mother, Mama Elena, refuses to allow her to marry Pedro, the man she loves. Partly her refusal is due to a family tradi-
tion in which the youngest daughter stays at home to care for
her mother. But partly Mama Elena doesn't consider Tita's
growth and chance to have a life. To this end she insists that
Pedro marry Rosaura, her eldest daughter, thus keeping Tita
from ever having any happiness with Pedro or from ever escap-
ing her mother.

When a mother leans on her daughter, she can stifle her
daughter's independence and individuality, and guilt her daughter into staying, as if she'll fall apart without her. A mother
who has done this and then wakes up to the problem can
reverse her pattern. Consider Dorrie, forty-seven, who has a
twenty-year-old daughter.

*My daughter was my crutch during my divorce and almost my
companion. She was young and I leaned on her, I know it. When
I had a boyfriend, it was different, but mostly, I wanted her to
be my support system. It's totally backfired and she's moving*

across the country to transfer to another college. I get her mes-
sage and I know the relationship should change and I should
leave her alone.

Lost Mothers/Lost Daughters. If the mother herself is unanchored in her life, she is often unable to nurture her daughter's
self-direction. Many mothers described themselves as "dysfunctional" while aware that their situation was hindering their
daughters. But full knowledge isn't effective in these cases, and
a daughter can become lost, too, much like her mother, who is
too impaired emotionally to do anything about it. A heartbreaking true-life story of mother-daughter entanglement is
dramatized in the HBO production of *Grey Gardens,* starring
Jessica Lange as "Big Edie" Bouvier Beale, and Drew Barry-
more as her daughter, "Little Edie" Bouvier Beale. Big Edie
had aspired to be a singer and hoped that her daughter would
be a dancer. Instead, when Big Edie's husband left, Little Edie
returned home permanently, as a young woman, to soothe her
lonely, forsaken mother. Impoverished, they became an eccen-
tric pair who found a twisted relief in their shared life together.
Although Little Edie tried to leave her mother several times,
she wasn't able to because of her love, respect, and sense of responsibility. Together, the mother-daughter duo (the aunt and
cousin, respectively, of Jackie Kennedy Onassis), ended up living in poverty with fifty-two cats in their rundown estate, Grey
Gardens. Consider Alicia, forty-nine, whose sixteen-year-old
daughter knows that her mother isn't very stable.

I think my daughter knows what I've been through and how
hard it is for me to stay on track. I try not to make her take care
of me or to fall behind with friends or schoolwork in order to
help me out. Sometimes I'm tempted, because she's such a good

soul, to ask her to be with me or to only apply to colleges nearby, but it won't be fair to her. I'd be very happy with her always with me, but I know how selfish this is and how she'd become as screwed up as I am.

Dragging a daughter down rather than encouraging her to spread her wings is not only a dangerous path but is blatantly unfair to the daughter, who deserves her own life. If a mother acknowledges her problem, seeks guidance, and speaks openly with her daughter, there is the chance for improvement.

Helicopter Mothers

According to an article that ran on CNN.com on August 19, 2008, "How to Ground a 'Helicopter Parent'" by Donna Krache, helicopter parents "hover over their kids, micromanaging every aspect of their lives." Krache describes them as flying "into school in attack mode, ready to confront the teacher or coach for "'unfair' treatment of their kids." The retired high school counselor whom Krache interviews believes that this parenting style stymies teenagers from developing their own "decision-making" abilities. The National Survey of Student Engagement found in 2008 that 86 percent of freshmen in college were in contact frequently with their mothers by e-mail or cell phone. These students had lower grades than those with more independence. If we look at mothers and daughters, the hovering is intensified, due to the nature of the bond they share.

Duking it out. A mother would rather fight *for* her daughter than *with* her daughter. The mother establishes a relationship where the daughter confides in her and depends upon her to take care of things. This type of mother will go to bat for her daughter, confronting anyone, from a driver's ed teacher to another mother to bosses, if she believes it can benefit her daughter. Consider Jamey, forty-two, who lives in New Mexico and is an artist with a seventeen-year-old daughter.

I know what my daughter does wrong, and I won't let her pay for it. When I'm angry at her, I'm still on her side. She knows I'm the go-to person if there's a problem, and I spend half of my time putting out the fires. My daughter recently was at a party that got busted. Some of the mothers grounded their daughters, others blamed the parents of the boy who threw it. I told my daughter that I knew she was innocent and that I'd see to it that there was no problem.

Living situations. Daughters may end up with a roommate problem in college and a mother will fight for her daughter, calling the school if she thinks it's necessary. Later on, the plot thickens; daughters are older, but the dependency lingers. A daughter may choose to live in an unacceptable area or her mother may disapprove of the roommate or the boyfriend with whom she's cohabitating. In these cases, a mother's hovering is not appreciated and there's friction between mother and daughter. For example, Alana, fifty one, who lives in Massachusetts, is a stay-at-home mother to three daughters, ages thirteen, sixteen, and twenty-one.

I've stopped myself from cleaning up my twenty-one-year-old daughter's mess. This is the third time she's lost a job and a share in a group house, and all of my friends' daughters are on track. But I'm not going to interfere this time. . . . She'll figure it out for herself or she won't know what she really wants or how to do it. It's weird, since I've always fixed it all and been there on top of issues, neither she nor I know quite what to do. So I'm trying to figure it out—be there for her but not intrude.

Returning home. Mothers should brace themselves for the day that their daughters return home after having lived on their own at college, grad school, or thereafter. This occurs when a romantic relationship fails, a roommate problem ensues, or a daughter loses her job (common in the downturn) and cannot afford her rent. Old issues replay themselves once the daughter is home, and the adjustment period for both mother and daughter is prolonged by the ghosts of the relationship past. Ironically, any hovering the mother has done would now be welcomed by the daughter, who is somewhat infantilized by her return. Indeed, Diana, forty-six, who lives in Texas and works in a family business, worries about her relationship with her daughter, twenty-eight.

It's been years since my daughter inhabited her room. This is the girl who left for college ten years ago and vowed never to return. But things have changed and she's in law school without any way to make money this year. So she just assumed I'd have her room ready. The trouble is her boyfriend, her hours, her music . . . And then I get too involved because she's there, I end up doing her wash, making sure everything is okay. But we're both beyond this. Or at least I thought we were.

Although helicopter parenting can be stifling and keep daughters from becoming independent and resourceful, it's important to note that mothers are not necessarily holding their daughters back by trying to help them. Mothers do best to preserve the closeness with their daughters while adjusting to new conditions that arise as the daughter grows older and her circumstances change. If mothers and daughters achieve equilibrium, it works well.

Squelching Personal Authority

In an article that ran on June 11, 2009, on People.com, "Chastity Bono Undergoing Sex Change," Stephen M. Silverman writes, "Political and social activist Chastity Bono—the only child of entertainers Cher and the late Sonny Bono—began undergoing a sex change shortly after her fortieth birthday on March 4." Silverman reports that "Cher is very supportive and has known about Chastity wanting to do this for a very long time." However, a 1998 *People* article details how, when Chastity announced to her parents she was gay in 1987, Cher "flipped out" because she'd imagined her daughter getting married, and having children. In the years to follow, it was Chastity's activism that caused her mother to recognize her "as a full person for the first time."

Because our culture is steeped in the importance of individuality, the very thought of repressing this in our daughters is chilling and, according to the majority of mothers with whom I've spoken, antithetical to their intentions. However, mothers not only want to be a refuge for their daughters, but also to see the results of their time and energy. Above all, mothers frequently imagine a specific result—and herein lies the problem. The mother's rationale is the following: I've told my daughter to be hardworking, to be inventive. I've raised my daughter to have all that I couldn't have. I'm so forgiving—I do so much for her and I'm less strict than my own mother. So why isn't she the way that I envisioned she'd be?

To play devil's advocate: What way would that be? Dependent but independent, created in her mother's image but with her own image? With a voice, but one that echoes her mother's sentiments? Ironically, the majority of mothers claim they never intended to squelch a daughter's voice and yet, by the time the interviews had ended, half realized that in some way they had done so, and the other half felt that their daughters had supremacy and authority, *not* the mothers.

The Good-Girl Syndrome

For those mothers who have attempted not to indulge their daughters, there remains the sense that both mother and daughter are interpreted by how they present to the world in terms of appearance, achievement, and social status. If a mother has all the right accoutrements, this reflects the daughter, and vice versa. Author Rachel Simmons writes in her latest book, *The Curse of the Good Girl*, that girls in middle school feel they must please others, be nice, do the right thing, not rebel or say how they really feel. Individuality is too intimidating and counterproductive. She warns that this keeps these girls from growing up as their own genuine self.

What is concerning, as we have seen in previous chapters, is a mother who wants her daughter to conform because she herself believes in the positive outcome of a daughter on this path.

Consider Juliet, fifty-one, who lives in Michigan, where she is a makeup artist and has a twenty-year-old daughter.

I raised my daughter to do everything that she was supposed to do and it backfired. After all the hellish stuff that happened in high school—I wasn't sure she'd graduate at times and she left a religious school to go to public school in the end—I see that she's very fragile. That's the problem now, and I try not to touch her hot buttons, so I don't push her to find work, I don't push her to be independent. Instead I think, if there's anything I can do, I'll do it for her. I've helped her move into a group house with some friends and she knows how sorry I am that I couldn't give her a happier home these past few years. I knew all along to let tensions go, but I couldn't. I keep trying to make it all okay for my daughter, for both of us.

In-charge Mothers

Abigail, fifty-two, who is a travel agent and lives in a small town in Connecticut, has two daughters, twenty-four and twenty-seven. Alice believes that her daughters having not asserted their own authority is a positive measure.

My girls were raised in a very formal way with a high level of politeness. No one could just go to the refrigerator and take food out without asking. They weren't allowed to leave home without announcing where they were going. I felt in charge as their mother and that meant that we had open conversations about feelings and they knew what I didn't approve of. There was tremendous respect from my girls toward me and from me toward my girls. Because I always listened to them and they listened to me, and as mothers and daughters go, there were no big fights, and few disagreements.

While I worked hard on everyone getting along and expressing themselves quietly, my two daughters are so different, and they fought tooth and nail at home. But both grew up in the same strict home and this has given them a sense of self and I

see it as they go forward in their lives. If some of my control ear-
lier on seemed a bit much, I look back and realize that it held up
when they hit those difficult teen years and beyond.

Catherine, like Abigail, justifies her decision to have the upper hand with her older daughter. At forty-eight, Catherine
lives in North Carolina, where she works in marketing. Her
daughters are twenty-five and twenty-two.

I've watched the mothers in my hometown suffer for their daugh-
ters and it taught me to accept my girls for who they are. My
younger daughter is so headstrong, it's her way or the highway,
and she was born this way. It took great effort on my part to
show her that it's not all about her. I didn't want to run scared
or for her to believe that she was in charge, and I let both girls
know it. They should be grateful—I'm married to their father
and it's a stable home. They have what they need but it's not
lavish. What I've taught them is to survive on their own and in
order to do that, to give them this confidence, I couldn't be per-
ceived as a wuss or a pushover.

When my older daughter had a problem with drugs—at
seventeen—I concentrated on that. If she had to have a problem,
at least it was while she was still under my roof and I could
confront it. I made the decision to commit this daughter and it
saved her. I didn't think that I'd done something wrong. I have
never wondered about what I did or why I did it.

Daughters at Full Gallop

Candace Bushnell's novel *One Fifth Avenue* features an in-
charge daughter who knows few bounds. Twenty-two-year-old

Lola Fabrikant, an only child raised in the Atlanta suburbs by a socially ambitious mother, exceeds her mother's aspirations after she arrives in New York City. Lola is more conniving, lazier, and more mercenary than anything her mother could have concocted. When she returns to Atlanta at her mother's behest, Lola cannot wrap her mind around her mother's crashing world.

On the way home from the airport, Lola's mother, Beetelle, tells her that her husband—Lola's father—has lost everything. Lola's response is to insist upon turning off her mother's "awful" seventies hits radio station. After years of what Bushnell describes as Beetelle having "adjusted to Lola's dismissive remarks," Beetelle hits her limit. Bushnell writes, "Beetelle took her eyes off the road for a second to regard her daughter, sitting impatiently in the front seat, her eyes narrowed in annoyance. An irrational anger overwhelmed her; suddenly, she hated her daughter. 'Lola,' she said, 'will you please shut up?'"

Indeed, Sonya, forty-two, who works as a freelancer and lives in Southern California, has a seventeen-year-old daughter who has recently rejected all of Sonya's life lessons.

I think I've been talking to the wall all these years. I remember how close my daughter and I were when she was small. I taught her to love books and music, the outdoors, to try out for cheerleading, to be a good student. It all made sense until about two years ago. Then it was all about her friends and what they wanted, what they were permitted to do. I found that anything I refused made me the enemy. When friends came over, I think they were whispering about me, quite honestly. She has sort of taken over—her room, her books on the table at dinnertime, her mess everywhere. Each of her actions is hostile and aimed at me.

My husband says nothing. He sort of shrugs and looks at me as if I haven't done the correct thing. My daughter listens to music all night long, she does her homework at the last minute, and she thinks because she's always been a good student that this is okay to do. Sometimes we fight, and other times, I not only give in, I supply her with the goods—a ride to school when she's overslept and missed the bus, money to go to the mall with her girlfriends, a yes instead of a no when she wants to go out on school nights.

Silencing a Daughter's Voice

Threaded through this book, in various circumstances, is the description of a mother's desire to protect her daughter when it comes to the trials and tribulations of life. The decision to spare one's daughter by placing her in a bubble or by discouraging her from taking risks often backfires. If a mother operates out of fear or memory of her own betrayals and teaches her daughter to do the same, the daughter feels unprepared for the world, including academics, workplace, and romance, and bears the weight of her mother's disappointments and worries.

The Cocoon Effect

"My sixteen-year-old daughter feels smothered by me, all the time," admits Angelina, forty-five. "She'll want to go to a rock concert or she'll want to go to a party and all I can do is worry about what might go wrong. None of the other mothers seem as worried as I am—I want to keep her home, safe with me."

If we keep our daughters from age-appropriate events, they'll not only be angry, but will sneak out to get there.

Daughters as Interpreters

"Every time I operate like a hysteric, my daughter, who is eighteen, calls me on it," begins Lara, forty-four. "She says I'm ruining her life. I can't help but worry, we live in a scary world. Should I let her go wherever she wants at whatever hour she chooses? She has no judgment, that's the problem."

Making a daughter anxious about her every move as a teenager will cause her to be nervous as an adult woman and lack confidence.

Disparaging Mothers

"Every thing I say seems to offend my twenty-three-year-old, and she thinks I'm giving her a hard time," says Sarah, fifty, "but it's more that I don't like her roommate and that she has to work harder on her graduate degree. I also don't like her boyfriend and I hope she'll meet someone else. When I say anything, she's defensive and then withdraws."

Imposing your values and style on your daughter makes her think that you are intolerant—and prohibits her from finding herself. It will also put a wedge in your relationship.

Silenced Daughters

"I realize how much I want to help my daughter," confides Anna, fifty-six, about her twenty-five-year-old daughter. "Why have others judged her when I know how she feels and why she acts like she does? One of my best friends tried to confront me, saying my daughter shouldn't be pushed by me, so I blew her off as meddlesome and nosy. Only recently did I start to think that I don't listen to what my daughter says, after all."

Mothers who don't take the time to hear their daughters and help them realize their dreams usually appear unsupportive and controlling to the daughters.

Acrobatic Feats

When a mother does somersaults for her daughter, her daughter's perception of the world becomes distorted. That said, plenty of mothers with several daughters say that their style of mothering their daughters has changed over the years. In this way, they are much milder and more inclined to say yes by the time the third or fourth daughter hits puberty. As Michelle Slatalla writes in her *New York Times* column on February 19, 2009, "My older daughters grew up in a family where candy was a controlled substance. . . . Sleepovers were restricted (one girl only, please, and not the one who gets homesick at two A.M.). I'm not that mother anymore." Slatalla's explanation for her change of heart with her third daughter, who came along years after the first two, is that she herself has become "the mother [she] wanted when [she] was a child." But is this younger/youngest daughter more independent, a freethinker, or simply the daughter who has a tired mother who's willing to say yes in order to get through the day?

Enough mothers in this study have remarked that birth order definitely had a place in how they dealt with their younger daughters. A group of mothers described themselves as world-weary and having seen it all by the time their last child hit the age of twelve. Some felt that their youngest daughter was the one who was most demanding. Yet because these mothers had been so careful with their older daughters and had tried to balance their own prerogatives with their daughters' need for autonomy, they were less daunted by what the youngest daughter expected and simply more inclined to give in.

There are also mothers with several daughters who have compromised with the first, in anticipation of the long road ahead. For instance, Hope, forty-six, who is a stay-at-home mother living in the Northeast with two daughters, understands the challenges set before her by her older daughter, who is fifteen.

I let my oldest daughter express herself through her makeup, how she dresses, and the friends she chooses. Her friends aren't my first choice, but I'm letting her find her way. This daughter uses impermanent tattoos on her forearms and I look at it as a phase. I let it come and go, knowing I need to pick and choose my battles. I believe that my daughter has a strong sense of responsibility, something I've taught her, and I allow her to travel by herself to visit friends in nearby towns by train. There are mothers who would disagree, but I'm confident that my daughter can do this and she has to find her way by my allowing her to have freedom. So when I'm uneasy or I give in, it's always with this feeling that she's coming around and that she's a real person. I know she'll come back to me with what's right for her.

Allowing a Daughter to Flourish

Do offer guidance to your daughter without stepping on her toes. This applies to her friendships, romances, and workplace experiences. It's best to tread lightly, giving your daughter the space she needs. A daughter hopes to be buoyed by her mother and at the same time recognized for her abilities.

Be conscious of how you address your daughter's self-worth, remembering how fragile her ego may be. Avoid being judgmental regarding your daughter's lifestyle, self-image, and interests. This will only push your daughter away. Rather, broach topics positively, even when expressing your concern.

Intervene and offer your opinion when your daughter asks for it or when she truly needs it. When you offer advice, be firm, wise, and understanding. Otherwise, allow her to learn on her own and bear in mind her distinct personality and style.

Stop enabling and excusing your daughter. Our daughters will never learn for themselves if we are always in the way. If a daughter faces her successes and failures on her own, she'll learn how to operate in the real world and how to express herself.

Know when to change your tune by listening carefully to your daughter. Many of the mothers were quite adamant about their beliefs and were immutable, despite their daughters' need for flexibility. If a mother can be open-minded, she will help her daughter to believe in herself and trust her own instincts.

Chapter 9

✽

Some of Us Pay the Price for Success

Sending Mixed Messages About Achievement and Ambition

- Are you preparing your daughter to work toward her goals?
- Do you push your daughter to do well academically?
- Have you moaned about glass ceilings and the second shift?
- Does your daughter consider you a success?
- Have you ever told your daughter that ambition is double-edged?

In any of these situations, your daughter is drawn to your missive *and* what the culture yields.

YOU WAKE UP at night and ask yourself what went wrong in terms of your guidance. After all, you taught your daughter, now twenty-six, to do well in school and to get into a good college and she did. Since she's been out there, in the work world for five years, she's made no headway and has no real career. Her interests—in art and music—couldn't translate into a moneymaking venture so easily, and she's had nothing but mediocre jobs and is becoming sort of mediocre herself. Had she listened to you, she would have gone to law school. This is something you know she would excel at and could also translate into success. She was resistant, probably because she has watched you working in the corporate world and sees how it takes everything out of you.

But what she must have missed is the idea of pushing ahead and hoping for some combination of loving work, loving oneself, and finally getting a break. Already she's gotten lazy and tired and, unfortunately, so have her two best friends from high school. They seem so . . . unanchored, uncertain. Secretly you believe that this is because she listened to how you complained and, more recently, to how her friends complain, and it's put her off. In fact, she has zero interest in a career. You suspect she's biding her time until something miraculous happens—the right job falls in her lap or she meets a successful young man who will sweep her off her feet. Can you blame her for hoping for a way out?

Ambition and Females

When a woman's ambition comes to light in our patriarchal culture, it reminds us that ambition is considered a male attribute; women who seek this are considered unfeminine. This was the case when Hillary Clinton sought the Democratic nomination for president in 2008 and the press circulated criticisms about her being too ambitious. While Hillary was damned if she did, damned if she didn't (remember when the press thought her neckline too low and her tone too harsh?), this underscores how our society interprets women who are smart, successful, and highly motivated. It's almost as if such women are encouraged to hide their M.O. because it makes them appear too tough-minded, unassailable, and aggressive (another quality considered positive for men and negative for women). In contrast, women who appear fragile are more readily accepted—thus when Hillary shed a tear at a roundtable discussion at a coffee shop in Portsmouth, New Hampshire, in January of 2008, it was newsworthy. Patrick Healy's piece in *The New York Times,* "On Eve of Primary, Clinton Campaign Shows Stress," describes the scene: "Her eyes visibly wet, in perhaps the most public display of emotion of her year-old campaign, Mrs. Clinton added: 'I have so many opportunities from this country, I just don't want to see us fall backwards. This is very personal for me—it's not just political, it's not just public.'" Women of all ages felt an affinity for Hillary Clinton's emotion and identified with the chink in her armor. It's as if her weakness made her one of us.

Other women in the news garner scrutiny, too, including Caroline Kennedy during her brief bid for the New York Senate seat left empty when Hillary Clinton became secretary of state in January 2009. There was speculation that Kennedy's three teenage children (Rose, Tatiana, and John) weren't happy with her decision. Yet when Caroline Kennedy was asked by Matt Lauer on the *Today* show on May 18, 2009, if her children were the reason for her withdrawal, she dismissed the idea. Edward Klein reported in the June 2009 issue of *Vanity Fair* that a few hours before Kennedy called Governor David Paterson to tell him she wouldn't seek the appointment, she was told by her daughter Rose, "You are above this." What is interesting is how Caroline Kennedy's decision stirred up emotions for women in terms of the age-old dilemma—achievement versus motherhood. In an editorial in *The New York Times,* "Coming Up Short as a Role Model for the Mommy Track," on January 23, 2009, Susan Dominus states, "To many women in midlife, one of the more appealing aspects of Ms. Kennedy's bid for public office was highly personal: Here was a woman poised to show that you could devote your thirties to raising children and yet have an impressive, challenging second act." Dominus also points out that the reason for Kennedy's withdrawal "suggested" it was due to a family emergency and that this is what employers "dread" they'll hear from their female employees.

Another famous woman (and a mother of two teenage daughters) under examination is Katie Couric, who left NBC for CBS in 2006 for an annual salary of $15 million. According to an article in *Elle* by Rebecca Traister, "Katie Couric: Reports of Her Demise Were Greatly Exaggerated," Couric's coverage of the 2008 presidential campaign, including an interview with Sarah Palin in June 2008, was "a stealthy combination of intelligence, approachability, and keen journalistic instinct."

And, of course, in terms of women in the spotlight, there are film stars and performers who garner great curiosity. When *Forbes* magazine published "The Celebrity 100," a "power ranking based on earnings and fame" in June 2009, the first four celebrities listed were women. Angelina Jolie topped the list, earning $27 million in the previous year, and was followed by Oprah Winfrey ($275 million), Madonna ($110 million), and Beyoncé Knowles ($87 million).

Educating Our Daughters to Achieve

Many mothers who push their daughters to do well academically believe that a daughter's education is tantamount to success. But the imprimatur of a daughter with the right test scores translating into the right schools and the right life starts at infancy, as reported by Melinda Beck in the "Health Journal" column of *The Wall Street Journal.* "How's Your Baby? Recalling the Apgar Score's Namesake" offers a brief history of the test created by Virginia Apgar in 1949, which grants a newborn a score for "how well they made the transition from womb to room." "Apgar" stands for appearance, pulse, grimace, activity, and respiration, and mothers, apparently, kick into achievement mode immediately, not only hoping that their babies will have high scores at birth, but also comparing the results with other mothers. Soon enough this translates to how well a daughter does throughout her career as a student—the sky is the limit when it comes to an achieving daughter.

More than half the mothers with whom I spoke admitted to aiding their daughters with their schoolwork at various junctures. Mothers who practically do their daughter's homework in grade school will hover over their assignments through high school and become the mothers who all but complete their daughters' college essays. These mothers are willing to confront administrators at any turn to explain why their daughters have been misunderstood and go unrecognized—another form of excuse making. Consider Kathleen, forty-six, who is a stay-at-home mother in a Midwestern town and has three daughters, twenty, nineteen, and twelve.

I admit, I've done the girls' homework since they were in third grade. If I hadn't it would have been bedlam. In our town, the mothers who didn't help were the bad mothers, and what I did was what any decent mother would do. There were times when I made a visit to the teacher, too, if I thought that any of my daughters was behind or being neglected. I also guided my older daughters when it came to college. I wanted to make sure they were looking at schools that fit with their plans. What else would I be here for but to do this? It's my job and I have to do it properly. I'd say I'm obsessed except that compared to the other mothers, I'm tame. I know my girls have benefited, the way anyone would benefit from having someone working for you 24/7. That's what it feels like, but I'll get very accomplished daughters out of this with solid careers and earning power—there's no other choice.

Single-Sex Schools

An ongoing debate of the past ten or fifteen years addresses the question of single-sex schools, with the salient question being how this promotes learning for girls versus boys. It isn't just a question of learning differences but one of eliminating the stereotypes that are a result of these differences—i.e., helping girls to improve in math and science and helping boys to do better with language—traditionally a female arena. According to "Where the Girls Aren't," an essay by Leonard Sax that ran in *Education Week* on June 18, 2008, girls who attend an all-girls school are "several times more likely to study subjects such as computer science, physics, and engineering, compared with girls attending coed schools." Mothers, as evidenced in the following two interviews, are divided on private versus public school education and single-sex versus coed education, all in the name of what suits their daughters.

Indeed, Dina, thirty-eight, who lives in a Northeastern city and works part-time in a hospital, chose a single-sex school for her daughters, nine, eight, and six, because she believed it would instill confidence.

I wanted my girls to have the best education, especially because I grew up in a small town without any private schools for miles, let alone single-sex schools. I have always worked and made money and appreciated it, but it's because of my college experience, not my grade school or junior high days, that I knew I could do it. There are different ways to be educated, and finding an elite private girls' school isn't about the social life for my girls, it's about learning. I want them to read the classics and to speak several languages and to love learning and have individual attention. My friends say that my girls should be in a coed classroom, coming from an all-female family, but I see it as just the opposite. The more all-girl environments, the stronger they'll be.

In contrast to Dina is Veronica, forty-eight, who lives in northern California and has taken her daughter, sixteen, out of an all-girls private school.

All that ever happens in these private girls' schools is that the social life is very fast and privileged. My daughter had lots of friends, but she also had lots of tutors. This annoys me since I thought the school spoon-fed the girls. So either it was too demanding or the girls didn't care about academics as much as boys and parties. I got tired of feeling that she couldn't keep up—I can only imagine how she felt about it. I decided, enough. Now she's at a public high school to complete these last two years and it's much better. Maybe in the private school system there are more ways to learn, but a regular public high school seems more normal. And the hope is that my daughter can learn anywhere.

Means to an End

A March 21, 2009, article, "In School, Michelle Obama Was Not 'Cool,' but Bent On Being Smart," reports that "Michelle Obama remembers being ridiculed for trying to be educated and getting good grades in school in Chicago's South Side." Her speech was a part of Women's National History Month at Anacostia High School. Other famous women who spoke to students in the Washington area included Alicia Keys, Sheryl Crow, Phylicia Rashad, Alfre Woodard, Fran Drescher, and the first female four-star army general, Ann Dunwoody. Michelle Obama remarked, "I wanted an A. I wanted to be smart. I wanted to be the person who had the right answer," and said she valued being an exemplary student and emphasizes this for her own daughters.

As Brendan I. Koerner notes in the *U.S. News & World Report* article "Where the Boys Aren't," there are three women for every two men attending college. What becomes of these women after college depends upon how influenced they are by their mothers, their friends, and the culture at large, and how motivated they are personally.

Consider Audrey, fifty-eight, who lives in a large town where she works as a high school administrator and believes that her thirty-one-year-old daughter has followed her advice about education and achievement.

My message was that I supported my daughter whatever she did, but I expected her to make decisions about what she could or could not do when it came to school and her career. I'd say I was very lucky—my daughter raised herself and I watched. But where she really understood my intentions was when it came to high school and college—there I encouraged her to do what she wanted and to become successful at it. She decided to go to law school and I knew she'd be good at it and it was a wise decision. I realized then that my daughter is someone who can take advantage of an opportunity and it's remarkable how well she's done. She's also left a job when she thought it was time and has been mindful always of being the best she could be and proud of it. It's fun to watch her land on her feet, and I feel that my example has made a difference.

Nicole, forty-nine, a physician in the Southwest, feels similarly about her twenty-seven-year-old daughter, a resident at a nearby hospital.

For all the craziness in our family, I know that the one thing my daughter has taken away is how important it is to have a career and to achieve. She went to a private school on scholarship and to an excellent college on scholarship. She always knew it was about getting ahead, and it's not only financial independence, but that she has interests and a focus. I didn't go to medical school until she was a baby, but she knew I had wanted to do it for years—I've told her about how long it took me. Through thick or thin, I've had this, and it makes me accomplished and someone who contributes to society. My daughter may have rejected my style of dress, my taste in music, but she really wanted this for herself, too. It is something we share and it's something that we respect in each other. Had she chosen another career, I would have been fine—as long as she made the commitment to it.

Hindering Mothers

Although both Audrey and Nicole believe that their deliberate modeling was well received by their daughters, there are mothers who are conflicted about their daughters' achievements. They know intellectually that their daughters should work hard to excel at school and establish a career, but they are often caught up in their ambivalence and cynicism about their own careers. As if this isn't difficult enough, the downturn and twenty-first-century job market has posed its own hurdles for young women today. Consider Viola, fifty-five, who lives in California and works as an interior designer. She has a twenty-three-year-old daughter.

My daughter is so talented, but she isn't lucky. She's twenty-three years old, she studied dance for years, and now she works at the Gap in our hometown. It's not the right job for her and the career she's chosen is so hard to break into. I feel like she's not equipped for anything but dance, and it's absurd that she's doing what she does. She's tired from a day that means nothing to her—after all her dance lessons. I tell her that it will work out and when she's upset, I try to give her some hope—remind her how talented she is. Since I was supposed to be a model and ended up designing, I am angry that history seems to repeat itself. When my daughter was younger, I called the shots, but now there's not much that I can say. Should I have pushed her toward something more practical, so that she could ignore her talent but make a living? Should I have let her have a more normal childhood, not one where we were so focused on her being in a dance troupe? I only know how unfair it is in the arts. I suppose she'll flit from job to job until maybe, if she gets a break, she ends up doing something rewarding.

As Sue Shellenbarger wrote in her *Wall Street Journal* column on work and family on June 10, 2009, "Raising Kids Who Can Thrive Amid Chaos in Their Careers," young people today

may change jobs up to fourteen times, and despite a fine education, there are few jobs available for graduates. The way to
"equip children for this," according to her research, is by teaching them three skills during childhood: adaptability, defined as
"helping children make logical choices when confronted with
many options" and teaching them how to "critique their own
work"; exploration, defined as "encouraging them to try new
things without fear or failure or shame"; and entrepreneurial-
ism, defined as "taking initiative and risks to put new ideas
into play" and to teach children to be resourceful.

If we apply this advice to daughters when they are younger
than junior high school, it stands to reason they'll be better
prepared for today's world. For daughters who are already in
college or in the workplace, it is worth discussing this method
so that they are better able to handle job searches or working
in a field that might not be their first choice. Yet when I mentioned this pathway to mothers who voiced concern about their
daughters' chances of landing a job, let alone forging a career,
some felt it wasn't imperative. Despite the economic climate,
this faction viewed their daughters as having more options
than they'd ever had and believed that their daughters would
exceed their dreams in terms of accomplishment and lifestyle.

Although mothers want their daughters to accomplish their
goals, a mother's complicated trajectory and her interpretation
of a situation might prove an impediment. The following are
ways in which mothers may inadvertently misdirect their
daughters:

Not teaching the necessity of practical skills. Mothers
who neglect the importance of this will not have daughters who
adjust easily to the outside world and the demands placed upon

them. Those mothers who teach the basics say their daughters are better equipped—and the daughters are grateful.

Interfering with scholastic endeavors. A mother who calls the school or fights her daughter's battles with teachers or administrators in high school or college isn't allowing her daughter to have a voice. This also limits her daughter's ability to integrate her personal style and the joy of learning, which can remain a problem when she enters the workplace.

Being an obstacle to a daughter's productivity and perseverance. The lamentable part is that the years of hovering and "helicoptering" have produced a daughter who finds the responsibility of the work week and the daily constraints of a job overwhelming. If the mother still fans the fire when her daughter complains that the boss isn't fair (much as she did during high school regarding a teacher), how will the daughter develop a work ethic or adapt to the environment?

Substituting beauty for achievement. As witnessed in Chapter 4, a mother who advocates beauty above brains positions her daughter precariously in terms of values, beginning at school and continuing in the years ahead. If a daughter is persuaded to trade on her looks rather than her academic abilities, she is denied the chance to develop an intellectual pursuit.

In all of the above scenarios, a mother's sense of herself plus how she's raised her daughter regarding skill set has impact. It's as if beauty, power, money, lost dreams, and work ethic—or lack thereof—are all being tested in this arena by the daughter, in part *because* of the mother. "These daughters have had so much, and were given 'trophies' every step of the way by their mothers," comments psychologist Seth Shulman. "They're both hopeful and ill-prepared for the real world—school and work—at the same time."

Self-Actualization

While Abraham Maslow's "need" for self-esteem is explored in the previous chapter, his fifth and last need is for actualization, a concept that is featured in this chapter. Maslow describes self-actualization as what an individual must do to be true to herself. For example, an artist must do her craft, a writer must write, and a surgeon must operate. If this doesn't happen, then Maslow views the person as on edge and restless. Because self-actualization is not a basic need, such as warmth or water, or an obvious need, such as the need to be loved and recognized, it becomes a bit trickier. Simons, Irwin, and Drinnien describe this in *Psychology: The Search for Understanding* as the importance of finding one's "vocation in life"—a "calling, fate, or destiny." This can apply to "finding the right career," where, unfortunately, we can be sidetracked by the expectations of society. As this applies to mothers and daughters, the mothers represent society, while the daughters are in search of their true identity. Ironically, mother and daughter alike can fall prey to the societal proscriptions to the exclusion of their inner selves.

Although we know that enough mothers have grappled with hitting their stride, the dream that one's daughter will exhibit leadership qualities and achievement is practically ubiquitous. That said, several mothers with whom I spoke admitted to feeling they were poor role models. Consider Tess, forty-three, who has never "found herself" and has a daughter she fears will follow this path. Tess lives in Virginia, where she practices dermatology part-time and believes that her younger daughter, seventeen, has already taken her cues from her.

I plan to pay for my two daughters to go to college and grad school. One daughter is conscientious and primed for success, and the other one looks at my schedule and figures she could be like me, which isn't such a good thing, but I'm over forty. I work limited hours, and to the outside world, I have a great profession, but I've never been totally into it. I did it because it seemed like the best idea in my day.

This daughter watches me and figures I'm not fully there, not at work, not in my love life, or in how I live. She's already more interested in going through the motions, too, and I know she will never be sure what she wants to do. So she's spoiled and could fill her days without having anything in the work world, but it isn't what I want for her. She seems confused about who she is and acts more like my peer than my daughter when it comes to this—as if she's earned it, which isn't her case at all. I worry that she won't shake this pattern of hers and I feel sort of helpless to say much. I know I should figure out what it is I want . . . and be a better role model.

Sleepwalking Daughters

More than half the mothers interviewed for this chapter expressed dismay that their daughters weren't paying attention to the trajectories of successful women or aware of illustrious women of a certain age. Nonetheless, these women, both boomer mothers, born between 1946 and 1960, and Generation X mothers, born between the early 1960s and late 1970s, are quite familiar with the significance of the workplace. They are equally aware that making one's own money is about independence, and know what it takes to be an achieving woman. Consider

Andrea, fifty, who lives in a small town, where she works part-time in administration and has two daughters, twenty-three and twenty-six.

I've told my girls that I've been responsible to educate them debt free and after that, it's their responsibility to take care of themselves and my responsibility to take care of myself. So they both know that they're out there building careers with the object being they're self-supporting. I'm fairly practical and logical and I've taught them to be the same about this. What I didn't do was make a fuss about women who had these great careers—women in the news—as role models. This all came from what we could afford and how much we could care for the girls after college. I'm a working mother, but it's part-time and I'm not the breadwinner because I have a very traditional marriage. What I did show them is that this isn't the best idea in today's world and that dual working couples do better with all that can go wrong or right. I didn't tell them they have to be married, but I did tell them they had to make their own money—and to do so they have to have drive. I assume they're hearing all this.

Unlike Andrea is Brett, forty-seven, who lives in a Southern city, where she works full-time at a corporation. She feels that her daughter, twenty-three, has no ambition.

My daughter doesn't admire how I've worked, and she thinks I only did it because I'm a single mother with two children I had to raise. I'm hardworking, but it isn't because I savor every moment of my job. It's a career, sure, and I've done well because I'm capable, but my daughter has somehow missed all this. What she sees is me stressed and tired and still not rich, just making ends meet. I'm not this innocent young thing I was when I ended up alone and I have become hardened. My daughter ignores this, as if she doesn't want to face who you become in the workforce. So she doesn't look at me and say, "Wow, it's great to be resourceful and make your own money." She looks at me and wonders how to escape this being your life. I'm not sure that she's wrong.

It appears that daughters don't see their mothers as having the final word on achievement and satisfaction, although they take it under consideration. In an interview, Anna Fels, the author of *Necessary Dreams: Ambition in Women's Changing Lives*, cautioned that our daughters are more influenced by peers, mentors, and the media when it comes to their ambitions. "There is a need for social fairness that hasn't been met for women in the workplace, and the daughters see this. While their mothers had the illusion that they could do it all, it's very difficult for these daughters—and they know it," said Dr. Fels.

Working Women

Despite that financial inequality and discrimination in the workplace still exists today, according to J. S. Eccles's model, women choose their occupation by predicting how successful they'll be at it and what kind of value it has. Long gone is the thinking that existed before the second wave of feminism and the women's movement of the mid-sixties, when nursing, teaching, and secretarial work were pursued as a fail-safe for those who either didn't marry or didn't marry a man who could support his wife. According to the U.S. Census, 72 million women are in the workforce as labor participants today and comprise 46.5 percent of the total U.S. labor force, as reported by the U.S. Department of Labor.

The mothers with whom I spoke for this chapter varied in their perspective of careers for themselves and for their daughters. A quarter of the women commented upon how driven their daughters were *despite* their mothers' ambivalence about careers and despite having heard their mothers describe work as an overrated experience. Seventy-five percent subscribed to the belief that having a career and the ability to earn money was of utmost importance. Curiously, virtually all of the mothers had encouraged their daughters to apply themselves along the way, i.e.: in high school, college, or graduate studies. Mothers and daughters shared the vagaries for women in the workplace, and mothers expressed how difficult it is to prepare one's daughter for the deterrents.

Rivalry Among Women

A mother who warns her daughter of the high rate of female rivalry in the workplace is surely preparing her. Seventy percent of the women interviewed reported feeling keenly competitive with women of all ages at work.

Consider Holly, fifty-four, mother of two daughters, twenty-seven and twenty-three.

First I stressed that business might be a good field for my daughters in college. Then I stressed that life was a long race and just because some schoolmates or colleagues might burn brighter for now, the situation would undoubtedly be different later in their lives.

Cutthroat Mothers

A mother's narcissism can rear its head here, as in other situations, when a mother wants her daughter to mirror her level of success rather than exceed her. This type of mother isn't open to her daughter finding her own area of interest. Consider, for example, Charisse, forty-eight, who has one daughter, twenty-four.

My daughter could have followed in my footsteps and studied pharmacology and worked with me. She didn't need to go for a Ph.D.—it isn't like there's a family business waiting for her. Did I do all this for her to turn away from my plan, turn her nose up at my job? I don't see the point of it, and I doubt I ever will.

Risk Takers/Determined Mothers

If a mother operates out of confidence, not fear, and encourages her daughter to do the same in the workplace, options open up. Indeed, Layla, fifty-nine, has advised her thirty-year-old daughter of this.

When one door closes, another opens. During the dot-com boom, my daughter was working for a tech company and feeling unfulfilled. I told her to leave immediately and look for the position that would launch her career, and she did.

Vicarious Thrills

It's difficult in a culture such as ours not to boast about one's daughter or embellish her success. There are those mothers who also feel a vicarious pleasure in watching their daughters. However, it isn't healthy for either woman when a mother thinks this is her victory as well. For example, Donna, forty-eight, believes her daughter, twenty-seven, has the chances she never had.

I got married young and pregnant and missed my youth. My daughter dates and works in a big company. She calls me every night to say how it went that day and I imagine it as if I'm there. She makes more money now per year than I've ever made. I keep thinking this could be my life. I talk about her to all my friends and it feels so real.

Preparing Our Daughters: Sexism

Because women at work are set up to compete for insufficient resources (and to compete only with other women), sexism remains a part of the work culture. Working mothers worry more that female coworkers and bosses won't treat their daughters fairly than they worry about a work environment that is male-dominated. Some mothers recommend their daughters protest any kind of unfair treatment. Consider Dee, forty-four, who works for a corporation and has two daughters, twelve and ten.

I am preparing my girls for the day when they'll face the same problems I face every day with my boss, who is ten years older than I am and so awful to me. My girls are great students and

*hope to have big careers, but unless the world changes by then, I
expect them to face the same problems. We talk about it, so they
understand and feel inspired to get into it and fight.*

Money and Work

According to the National Committee on Pay Equity, women
are paid 77.1 cents for every dollar a man earns, still today.
Mothers who make their daughters aware of this are preparing
them for the realties of the workplace for women. For example,
Lynnie, thirty-eight, has just left her position as an in-house
attorney. She has three daughters, six, three, and two.

*I left my job because once I had children, I couldn't stand the un-
fairness anymore. It's as if thinking about what the world would
be like for the girls just made me want to quit work. But I plan to
share very early how fabulous it is to work and make money even
if the system is unjust in terms of equal pay for equal work.*

Leslie Bennetts, author of *The Feminine Mistake,* believes
that there hasn't been enough emphasis placed on the rich rewards of a woman's career. In an interview, Bennetts remarks,
"There's a real taboo against women tooting their own horns
and boasting about achievement, so they often feel inhibited
from saying, 'I did this, I did that—aren't I fantastic?' the way
men do. As a result, there's been a crucial failure in communication from older women to younger women about how satisfying it is to be successful in your own right, so that many
younger women have focused on the stress of the juggling act
between family and work, instead of the joy, pride, and the power
women enjoy with success."

Marriage as a Driving Force

In the feature film *Mona Lisa Smile*, Julia Roberts plays Katherine Watson, a professor at Wellesley College, an all-female institution, in 1953. Katherine Watson strongly suggests that her female students, played by Julia Stiles, Maggie Gyllenhaal, and Kirsten Dunst, consider careers and not just aspire to marriage. In spite of how trapped a few of her students might secretly feel, no one has the courage to follow her advice, let alone entertain such notions. During this era in America, post World War II, a woman's ambition was to be satisfied by whom she married. Marrying up or marrying rich was embraced by mothers and daughters alike. It was practically a career to land a husband and to keep him happy.

This was a decade before the second wave of feminism would begin, close to twenty years before women would actually march to the workplace. Paradoxically, fifty years hence, the millennium would have a faction of highly educated women "opting out" of powerful positions to be with their children. Indeed, Betina, forty-three, who works in advertising, lives in Florida, and has two daughters, thirteen and eleven, feels pressured by her family to work less, in order to "wife and mother" more.

I have worked so hard to have my career and to have my girls satisfied that I'm around. My mother never worked a day and was unhappy. In my opinion, she cared more about who I married than what I did in the work world. That's because she married well and has had a very comfortable life, but what if it hadn't gone according to plan? I knew I needed to have a job because life isn't that neatly packaged—you can't count on that.

I want my girls to marry for love, not money, and to have ca-
reers, regardless of what their husbands do, and I'm at odds
with my mother on this.

My girls are only in junior high and grade school, but we talk
about careers and marriage. My older daughter thinks I'm a
dishrag because I work and she wants a life like my mother's.
She cares about her social life, not her grades, and she's very
popular. I tell her this isn't as important as learning, and she
and my mother laugh about it.

Betina's daughter's take on her future and her identification
with her grandmother's life is not unique. Enough mothers report that their millennial daughters, born between 1982 and
2000, would prefer to emulate their grandmother's stress-free,
work-free marriages than their mother's marriages, replete
with glass ceilings, divorce, remarriage, and stepfamilies (more
on this in Chapter 10).

Motherhood + Other Ambitions

As I was wrapping up this chapter, an article about Christy
Turlington in the August 2009 issue of *Vogue*, "Beauty and Soul,"
by Joan Juliet Buck, caught my eye. Buck describes Turlington
as "the most beautiful thing that ever lived, an angelic being, a
freak of nature," who "turned forty last January." The journal-
ist emphasizes that Turlington likes to be challenged, and to
this end, although the mother of two young children, the wife of
actor Ed Burns, and a supermodel, she has a heightened social
conscience and is presently attending Columbia University for a
master's degree in public health. What we can take away from

this article is that motherhood, career, and personal growth are all possible, if we set our sights on it.

Consider Deirdre, forty-five, who works from a home office in Maryland and appreciates both marriage and work.

I have shown my girls that motherhood and careers can coexist as long as one has the attitude "I'll do what I can do." Biting off too much can mean real stress for the working mother, who may also be dealing with other personal issues such as family problems, financial problems, and aging parents. I believe that my daughters, when they marry, should modify the pace of their careers and choose partners who get what that's all about. Marriage is a great experience and my girls are so pleased that I'm still married to their father and that he and I still like one another. So many of their friends' parents are divorced and the mothers aren't thinking about marriage or about career but about how to make ends meet. I don't want my daughters to feel this is their fate, and I hope that I set an example in terms of what's important—marriage and a career.

While Deirdre is determined to teach her girls how to balance marriage, motherhood, and a career, there are those married mothers who have made an unequivocal decision to give up their careers for their children's sake and to preserve their marriages. For those daughters of all ages whose mothers are stay-at-home mothers, there is another form of mothering: the highly motivated, extremely involved mother who micromanages her daughters' lives. If we consider Natasha's take on this, as a thirty-eight-year-old stay-at-home mother living in upstate New York with two daughters, eight and five, we realize that the dichotomy between working and nonworking mothers remains an issue and informs the daughters.

I've already told my girls they have to marry a good man and to work if they want to. They don't have to—that's the thing, but they must have children, must marry, and keep the marriage happy. That's enough work, I know this for sure and already, I think, they get it. They're young but I bet that what stresses out working mothers today will stress my girls out in twenty or twenty-five years. I see working mothers who look exhausted, with their marriages on the brink. I've made this decision for my girls and for myself. I'm doing it in a way that they can follow in my footsteps.

When addressing mothers, daughters, and achievement, marriage and motherhood loom large. Daughters are at an advantage when their mothers encourage them to have careers and autonomy, regardless of how their personal lives play out. Christine B. Whelan, social historian and author of *Why Smart Men Marry Smart Women,* and I discussed the mother's role. Dr. Whelan observed, "Those women who grew up in the fifties and sixties were excited about a bigger and better future, and were not interested in marriage being their ambition. How their daughters, ages eighteen to thirty, will decide what to value can go either way. These daughters are being pushed academically to do well and socially about whom to marry by their mothers."

Our Goals for Our Daughters

Embolden your daughter, from an early age, as it applies to any of her pursuits. Be it ambition of any kind: academics, the arts, career, marriage, or motherhood, it's important that a mother be positive, not negative, about her daughter's chances of success.

Encourage tenacity at school, at work, and in relationships. It is important for mothers to teach their daughters that perseverance pays off. Don't allow excuses to enter into the equation, and cheer your daughter on when she's losing faith. Teach your daughter that giving up isn't an option until she's given it her all.

Consider your daughter's strengths and her individual talents. While we all attempt to strive for excellence, it also matters that a mother understands her daughter's capacities.

Don't bombard your daughter with your sour grapes or look to her as your only hope. Pressuring your daughter to do what you did or didn't get to do isn't fair to her and is discouraging. Also, while some of your daughter's experiences may be similar to yours, much of it is all hers, with her own hopes and ideas for her future.

Teach your daughter to be responsible to herself. It is very important that the daughter realizes her own motivations when it comes to her work and her relationships. And as we have seen in the previous chapter, a strong ego and firm footing from an early age provide a great advantage.

Chapter 10

✳

Sure, We're Just Like
the Brady Bunch

How Family Life Today Confuses Our Daughters

- Have you presented your family as "ideal"?
- Do you worry about what people will think of your family?
- Do you carefully guard a family secret?
- Do you feel that your family life has somehow harmed your daughter?
- Have you put your family's image ahead of your daughter's needs?

If your answer to any of the above is yes, your daughter is part of a complicated family life.

WHO COULD HAVE IMAGINED that your family life would turn out this way? You've been divorced since your third daughter was five—when you were forty—and before that it was an uneasy truce. Your

ex-husband had a bad temper and you rarely agreed about anything. While you wanted to keep all this private and put on a good
show for your closest friends and relatives, once your husband had
an affair and then divorced you to marry this woman, your cover was
blown. Not only were you humiliated but you were also worried
about your daughters' well-being in the face of divorce—as well as
your finances, status in the community, and whether you'd ever meet
anyone else. Although your ex-husband got on with his life very
quickly, and thankfully his new wife is decent to your daughters, all
the back-and-forth—adhering to a schedule for daughters of
divorce—has been taxing for the girls, especially when they were
younger. It's bothered you that their happiness as a family was compromised by a failed marriage—and you've gone out of your way to
please them.

Ten years out, everything seems to have quieted down and your
daughters, now ages twenty-one, eighteen, and fifteen, are nice to
your present boyfriend, his daughters, their two young half brothers
(on their father's side), and all the in-laws and extended family that
come with the package. What has also made you feel less guilty
these past ten years is how many other mothers have ended up divorced. You no longer ask yourself if you drove their father away, if
that's why he had an affair, if it was your fault that the family fell
apart, or what you could have done differently. Suddenly it's everywhere, and your daughters understand this. Thus, you don't feel as
defensive and as scrutinized, as if you have to pretend that the fall-
out of divorce has been a piece of cake for your three daughters.

Family Life as Destiny

Getting family life right looms large as the tenth and final
"wrong" to be righted in how we conduct ourselves as mothers.

Few mothers or daughters escape the importance placed on family, or how much the culture judges this in the outcome for children in terms of their upbringing. It's virtually impossible for a mother, whether married, divorced, or widowed, not to have endured some sort of family issue, or not to be in denial about an aspect of family life. And so we're brought full circle, back to Chapter 1, where we began with mothers making a variety of excuses for their daughters; these include the myth that family life is a bowl of cherries, and that one's family is normal.

The Many Faces of the Twenty-First-Century Family

What has been held up to us since the postwar baby boom era of the 1950s is the ideal of the flawless nuclear family. This was exemplified through television shows that ran from the early to mid-fifties to the mid-sixties, such as *Ozzie and Harriet, The Donna Reed Show, Leave It to Beaver,* and *Father Knows Best.* In these weekly series, the hierarchy of the parent-child relationship was fully realized and family was glorified. Parents were in charge, children were obedient, and any minor crisis was entertaining and resolved by the end of the episode.

As the world rapidly evolved in the 1960s and 1970s, it was reflected in a new kind of television series about family. *The Brady Bunch,* which ran from 1969 to 1974, legitimized stepfamilies, albeit both Carol Martin and Mike Brady were widowed, not divorced. The idea that a mother and her three daughters could "blend" with another family, one comprising three sons and a father, nonetheless underscored the idea that stepfamilies are a form of family. The spillover effect of legitimizing remarriage among parents with children extended to divorced families, making daughters everywhere who were a part of such families feel less stigmatized and awkward.

If we fast-forward to 2004, when *Desperate Housewives* first aired, the theme of family obstacles still prevails. In the first season of the series, we are introduced to a much edgier, more unsettling view of mothers and daughters (this certainly isn't *Gilmore Girls*). We observe Teri Hatcher's character, Susan Mayer, a single mother, depending upon her overly responsible teenage daughter, Julie Mayer, played by Andrea Bowen, and Marcia Cross's character, Bree Van De Camp, steer her nuclear family, comprising a teenage son, teenage daughter, and physician husband, toward her perception of perfection. When Bree ends up widowed and remarried several seasons later, we empathize with the arduous task of mothering a daughter who defies her, despite her best efforts to hold her family together once they are fatherless.

The ABC series *Brothers and Sisters,* which first aired in 2006, revolves around the machinations of adult siblings in their ongoing twenty-first-century-style, upper-class dramas. The show features two daughters, played by Calista Flockhart and Rachel Griffiths, and three sons, with Sally Field as the widowed matriarch of the Walker family. In terms of the mother-daughter bond, both adult daughters recognize their mother's power and impotence at once. Family life for the Walkers is an ongoing soap opera with their mother at the helm as each family member absorbs their late father's duplicitous nature (illegitimate offspring plus former lovers).

Each of these shows reflects the current social climate of the times and soothes female viewers who have tuned in to feel less alone in their plight. The most recent shows remind us that mothers today are not as buttoned-up as those in mid-century American television. However, circumscribed roles exist nonetheless. Mothers are still evaluated for their roles in the family, be it on television or in real life.

Consider Candace, forty-three, who lives in Nebraska, where she is a stay-at-home mother to two daughters, thirteen and five, from her first and second marriage, respectively.

My relationship with my older daughter would be the way it is whether I was married to her father or not. Still, I see how she's suffered for the divorce and the years that I was a single mother when she had little contact with her father. She wanted to be daddy's little girl and he's very distant but I don't pry or give my opinion about it. I know that the family unit that we've built here, with my present husband and his three sons, works well for her, and I feel that's the best I can do. It matters to me that we are a real family, and it helps me when I think of the divorce and how much that has hurt my daughter, much more than my son. So I tend to overcompensate. I'm the mother who carpools and invites all the girls over. I make an effort to make her happy. Most of my guilt has to do with what followed after the divorce. I don't want my daughter to be disappointed or think she won't have what she needs or that she won't find the right partner the first time around. And it's complicated by my younger daughter, who has the advantage of being in the new family and is at the center of it. Mothers in town watch—that's another thing—trying to figure out how our family works.

More than 90 percent of mothers interviewed for this project expressed a sense that the world is harsh toward females, and for this reason, they've worried more about their daughters than their sons from infancy onward. Their worry is for their daughters' family life, as well as for the concerns voiced in previous chapters. More than 70 percent of mothers were apprehensive about their daughters repeating the past, unable to shed a family pattern. Daughters of women who are "stuck" and disappointed in their family life frequently express their hesitations about this when starting their own families.

Daughters of Divorce

A parent's divorce and life after divorce become a focal point in the girls' own lives. According to E. Mavis Hetherington's longitudinal study in the *Journal of Family Psychology*, daughters have more trouble adjusting to a divorce than do sons. What has transpired colors their future decisions about romance, family, and commitment. The blow of divorce shakes a daughter's identity, and she is often torn between both parents to varying degrees. Dawn Bradley Berry, author of *The Divorce Recovery Sourcebook,* points out how the suffering continues after a divorce has occurred. Both mothers and daughters may be angry, afraid, and anxious, but for adolescents, these emotions are more pronounced. So while the stigma of divorce has waned in the past thirty years, for mothers and daughters, the repercussions of divorce, and the subsequent adjustments, can be profound.

Money in Divorce

Once the marriage has dissolved, both mothers and fathers can be culpable of "buying their children's love." Usually the father ends up on top, as reported by David Popenoe's article "Debunking Divorce Myths," since the father's income typically ascends while the mother's descends in divorce situations. Mothers with whom I spoke felt that they were compromised because they couldn't provide the lifestyle their daughters had known before the divorce, while their ex-husbands could. In addition, many of the mothers sought to please their daughters through material goods and luxuries. One mother described herself as "stretched to the limit." She said, "I bought my daughter everything she wanted—because I was so worried that I'd lose her if I didn't. The truth is, I can't keep up, and her father can do whatever he wants for her. I don't have the cash anymore."

Consider Tina, forty-one, who lives in a Midwestern city, where she works part-time as a waitress and full-time at a bank. Her daughters are eight and eleven.

I see my ex-husband using the money as this sort of weapon against me. He knows that it isn't easy for me, working on weekends and during the week to make ends meet. He's gleeful that I'm doing all this and he'll take the girls on great vacations and buy them the latest cell phones. I don't even think they need cell phones and iPods at their age. But their father would never miss this opportunity, and his ego is so gratified. I look like the strict one and I'm simply not giving in. It isn't what I want for my daughters. So basically, because I'm divorced, I have two daughters who have things I don't want them to have and stay at four-star hotels with their father when it isn't necessary. The worst part is how they act out after a weekend with their dad and all the fun they've had. I look like the bad guy and I look so weak.

If Tina believes that she appears to be less by not offering her daughters enough, Katherine, forty-seven, realizes that she's jealous of her daughter's shopping sprees with her ex-husband. Katherine lives in Atlanta, where she works in public relations and has one seventeen-year-old daughter.

For the past five years, since my divorce became final, my daughter has come home after being with her father with the most amazing stuff. This reminds me of the life I left behind and how much fun it was to have designer clothes or go to the ballet without having to worry about the price of the tickets. I remember how he would buy me wonderful things and it's not enough to make a relationship work, obviously, but it was a good part of it. I worry that my daughter is so happy to see her father because there's always a visit to the mall, and that the relationship isn't happening on other levels. At the same time, I think it's nice that he wants to buy for her—I have a friend whose ex-husband spends all his money on his new wife, and her daughters are nickeled and dimed. So at least he's not doing that. Instead, my daughter and her stepmother shop with him on weekends and sort of bond over these sprees. I can't say that it causes friction between us, but sometimes I feel angry about the whole thing— and sorry I can't do more for her.

Despite a mother's core beliefs, in a divorce situation she may feel unnerved by her daughter's material life compared to her own. It helps if a mother is aware that none of this is due to her daughter's decisions or actions. Notwithstanding this, daughters may be dealing with mothers who feel denied and resentful or regretful, as if they'd made a mistake leaving the marriage, because they've come upon hard times since the divorce.

Some mothers are bitter and overcome with worry; they lack a support system, and their daughters sense this. The mother doesn't appear strong and the daughter worries about wanting to see her father when she knows that may make her mother angry or jealous. What the daughter yearns for is to have a relationship with both parents, free of constraints and friction about finances and lifestyle. Mothers who respect this are helping their daughters out.

Stepmothers in the Mix

According to the National Center for Health Statistics, for every one thousand divorces, 1,175 children are involved. For daughters, who are keenly affected by the machinations of shuttling between two homes and contending with a stepmother, the power plays between the two parents can be overwhelming. It can take years for a daughter to adjust to having a stepmother and being a part of a stepfamily. Much of how a daughter responds to her stepmother is a reflection of her mother's messaging. If her father had an affair and divorced her mother, the daughter maybe believes that she's disloyal to her mother if she likes her stepmother. If the mother initiated the divorce, it might make it easier for the daughter to forge a relationship without her mother's wrath toward the stepmother.

Still, there are daughters who have a strained relationship with their stepmothers and resent her place in their father's life, emotionally, financially, and physically—an anger often fueled, as we have observed, by the mother. Conversely, there are daughters who want a relationship with their stepmothers and a family life that encompasses the father and stepmother. The idea that a stepmother might wield any amount of influence is infuriating to enough mothers in these circumstances that some take action. For example, Georgia, forty-one, who lives in the Midwest and works in retail, has alienated her daughters, ten and eight, from their stepmother.

Their father was never here and now he's remarried and he expects the girls to jump high for his new wife. I have done everything for these girls—sheltered them and supported them since he walked out on me—and I'm not going to send them over to his house for a weekend where they're with this young babe. So we fight about it and the girls cling to me. There's a chance that this woman is decent, but so far it hasn't been anything the girls or I know about. So I try to keep them away and they know what I think of her. She tries to buy them things and to take them to their favorite stores. But she isn't their mother and the girls know it—no matter how hard she tries. I guess the girls already wonder why I'm not there, in her shoes. And this will go on for years, my girls are young.

Unlike Georgia, there are mothers who subscribe to the "greater good" theory—that everyone has to get along and that their daughters' desire for a home life and secure family is more important than any animosity or tension between exes. Indeed, Denise, forty-seven, who lives in Southern Florida, and works part-time as a physical therapist, has implemented this way of thinking as a way to help her two daughters, nineteen and sixteen.

Both my ex and I are remarried, and the rule here is that everyone has to make do and everyone has to be civil. I won't have any problems and I have befriended their stepmother and included her and vice versa. We both have girls from our first marriage, close in age, and we all work together. It's the new way—and my daughters and her daughters can only learn from it. No one is trying to one-up the next person and we work at this—there's no way it can happen easily. I don't want my girls to suffer and she feels that way about her girls. So everyone has to act like a family member and give the girls a family life.

Single Mothers/No Father Figure

For those daughters who are fatherless, whether due to a death of the father, a never-married mother, or a father who abandons his family, there are similarities and differences in approach to that of daughters whose parents are divorced. As reported by the U.S. Census Bureau in August 2007, close to 13.6 million single parents in the United States are raising 21.2 million children. Of this population, approximately 84 percent of the custodial parents are mothers and 16 percent are fathers. The single mother has unrelenting responsibilities beyond what most mothers in a family of divorce experience. A strong image of a capable mother is a fine role model for a daughter, and the mothers who fit this category remark upon how connected they are to their daughters. At the same time, these mothers also have expressed that daughters do not have a sense of what traditional family life is like, and they worry their daughters may be missing out and obligated to one another because of their family setup. This mother-daughter bond can be intense, as shown to us in Mona Simpson's novel *Anywhere But Here,* which portrays a mother so closely linked to her daughter that the daughter's hope to attend a college in another part of the country becomes an issue.

For Florence, forty, who lives in California and works in a health clinic, her twelve-year-old daughter's dismissal of men is a concern.

There aren't any men around and I worry about it although my daughter is okay with it. I want her to know that having a husband and kids is important and probably a better life. But then again, I don't have a husband or other kids. She thinks we're fine, only the two of us, and that she isn't missing something. We are very close, sometimes too close, and I feel guilty but I also see how happy we are. My daughter respects that I work and that I've raised her by myself. She also doesn't want a boyfriend or a husband one day and looks to all the women in our family who take care of her—my mother, my sister, my cousin. We are all strong enough, and there's no doubt in her mind it will work out fine. When kids at school ask her why she doesn't have a father, she says she never needed one.

A mother's approach is meaningful, and the better adjusted she is as a single mother, the better off her daughter is. It is wise for mothers to be cautious and thoughtful of their daughters' feelings in a divorce situation, including how they feel toward their stepfamilies. Whether a mother is widowed, divorced, or never married, her independence and open-mindedness to new experiences is also a model for her daughter.

The Traditional Nuclear Family

What has been held up to us as the model for the modern intact family is the traditional family. This consists of a father as major breadwinner, a mother who stays at home or who brings in a secondary income at a pink-collar job, and children all in one household. Idealized since postwar America, this concept has recently been overshadowed by a variety of family units. However, mothers interviewed for this chapter often lamented that theirs was not the traditional family unit that once prevailed. These mothers felt they were less than the gold standard and that there is more respect for traditional families than for mothers and daughters of single-parent families. Indeed, Tory, thirty-four, a stay-at-home mother who lives in Rhode Island with her two young daughters, ages seven and ten, is very comfortable with her lifestyle and marriage.

It's easy to be at home, to get involved with community work, and to be there for my children. I know it sounds lame and lots of people would wonder about it, but I've made friends with so many mothers who are like me. We do work at the school and volunteer in town. There's less stress on my marriage because my job is taking care of the girls and the house. My girls are growing up in a world where women work more and more, but I don't think it's best for a marriage. I am proud of the kind of comfort and security I offer my children, and the kind of family we are—my husband and I talked about all this before we got married. I signed on for this, and I see how much better off they are than with divorced parents or mothers who work 24/7. I'm already telling them this.

As Walters, Carter, Papp, and Silverstein note in their essay "Toward a Feminist Perspective in Family Therapy," in the "patriarchal family organization . . . earning money through work [is] the province of the male, and emotional tasks such as nurturing, building, and maintaining relationships, and childrearing [are] the province of the female." So while in traditional families, there are mothers who work, as well as stay-at-home mothers, many of my interviewees commented that part of being in a "traditional family" was the decision to give up their careers to care for their children. These mothers justified their decision, saying that their children are secure because they are physically present. In spite of the justifications stay-at-home mothers offer, their unrealized ambitions are often tied up in their children, and the message they give their daughters as they grow older is mixed. On the one hand, these mothers have made a pledge to their daughters' needs, but as the years go on, their daughters lack a role model with ambition.

However, if there is strife and tension in the marriage, daughters not only take sides (often with their mothers), but also are anxious about the state of their parents' marriage and about bringing home friends under these conditions. This, too, can cause tension in a daughter's life. Consider Grace, forty-five, who lives in Arkansas, where she is a stay-at-home mother. She has held on to her marriage for her fifteen-year-old daughter's sake.

Once I had my daughter and my sons, I stopped thinking about what I wanted in a marriage. I thought it would be better to raise them in an intact family, and that's what I did. For my daughter, this has made all the difference, and she's always saying how her friends' parents are divorced and the mothers seem so beaten down. I work part-time, and I run the family—it's exhausting. Then I tell myself that my daughter has the safeness of parents who haven't split. Until recently, this was the case, but now I think she is starting to notice how I feel about being married to her father, and she listens when we fight at night. I wonder when I can leave and if this sacrifice is worth it. I wonder what it will actually do to her.

Conventional Values

The effect of holding up the model of the traditional nuclear family—father at work, mother at home—as one to emulate is the perpetration of sexist values, a situation that reflects mid-century American male supremacy, not present-day attitudes. Such a family may take pride in its construct even as it robs the mother of her voice—a limitation that has a profound effect upon her daughters. Daughters today are keenly aware of their mother's situation, and this can play out in one of two ways. In the first scenario, the family is so deeply invested in this system that the daughter may not be strong enough to discuss anything with her mother, let alone break the pattern when she becomes an adult. Molly, thirty-seven, who has two daughters, four and three, already worries about their future.

I know that I'm not a good model for happiness, and my daughters have a father who wishes he had boys. I work doubly hard to make them feel special, but I fear my older daughter won't ever get out of this lifestyle. It's partly our religion and it's also our family values. We think that family comes first and that means we're back in the dark ages. My marriage is very much like my mother's was, and my daughters will have the same. I wish it could be different for them. As little girls they are in a great environment, filled with love and attention. But when they're grown girls, it won't be like that—they'll feel trapped. I wish that I could do more for them, let them know what choices they could possibly have. I'm sort of scheming to make it happen one day for them.

In the second scenario, a daughter roots for her mother to cut free and to be all that she can be. Helene, forty-six, who lives in a rural area, views her sixteen-year-old daughter's perception as a red flag for her "escape" one day.

She sees how her father is with me and with her, and she isn't interested in the least in having this sort of male in her life. The idea that I believe in marriage and commitment must strike her as odd—she knows I'm secretly wild and that I act this way because it's easier than rebelling. She's been asking me about how I really feel and has suggested that I get divorced and pursue my own life. I tell her I'm not ready, but I'm not sure she believes that. And then what kind of heavy is it to know someone has sacrificed so much for you? Is that what I should say? I don't think so. I've done this for my daughter and she knows it, and she feels the weight of it. So I say nothing but she gets it anyway.

Smug Status-Conscious Families

In traditional families whose patriarch is respected in the community, there is an exclusivity that the mothers and daughters in such units sense as well, with the implicit message being that this family is special and it's an honor to be a part of it. In the movie *The Wedding Crashers,* starring Rachel McAdams, Isla Fisher, Owen Wilson, and Vince Vaughn, the father of the daughters is a senator, and the mother is a sophisticated wife. This family is impressed by their own form of nobility and not in touch with their feelings. The expectation placed upon McAdams is that she'll marry "one of their kind," and nothing less will do (until she meets Owen Wilson's zany character). This smugness affects everyday families as well. Corrie, fifty, lives in a Midwestern city and has one daughter, eighteen.

My daughter has seen how I live, how I dress, my friends. Every-one is sort of bohemian and artistic. She's my daughter and her life will be similar when it comes to this. I hope she isn't divorced and that she has a great career, but mostly she should be with a man who is interesting and who loves theater and film, because that's what her father and I care about. It isn't about money but about books, art, literature. She should have an exceptional life, in every other way. This is what I've encouraged, it's what I know is best. So far she's been taken by what I've shown her, but I worry that she'll give this up one day.

Corrie's concerns also underscore the reality that not every daughter will sign on for her mother's type of life. For example, Valerie, forty-one, who works for a large corporation, perceives her thirteen-year-old daughter as dead set against her choices.

My daughter already has made it clear she doesn't need my lifestyle and plans to save the world. I try to tell her that it isn't like this, that her father and I are lucky and also destined to live this way. Of course she should have a circle of friends who do good deeds. Mostly I'm just frustrated by how little she cares about her upbringing and how little she seems to respect what I do and what my marriage is like. I want us to be close because she'll have my life and her husband will be like her father. If not, I'd be very upset with her, and it wouldn't be acceptable.

Daughters who wish to break free and who don't subscribe to their mothers' narrow worldview might be misunderstood—even shunned—and uncertain of how to cross over to a broader spectrum. Mothers who are conscious of how their daughters wish to proceed socially, including whom they choose for a partner, will respect the daughters' decision, although it doesn't reflect their experience.

Scripts for the Twenty-First-Century Family

With the twenty-first-century family consisting of stepfamilies, single-parent families (divorced, widowed, or never married), gay couples, or fictive family units (composed of friends as family), the traditional nuclear family is no longer the only recognized family component. Girls today are born into a variety of family structures and are profoundly affected by the style and values system within their families. This plays out on two levels: identifying her family by type and then navigating the machinations within the structure, i.e., happiness, strength, narcissism, competition, or addiction. As one mother of a twenty-four-year-old daughter explained, "I'm trying so hard to make it all work for my daughter. Why should I let her know about the drinking problems her father had? Why should she know that I fight depression if I can keep this from her?" Another mother, who is divorced and has financial problems, believes that her full disclosure has made her twenty-six-year-old daughter more motivated to make money. "My daughter has seen me worried all the time, and she knows the only way out is through a job. She knows what to do." Meanwhile, there is little that goes unnoticed by the daughter, whatever the mother's plan, and the idea of a "perfect family" is frequently shattered by assorted realities.

After listening to mothers describe their families and how they present to their daughters, the following patterns emerge:

Only Daughter/Several Sons

Many times, the mother, so intent on gender identity, lavishes attention upon her daughter in female rituals such as shopping, hair care, lunches, manicures, specific books, and films. This mother and daughter can also be clannish toward outsiders, including friends, love interests, and at times to the boys in the family. In the 2005 film *The Family Stone*, Rachel McAdams plays the only daughter of Diane Keaton. Together they are unkind to Sarah Jessica Parker's character, the love interest of an older brother.

Dawn, thirty-seven, who has one five-year-old daughter and twin sons who are ten, believes that her daughter evokes another kind of mothering experience.

I was fine with my two boys until I had my girl. Now I know it isn't the same at all and that my daughter is my future, she's part of me. I imagine as she gets older it will only get better. I hope we won't fight or have the usual battles. I can see us being all about each other.

Celebrity Families

Although celebrity families are in another sphere altogether, whatever they do is intriguing and appears bold to everyday mothers and daughters. The weekly magazines offer details of Angelina and Brad's family life, Katie and Tom's, the Gosselins and their eight children and subsequent breakup. We are cognizant of famous mothers with daughters, including Halle Berry, whose daughter is Nahla; Jennifer Lopez, who has a daughter, Emme; and Denise Richards, who has two daughters, Sam and Lola. Mothers who are exhausted and at odds with their daughters imagine that celebrities never have these issues. Their form of motherhood is enticing, glamorized, and celebrated. Eva, thirty-three, who has four-year-old twin daughters, remarks upon how swayed she is by this.

I feel like I'm a young mother who is married to a cute guy. So are some of these famous women and we all have daughters. It makes me think it's not just another day for me with my girls but for all these stars, too. My girls already know fashion and who is famous and how they're supposed to be. I bought them matching dresses that look like Suri Cruise's wardrobe in pictures. I pretend our family is as hip and lucky as they are.

Mothers as Matriarchs

The new spin on the matriarchal family is that whether a mother is single or married, working outside the home or not, she is there to run her daughters' lives (and son's and husband's, as the case may be). As the leader of the family, she exudes power and is the decision maker. Her daughter feels enveloped in love and safeness with such a strong mother figure, but she also depends upon her mother, who can be enabling. Consider Angie, forty-one, who has a twenty-year-old daughter.

It's just been the two of us since she was born. I am in charge of her life and she knows she is fine in the world because of me. What more should I do for my daughter? I do worry about the day that I can't help her, but it hasn't happened yet. I am her

provider financially, physically, and emotionally. I try not to over-
whelm her but always to protect her.

Favorite Daughter Syndrome

In the recent Broadway revival of the musical *Gypsy*, Patti
LuPone played the stage mother Gypsy Rose Lee. This domi-
neering mother has her sights set on her daughter June becoming a star, but when that plan fails, she finds that her less
favorite daughter, Louise, is the one who can fulfill her dreams.
When a mother favors one daughter over others, it creates havoc
in the family and stirs up rivalry among sisters. Perhaps a fa-
vored daughter reminds the mother of her own youth or satisfies
her fantasy of what she might have been like. In a divorce situation, one daughter may be on the outs with her mother or may
remind the mother of her ex and is penalized for this. A daughter who reaps the praise, affection, and attention initially basks
in this, but at the risk of hurting her sisters. A rift between the
favorite daughter and her sisters may even form. Deb, forty-
eight, has three daughters—twelve, nine, and six—but favors
her youngest.

My youngest daughter is the best in the family, and already I
relate to her totally. She is smart and funny, filled with curios-
ity. I know she's going to have an exciting life and my other two
girls will not. My oldest daughter is drippy and my middle
daughter is too bossy. I try not to show my favoritism, but my
youngest is so unlike the other two, so charismatic.

Mother and Daughter in Cahoots

When there is a problem in the family—a father who gambles, a mother who abuses painkillers, an unhappy mother, troublesome financial matters, a difficult child—some mothers confide in her daughters. Although a mother might find it helpful, this divides the family and encumbers the daughter. A daughter is flattered if she's sought out to discuss adult issues, but then worries about what will happen next in the family and becomes insecure. Consider Dolly, forty, who has conveyed her concerns to her nine-year-old daughter.

My daughter is very reasonable and can listen objectively. I say how hard it is being without a job and how her father now works a double shift and she hears it. She's sympathetic and also a little worried. She and I sit and talk about money and what we'll do if I don't get some work. I don't say much to her father, I say it to her.

Older Mothers

Across the country, there are women who have postponed motherhood to develop their careers and to explore the world. And with medical treatments such as in-vitro fertilization and the use of donor eggs, waiting until forty-plus has become a viable option for a broader spectrum of women. The number of mothers in the United States giving birth at age forty or older has doubled in the last several decades, as reported by the National Center for Health Statistics. There is a maturity factor in older mothers, who have sown their wild oats and who welcome motherhood without any regrets. However, both mother and daughter are conscious of the mother's mortality, and this can become a caregiving that goes both ways fairly early in the daughter's life. For instance, Jesse, fifty-six, who has one ten-year-old daughter, believes that her daughter is being raised to care for her one day.

My daughter knows that I'll be old when she leaves for college, and she's prepared for it. She has friends whose mothers are ten or fifteen years younger than I am and sometimes that makes her worry about me—as if I'll be enfeebled so much sooner. Or that I'm too old for what's ahead. I'm trying to stay healthy, but we both know what age can do.

Working Mothers

According to the U.S. Census, nearly two-thirds of wives with young children are employed. For those women who are on the career path, the commitment to their work is important, as well as their commitment to their children. In contrast to the stay-at-home mother, the working mother straddles home life and work life, and offers her daughter another model. It is striking that enough daughters would not repeat their mother's choice, however, and view her as being spread too thin. A working mother's exhaustion can deter the millennial daughters who are not quite as driven to achieve, as noted in the previous chapter. Consider Sandra, forty-nine, whose daughters, twelve and fourteen, are unimpressed with her career.

My girls see me as a loser who hasn't a moment to spare. They think I'm stressed, underpaid, and underappreciated. But they don't appreciate me more for this; they lean on me as a way to prove I've made the wrong decision. I guess I haven't given them the right impression, but one thing they know is that I earn my own living and nothing can take away what I've accomplished in my office. Maybe when they get to college they'll get it.

Mothers and Daughters in a Fog

The phenomenon of mothers and daughters who aren't aware of how they are living and what choices are theirs is a modern-day problem. In the 2000 film *Traffic* Michael Douglas plays Robert Wakefield, a judge who is appointed to head the President's Office of National Drug Control. When his honor student daughter, Caroline, played by Erika Christensen, is arrested for drug use, his wife, Barbara, played by Amy Irving, already knows that she uses. Why, then, hasn't she said anything to her husband? Might she not have "awakened" had their daughter not been in trouble? Many mothers, as we have observed, make excuses and choose to camouflage serious issues that affect the entire family. And while a small percentage of mothers report having gotten lucky with this approach—their daughter straightened out on her own—in the long run, it will harm the daughter and the mother. It requires courage to be wide-awake and take responsibility for our daughters and for our own complicity.

Marla, forty-six, already knows (but doesn't want to know) that her fifteen-year-old daughter is cutting school.

I can't stand what my daughter puts me through, so I keep pretending it's okay. I say that the next week will be better and I wait for that to be true. I try talking to her, but she's in her own world and I can't make any headway. We look like a great family but we're not, and I can't face it. So I keep saying it's a phase and she keeps letting me think that she's still doing what she's supposed to do.

It seems fitting to end this book with a chapter about family and to realize how many mothers subscribe to a variety of new and complex family models, filled with excuses and hopes that it could be better. Although a third of the mothers I interviewed say they feel unable to break free of the constraints of family, a third felt that both they and their daughters had to be almost acrobatic to make it work, and a third believed that the outcome was a positive one. This last group believed that they'd made the best of it or had broken an old pattern for a fresh paradigm. In this way, the hardships of family as well as the safety and progress of this unit are offered to our daughters.

Prescriptive Family Measures

Encourage your daughter to learn from your "type" of family. Let your daughter know that your family style counts but also that she is entitled to her own kind of family one day. For example, she might choose a career despite coming from a traditional family with a stay-at-home mother.

Even if your family isn't exemplary or conventional, emphasize its strengths and what it has taught you. Show your daughter that your "crazy family" is filled with love and support and, while not picture-perfect, has great strengths and individuality.

Have the courage to be honest about your family situation. If you allow your daughter to believe that all is well when there are inherent problems, she will begin to make excuses for the family herself or will feel she's living a lie.

Avoid drawing your daughter into a contentious divorce and the aftermath. Your daughter deserves to feel safe and stable, and this can only be achieved if both parents are civil and respectful in a divorce situation. Don't allow your daughter to suffer or be the victim, and don't ask her to choose one parent over another.

Instill family values. Whatever kind of family unit you and your daughter are a part of, make sure that she learns to have values and trust as a result. It isn't what kind of unit you offer but that you offer a unit to your daughter.

Let your daughter know the safeness of family, even during rocky times. Daughters of all ages should be aware that they have the unconditional love and security of their family, regardless of circumstances. In this way, they know that together you can work through problems.

Conclusion

※

Lessons Learned

From the early stages of this project, as I gathered research and listened to a diverse group of mothers, I understood that there is something very unsettling about mothering daughters today. Although a mother may have great purpose, high hopes, and steadfast dreams for her daughter, it is her execution and approach that complicate matters. Daughters today, whether four years old, sixteen, or twenty-eight, navigate an unprecedented universe, a crazy salad of pop culture, high tech, fractured families, media frenzy, and competition among peers. Yet what remains the same as in generations past, despite the modern-day daughter's experience, is a mother's unconditional love for her daughter and her goal for her daughter to have as many options as possible.

Mothers, like their daughters, exist in the fast lane, cramming the many aspects of their lives into a twenty-four-hour day. *All* mothers are tugged in many directions, compounded by their children's schedules and expectations. So when it comes to an altercation with our daughters of any age, it's not a surprise that many mothers are too depleted to put up a fight. When an argument ensues, both mother and daughter suffer, but it's the mother who begins to question what she has said or done and readily looks for a way to assuage her daughter's discomfort. The mother is perplexed as she asks herself, How did my daughter get like this? Haven't I always worked double-time for her, moved mountains, put her on a pedestal?

Best Intentions Versus Poor Execution

At every stage, a mother plays a crucial role in her daughter's life, yet as we have witnessed repeatedly, her efforts to support her daughters may not magically fix anything. More likely this approach will result in not enough limits, too many indulgences, an overemphasis on looks and weight, misunderstood sacrifices that have been found to evoke tensions and arguments. However, toughing it out, as many mothers do, reminds us that this is a fluid and evolving relationship, one that ultimately moves forward. Unfortunately, at many steps along the way, a mother's quest yields frustration and human error that we all know too well.

In this book we've recognized the pros and cons of our mothering styles, the common scenes that haunt, the self-doubt at these junctures, and the overwhelming sense of obligation and discouragement that so often accompanies the mother-daughter bond. Mothers have remarked—as if only there was a way to ensure the equation—"If you are the best mother possible, you will get the right result." In reality, we know that it is a rocky road to a healthy, rewarding relationship with our daughters, and we intend to provide guidance, wisdom, and the right examples. More than 70 percent of the mothers interviewed said they didn't feel prepared for the demands of raising a daughter. These mothers were particularly surprised by what their daughters expected materially and socially, and never believed their daughters could be unkind, belligerent, and irrational. These mothers described themselves as alienated from their daughters on occasion, hesitant to talk about the situation with other mothers, and engulfed by frustration and a sense of failure.

Enabling Habits

One theme examined in this book is how mothers facilitate their daughters' requests rather than put their foot down—an act that affects their daughters in the long run. A mother's M.O. is to keep her daughter safe, but when she doesn't trust her own instincts or hasn't the courage of her convictions, her actions are detrimental to her daughter and can undermine her daughter's confidence in her mother's parenting.

Operating out of fear. Early on, mothers realize how easy it is to lose their power and cave in to their daughters. More than 80 percent of my interviewees described this sensation, and 50 percent felt they took charge at some point along the way. The daughters benefit when the mother presents herself as assured and secure.

Brigette, thirty-seven, who has three daughters, ages eight, six, and three, began putting her foot down.

Recently I saw that my oldest daughter was doing things I didn't like. I didn't want to rock the boat and said nothing. Then it occurred to me: I don't have to be afraid of her, I have to raise her properly.

Here to please. If the mother believes it's best for her daughters to have whatever they desire, the daughters won't adjust to being told no. It's better to have limits and to instill boundaries.

Violet, forty, who has a fourteen-year-old daughter, accommodates her daughter's every desire.

I will shop with her, help her with her homework, bend over backwards to make sure her weekend is the way she wants it. I feel it's the least I can do so she's not unhappy.

Cover-ups. Spinning yarns to help daughters out of sticky situations makes the mother into the fall guy. Mothers should insist that their daughters take responsibility for their actions.

Beth, forty-six, who has an eighteen-year-old daughter, makes excuses for her daughter repeatedly.

Every time she gets into trouble, I'm there to tell a better story than she does. I don't want any trouble. I wish she was more together . . . but I say what needs to be said.

Dancing forward/stepping back. Mothers are selfless and giving, despite that they often feel betrayed by their daughters by the time the daughters reach high school. More than 80 percent recoil briefly and then continue to try to please their daughters. It is much more effective to call a daughter out on her behavior than to ignore it.

Roya, forty-nine, who has a seventeen-year-old daughter, doesn't address her daughter's behavior toward her.

My daughter and I have been close all her life. Now what she
says to me, the way she looks at me, cuts me like a knife. I'm not
sure who she is anymore . . . but I don't say anything, I act like
we're the same as we used to be.

Taking a Stand

The mother who understands her own intentions and her daughter's intentions, who has introspection and a strong sense of
self, and who is able to separate her identity from her daughter's has the key in achieving the right balance.

Shaping their view of the world. When mothers stick to
their values and remain consistent—even when it's tempting
to give up—they are more gratified in their mothering and
their daughters are less skittish.

Ava, forty-three, whose daughters are fourteen and twelve,
sticks by her convictions.

I've taught these girls what I know and believe in since they
were born—about love, family, money, school, friends. I won't
stop because they might not like what I say or think they know
more. I figure they'll respect this later.

Emphasizing achievement. Mothers who prepare their
daughters to achieve on their own, and to have the practical
skills to do so, are placing them at an advantage.

Marcie, fifty-one, has been preparing her twenty-six-year-
old daughter to be financially independent.

I could just as easily have let my daughter drift, but I kept hammering into her that making my own money mattered and that she had to have this in her life. She finally listened and enrolled in business school.

Keeping daughters safe. A daughter's security is of enormous concern to mothers, from the time they walk home from school alone to when they live alone—on campus and after college. While no one wants to instill fear, a daughter should be taught how to protect herself against potentially threatening situations.

Drew, thirty-eight, encourages her daughters, eleven and nine, to be vigilant.

I wait at the school bus in the morning and in the afternoon. I don't care what other mothers do or that it embarrasses my eleven-year-old. I just show up—and I talk to the girls about strangers and what the world is like and how to react if something happens. I want them to be prepared.

Degrees of Expectations

We keep thinking that we are close to our daughters and that it all goes so smoothly because we are the same gender with similar styles (despite the generation gap). However, it is more complicated than that, and a healthy mother-daughter relationship can't exist in a vacuum. The majority of mothers interviewed described themselves as eager to have this bond with their daughters, but said they walk a fine line between safekeeping and fostering independence. Once a daughter goes off to college, the relationship continues but the day-to-day involvement is no longer present. Many mothers find relief at this point, while others lament how quickly their daughters have grown up and second-guess some of the challenges of the recent past.

Avoid estrangement. Keep the lines of communication open. Although the stakes are raised and mothers describe themselves as "ready to throw in the towel" on occasion, communicating with one's daughter makes all the difference.

Avoid trying to make her fit the mold. Respecting a daughter's individuality can be taxing to some mothers, especially if the direction the daughter is choosing doesn't seem satisfying. However, if the daughter is not doing something that would endanger her (drugs, drinking, indiscriminating sex), it's best to honor her choice.

Take your ego out of it. If a mother looks to her daughter to fulfill her dreams or views her daughter's career as a reflection of herself, it's unfair to the daughter, and puts too much pressure on the relationship. The mother and daughter are separate, each with her own distinct style.

Keep mother-daughter competition away. Daughters contend with enough rivalry among their schoolmates and female coworkers, and mothers among their friends and coworkers. Mother-daughter competition stirs up an atmosphere of doubt and tension and should be avoided.

The Ideal Mother?

In Neil Gaiman's novel *Coraline,* Coraline finds her parents rather dull and somewhat inattentive. And so she wanders beyond a locked door in her home and discovers "the other mother," who seems strangely like her mother but has buttons for eyes, an ability to imitate, an evil spirit, and plans to kidnap Coraline. Coraline escapes this harrowing experience and realizes that her own mother, quirks and all, is the winner, despite her flaws.

The ideal mother can't exist in a bubble but in real time, in tandem with her ideal daughter. So in reality, there is no ideal mother, but the understanding that a mother and daughter are there for each other, giving what they can as they can. In the recent remake of the feature film *The Women,* Candace Bergen plays the mother of Meg Ryan's character, whose husband has left her for his lover. Bergen's character understands and comforts her daughter, having seen it all herself, and is there for her in an unprecedented way. Ultimately, when Ryan's character wakes up as a mother (to a slightly belligerent preadolescent daughter), wife, daughter, and career woman, her mother is her cheering squad. At last, the mother and daughter, adult women who have both endured, appreciate their commitment to each other.

Shedding Preconceived Notions

Give up control. Mothers fear that they are judged and blamed when any trouble arises, not only by their daughters, but also by other mothers, family members, and friends. Controlling their daughters (frequently since they were small) may seem a way to fend off this criticism, but in fact, it is harmful to both daughters and mothers.

Don't force your daughter to conform. Your daughter may be a late bloomer, a renegade, a jock, the "It girl," or the brain, among other types. Don't impose your vision of her. Allow her to be herself and encourage her to seek out her own interests on her own timetable.

Let her spread her wings. Fostering independence is tan-tamount to our daughters achieving their own style and interests. We want our daughters to have confidence, self-esteem, options beyond our own experience and to soar.

Keeping It Honest

Because mothers are so close with their daughters today, sharing their feelings, the desire to please exists for both mothers and daughters, and is inextricably tied to a woman's place in our society. This can trip up any truth telling and bury our emotions.

Talk openly about choices, self-awareness, and self-esteem. Mothers should discuss these with their daughters and encourage them to set their own goals and be confident of their decisions.

Discourage certain behaviors and attitudes. If you are unhappy with your daughter's choice of friends, boyfriend, spending habits, value system, communicate this directly. A daughter will benefit from a mother who is up front.

Show responsibility. Mothers who define their responsibility as mothers are teaching their daughters appropriate boundaries. Daughters whose mothers have shown them this model will become self-reliant and responsible.

Creating the Best Mother-Daughter Bond

Now that we've reviewed the ten ways that we as mothers have "created our own monsters," the ways to raise daughters who cope with the world at large as strong, self-sufficient young women are now apparent. By breaking our old patterns, offering a worldview, and providing the right modeling, we cull more successful mother-daughter unions and better acclimated, better prepared daughters. In this way, both mothers and daughters sense their own power.

The mother-daughter link is layered; relationships are intricate, vulnerable, and significant. Sometimes our hopes and output for those dearest to us result in confusion, agony, and despair. Easing the way for our daughters is a pervasive desire, and to this end a mother frequently justifies her daughter's actions when it would be better to call her daughter out. Mothers, in their vigilance to protect, aid, and provide for their daughters, aren't always logical and may put the daughter at a disadvantage. For mothers, this process may feel endless.

It begins with young daughters, during idyllic, promising times when it seems impossible that a daughter would be anything but sweet and innocent, and moves into a befuddling stage when her daughter becomes adolescent, hostile, and alien. Mothers and daughters plow through those precipitous years to the early twenties, when the daughter usually returns to the fold with her own distinct style and inflection of her generation. Thus is the reward: A brave new path is offered to mother and daughter as adult women a generation apart, weathered by their shared journey, awakened by what they've done right and wrong in the relationship. The arduous task of facing these issues provides an improved communication between mother and daughters, a heightened awareness of ourselves, and a clearer understanding of what our daughters' lives entail.

Susan with her daughters in 2009.

Questionnaire

✳

1. Please state your age and that of your daughter/s
   Age of mothers
34–49 years	36 percent
50–59 years	40 percent
60–71 years	24 percent

   Age of daughters
8–22	36 percent
23–30	40 percent
31–38	24 percent

2. Do you worry about how to raise your daughter/s?
Yes	75 percent
No	13 percent
Not applicable (already raised daughter/s)	12 percent

If so, please explain the reason.

Instilling morals and values	46 percent
Keeping her safe	16 percent
Having enough control	14 percent
Peer pressure	12 percent
Instilling independence	12 percent

3. Do you feel it is more difficult dealing with a daughter today than it was for your mother when you were growing up?

Yes	74 percent
No	24 percent
Yes and no	2 percent

4. Do you ever cave in to your daughter's demands?

Yes	69 percent
No	31 percent

If so, why?

You feel worn-out	45 percent
You want to avoid confrontation	51 percent
Your daughter is so persuasive	45 percent

5. Are you aware of treating one daughter differently from another?

Yes	92 percent
No	8 percent

6. What are your biggest issues with your daughter/s?

Establishing boundaries	53 percent
Respect	37 percent

A value system   32 percent

Materialism   24 percent

7. What indicates the biggest obstacle to your daughter's ability to be on the right path?

Peer pressure   50 percent

Boyfriend   25 percent

Media influences   25 percent

8. Is your daughter presently adversarial, or has she been in the past?

Yes   65 percent

No   23 percent

Unknown   12 percent

If yes, at what age did she become adversarial?

10 years   10 percent

11–13 years   42 percent

14–17 years   36 percent

18 years   12 percent

9. Do you consider yourself a role model for your daughter?

Yes   42 percent

No   58 percent

10. If you feel that you and your daughter are competitive, in what areas do you compete?

Achievement   82 percent

Looks   55 percent

Social life   55 percent

Finances   27 percent

11. Is your daughter competitive with her friends and colleagues?

    Yes   58 percent
    No   42 percent

12. If you are a single mother, do you believe that your divorce and life after divorce have affected your daughter's view of romance?

    Yes   33 percent
    No   60 percent
    Not applicable (daughter married prior
        to parents' divorce)   7 percent

13. If you are married to your daughter's father, do you feel that your marriage has been an influential example for your daughter?

    Yes   80 percent
    Yes and no   9 percent
    No   11 percent

14. As a working mother, do you believe that your career has shown your daughter what women can achieve, or do you believe it has had a negative effect upon her?

    Shows women can achieve   89 percent
    Had a negative effect   2 percent
    Both   2 percent
    Neither   7 percent

15. If you are a stay-at-home mother, what sort of message do you believe this has been for your daughter?

Positive message   85 percent

Negative message   0 percent

Mixed message   15 percent

16. Do you feel you've been too lax with your daughter regarding her schoolwork, choice of friends, and lifestyle?

Yes   22 percent

No   78 percent

17. In what areas do you attempt to be strict?

Schoolwork   66 percent

Your daughter's choice of friends   63 percent

Family time   47 percent

18. Do you ever feel as if you have little impact (which is why
you've become lax)?

Yes   29 percent

No   71 percent

19. Do you ever feel at a loss with your daughter in terms of
guidance and influence?

Yes   44 percent

No   56 percent

20. Do you feel that you've pressured your daughter to excel
academically and socially?

Yes   43 percent

No   51 percent

Academically only   6 percent

21. Does it ever seem that you are overburdened by the responsibility of raising your daughter?

Yes   34 percent
No   67 percent

22. Does your daughter exhibit interests that you never had?
    And do you encourage this?
    Yes   85 percent
    No   15 percent

23. Do you believe that you compensate for your daughter at
    times?
    Yes   67 percent
    No   33 percent

24. Do you believe that you enable your daughter?
    Yes   77 percent
    No   23 percent

    If so, in what capacities?
    Financially   92 percent
    Emotionally   58 percent
    Physically   32 percent

25. How would you describe yourself as a mother?
    Balanced (loving and realistic)   35 percent
    Perfectionist/high expectations/
        too involved with appearances   30 percent
    Busy/supportive   30 percent
    Loving/caring   29 percent
    Overprotective and overbearing   20 percent
    A+/solid   16 percent
    Inadequate/work in progress   10 percent

26. If there is one issue you wish you had addressed differently with your daughter long ago, please state what it is.

Being more consistent/less reactive   29 percent

Not indulging her/better boundaries   29 percent

Her individuality/self-esteem/confidence   28 percent

Being more involved with her life   14 percent

Situation with ex-husband   12 percent

Being more protective of her   7 percent

27. What is your deepest regret with your daughter/s?

More time or intimacy   33 percent

Better boundaries   24 percent

Couldn't get across values/morals   22 percent

Physical issues (health/weight loss)   10 percent

Divorce affected relationship   10 percent

Being absent too much   12 percent

Wish lived closer   3 percent

28. After distance and misunderstandings, did your daughter "return" emotionally to you?

55 percent responded that their daughter never "left."

45 percent responded that their daughter had "left" and did "return."

Of the 45 percent who said their daughters had "left," she returned at the following age:

17 years   11 percent

18–24 years   56 percent

25–29 years   24 percent

Never returned   9 percent

29. For those who did "return," how did this occur?
     Daughter married, started grad school, got pregnant,
          became a mom, or got a job   29 percent
     Boyfriend/father or other issues
          in her life   29 percent
     Change in mother's or daughter's attitude 29 percent
     For support   20 percent

30. How would you describe your relationship with your daugh-
     ter today?
     Positive   60 percent
     Mixed   40 percent

References

�֍

American Psychiatric Association. *Diagnostic and Statistical Manual of Mental Disorders DSM-IV.* Arlington, Va., 1994.

American Society for Aesthetic Plastic Surgery, "Cosmetic Procedures in 2007: American Society for Aesthetic Plastic Surgery Reports 8% Increase in Surgical Procedures." New York, February 25, 2008.

American Society for Reproductive Medicine, http://www.asrm.org/.

Apter, Terri. *You Don't Really Know Me: Why Mothers and Daughters Fight and How Both Can Win.* New York: W. W. Norton, 2005.

Asian News International. "In School, Michelle Obama Was Not 'Cool,' but Bent On Being Smart." *Thaindian News,* March 20, 2009. www.thaindian.com/newsportal/world-news/in-school-michelle-obama-was-not-cool-but-bent-on-being-smart-re-issue_100169354.html (accessed February 1, 2010).

Austen, Jane. *Pride and Predjudice.* New York: Penguin Classics, 1996.

Ball, Aimee Lee. "Everyone's Doing *What?*" *O, The Oprah Magazine,*
    May 2009.

Beck, Melinda. "How's Your Baby? Recalling the Apgar Score's Name-
    sake." *The Wall Street Journal,* May 26, 2009. http://online.wsj
    .com/article/SB124328572691452021.html (accessed February 1,
    2010).

Begley, Sharon. "Inside the Shopping Brain." Newsweek.com, Decem-
    ber 6, 2008. www.newsweek.com/id/17592 (accessed February
    1, 2010).

Belluck, Pam. "Yes, Looks Do Matter." *The New York Times,* April 24,
    2009, New York edition, ST1.

Bennetts, Leslie. *The Feminine Mistake: Are We Giving Up Too Much?*
    New York: Voice, 2007.

Berry, Dawn Bradley. *The Divorce Recovery Sourcebook.* New York:
    McGraw-Hill, 1999.

Bloom, Alan. *Love and Friendship.* New York: Simon and Schuster,
    1993.

Bloom, Amy. "The 'EEW' Factor," *O, The Oprah Magazine,* April 2009.

The Brady Bunch. Created by Sherwood Schwartz. A Sherwood
    Schwartz Production, Paramount Television, 1969–1974.

Branden, Nathaniel. *The Six Pillars of Self-Esteem.* New York: Bantam,
    1995.

Brothers and Sisters. Created by Jon Robin Baitz. ABC, 2006–.

Brown, Lyn Mikel, and Carol Gilligan. *Meeting at the Crossroads:
    Women's Psychology and Girl's Development.* New York: Ballan-
    tine Books, 1992.

Buck, Joan Juliet. "Beauty and Soul." *Vogue,* August 2009. www.style
    .com/vogue/feature/2009_August_Christy_Turlington (accessed
    February 1, 2010).

Bushnell, Candace. *One Fifth Avenue.* New York: Voice, 2009.

Campbell, Susan. "The Mother-Daughter Bond." *Psychology Today,*
    May 1, 2001. www.psychologytoday.com/articles/pto-20010501
    000010.html (accessed February 1, 2010).

Caplan, Paula J. *The New Don't Blame Mother: Mending the Mother-
    Daughter Relationship.* New York: Routledge Publishing, 2000.

Carey, Benedict. "Some Protect the Ego by Working on Their Excuses

Early." *The New York Times*, January 6, 2009, New York edition, D5.

CaringOnline. "Eating Disorder News: Celebrities with Eating Disorders." 2010, The Center Inc. http://www.caringonline.com/catdis/people.htm

Carlin, Peter Ames, and Vicki Sheff-Cahan. "Out and About." *People*, October 12, 1998.

Center for Adolescent Health and Development. "Protecting Teens: Beyond Race, Income and Family Structure." 2000, University of Minnesota.

Center for Disease Control and Prevention. "Fast Stats: U.S. Marriage and Divorce." 2008. CDC/National Center for Health Statistics. December 22, 2009. http://cdc.gov/NCHS/fastats/divorce.htm.

Chodorow, Nancy. "Family Structure and Feminine Personality." In *Woman, Culture, and Society,* edited by Michelle Zimbalist Rosaldo and Louise Lamphere, 43–66. Palo Alto, Calif.: Stanford University Press, 1974.

Cohen, Rich. "The Jessica Question." *Vanity Fair,* June 2009. www.vanityfair.com/ culture / features/2009/06/jessica-simpson200906 (accessed February 1, 2010)

Colman, David. "The Great Sale of '80." *The New York Times,* December 11, 2008, New York edition, E1.

Cosgrove-Mather, Bootie. "Girls Getting Increasingly Violent." CBS News.com, April 29, 2004. www.cbsnews.com/stories/2004/04/29/national/main614781.shtml (accessed February 1, 2010).

Crocker, Jennifer, and C. T. Wolfe. "Contingencies of Self-Worth." *Psychological Review* 108 (2001): 593–623.

Dargis, Manohla. "One Word for What's Happening to Actors' Faces Today: Plastics." *The New York Times,* January 23, 2005, New York edition, A1.

Desperate Housewives. Created by Marc Cherry. ABC, 2004–.

"Determination of the December 2007 Peak in Economic Activity." National Bureau of Economic Research Business Cycles and Recessions, (December 11, 2008): 1–7.

Dirty Sexy Money. Created by Craig Wright. ABC, 2007–2009.

Dominus, Susan. "Coming Up Short as a Role Model for the Mommy Track." *The New York Times,* January 23, 2009, New York edition, A22.

Dweck, Carol. *Mindset: The New Psychology of Success.* New York: Ballantine Books, 2006.

Eccles, J. S. "Understanding Women's Educational and Occupational Choices." *Psychology of Women Quarterly* 18, no. 4 (December 1994): 585–609.

Ephron, Nora. *I Feel Bad About My Neck: And Other Thoughts on Being a Woman.* New York: Vintage, 2008.

Esquivel, Laura. *Like Water for Chocolate.* New York: Anchor, 1995.

Etcoff, Nancy, Susan Orbach, Jennifer Scott, and Heidi D'Agostio. "The Real Truth About Beauty: A Global Report." StrategyOne and Dove Campaign for Real Beauty, September 2004, Web.

The Family Stone. Directed by Thomas Bezucha. Fox 2000 Pictures, 2005.

Family Violence Prevention Fund, 383 Rhode Island St., Suite 304, San Francisco, CA 94103-5133.

Fels, Anna. *Necessary Dreams: Ambition in Women's Changing Lives.* New York: Pantheon Books, 2004.

Fingeret, Michelle Cororve, and David H. Gleaves. "Social, Cultural, Feminist and Psychological Influences on Women's Body Satisfaction: A Structural Modeling Analysis." *Psychology of Women Quarterly* 28, no. 4 (December 2004): 370–80.

Fisher, Helen. *Why We Love: The Nature and Chemistry of Romantic Love.* New York: Henry Holt, 2004.

Fitch, Janet. *White Oleander.* Boston: Little, Brown, 1999.

Flax, Jane. "Forgotten Forms of Close Combat: Mothers and Daughters Revisited." In *Toward a New Psychology of Gender: A Reader,* edited by Mary M. Gergen and Sara N. Davis, 311–24. New York: Routledge, 1997.

Friedan, Betty. *The Feminine Mystique.* New York: Dell Publishing, 1983.

Friedlin, Jennifer. "Gaining Weight Cost Me My Job." *Marie Claire,* October 1, 2005. http://www.accessmylibrary.com/coms2/summary_0286-11567991_ITM.

Gabe Kapler Foundation, www.prolebrity.com/the-gabe-kapler-foundation.

Gaiman, Neil. *Coraline: The Graphic Novel,* illustrated by P. Craig Russell. New York: HarperCollins Publishers, 2008.

Georgia Rule. Directed by Garry Marshall. Universal Pictures, 2007.

Gilmore Girls. Created by Amy Sherman. Warner Bros., 2000–2007.

The Graduate. Directed by Mike Nichols. Embassy Pictures Corporation, 1967.

Grall, Timothy S. "Custodial Mothers and Fathers and Their Child Support: 2005." U.S. Census Bureau, March 17, 2008. http://www.census.gov/prod/2007pubs/p60-234.pdf.

Grey Gardens. Directed by Michael Sucsy. HBO Films, 2009.

Grimm, Wilhelm Carl, and Jacob Ludwig Grimm. *Cinderella.* New York: Parragon Books, 2006.

Gypsy. Book by Arthur Laurents, lyrics by Stephen Sondheim, music by Jule Styne. 1959.

Hamermesh, Daniel S., and Jeff E. Biddle. "Beauty and the Labor Market." *The American Economic Review* 84, no. 5 (December 1994): 1174–94.

Hamkins, SuEllen, and Renée Schultz. *The Mother-Daughter Project: How Mothers and Daughters Can Band Together, Beat the Odds, and Thrive Through Adolescence.* New York: Penguin Group, 2008.

Healy, Patrick. "On Eve of Primary, Clinton Campaign Shows Stress." *The New York Times,* January 8, 2008. www.nytimes.com/2008/01/08/us/politics/08clinton.html?scp=1&sq=%22On%20Eve%20of%20Primary,%20Clinton%20Campaign%20Shows%20Stress%22&st=cse (accessed February 1, 2010).

Hetherington, E. Mavis et al. "An Overview of the Virginia Longitudinal Study of Divorce and Remarriage with a Focus on Early Adolescence." *Journal of Family Psychology* 7, no. 1 (June 1993): 39–56.

Hill, John P., and Grayson N. Holmbeck. "Disagreements About Rules in Families with Seventh-Grade Girls and Boys." *Journal of Youth and Adolescence* 16, no. 3 (June 1987): 221–46.

Hinshaw, Stephen, and Rachel Kranz. *The Triple Bind: Saving Our Teenage Girls from Today's Pressures.* New York: Ballantine Books, 2009.

Hoffman, Jan. "Bingeing on Celebrity Weight Battles." *The New York Times,* May 31, 2009, New York edition, ST1.

———. "If They Can Find Time for Date Night . . ." *The New York Times,* June 7, 2009, New York edition, ST1.

Hrdy, Sarah Blaffer. *Mother Nature: Maternal Instincts and How They Shape the Human Species.* New York: Ballantine Books, 2000.

Hsu, L. K. George. *Eating Disorders.* New York: Guilford Press, 1990.

InfoNIAC.com, www.infoniac.com/press-releases.

Isadore, Chris, "It's Official: Recession Since Dec. '07." CNNMoney .com, December 1, 2008. http://money.cnn.com/2008/12/01/news/ economy/recession/index.htm (accessed February 1, 2010).

Jacobs, Tom. "Economic Expansion: Teen Girls Gain Weight During Downturns." Miller-McCune.com, May 6, 2009. www.miller mccune.com/news/girls-gain-weight-during-downturns-1198 (accessed February 1, 2010).

James, W. "The Self." In *The Self in Social Psychology: Key Readings in Social Psychology,* edited by Roy F. Baumeister, 69–77. Philadelphia: Psychology Press, 1999.

Jerome, Richard, and Carole Glines. "Inside Robert Pattinson and Kristen Stewart's *Twilight* Love Story." *OK! Magazine,* June 15, 2009.

"Jessica Alba's Style: Go Behind the Cover Shoot and Get Her Look." *Elle,* March 2009. http://www.elle.com/Pop-Culture/Cover-Shoots/ The-Changeling2.

Kaiser Family Foundation, www.kff.org.

Kelton Research, 25 W. 45th St., New York, NY 10036–4902. www .keltonresearch.com.

Kershaw, Sarah. "For Teenagers, Hello Means 'How About a Hug?'" *New York Times,* May 27, 2009, New York edition, A1.

KidsGrowth.com. "Stages of Adolescent Development." 1999–2010. KG Investments LLC. http://www.kidsgrowth.com/resources/articledetail.cfm?id=1140.

Klein, Edward. "The Lion and the Legacy." *Vanity Fair,* June 2009.

Koerner, Brendan I. "Where the Boys Aren't." *U.S. News and World Report* 126, no. 5 (February 8, 1999): 46–50, 53–55.

Koran, Lorrin, M.D. "Complusive Shopping Research at Stanford

Seeks to Treat Mysterious Disorders." Stanford School of Medicine News Releases (December 16, 2002): Web. 12, March 2010.

Krache, Donna. "How to Ground a 'Helicopter Parent.'" CNN.com, August 19, 2008. www.cnn.com/2008/LIVING/personal/08/13/helicopter.parents/index.html (accessed February 1, 2010).

Kreamer, Anne. *Going Gray: What I Learned About Beauty, Sex, Work, Motherhood, Authenticity, and Everything Else That Really Matters.* New York: Little, Brown, 2007.

La Ferla, Ruth. "Even in Recession, Spend They Must: Luxury Shoppers Anonymous." *The New York Times,* December 11, 2008, New York edition, E1.

Lamanna, Mary Ann, and Agnes Riedmann. *Marriages and Families: Making Choices in a Diverse Society,* 10th ed. Florence, Ky.: Wadsworth Publishing, 2008.

Legally Blonde. Directed by Robert Luketic. Metro-Goldwyn-Mayer, 2001.

Lennon, Christine. "Your Changing Ideal of Pretty." *Marie Claire,* October 2005.

The Light in the Piazza. Directed by Bartlett Sher. Lincoln Center Theater, 2005–2006.

Lipton, Lauren. "Get Bobbed, but Don't Get Clipped." *New York Times,* December 11, 2008, New York edition, E1.

Mad Men. Created by Matthew Weiner. AMC, 2007–.

Madsen, Stephanie. "Parents' Management of Adolescents' Romantic Relationships Through Dating Rules." *Journal of Youth and Adolescence* 37, no. 9 (October 2008): 1044–1058.

Major, B., L. Barr, J. Zubeck, and S. H. Babey, "Gender and Self-Esteem: A Meta-Analysis." In *Sexism and Stereotypes in Modern Society: The Gender Science of Janet Taylor Spence* (223–254), edited by William B. Swann Jr., Judith H. Langlois, and Lucia Albino Gilbert. Washington, D.C.: American Psychological Association, 1999.

Mamma Mia! Directed by Phyllida Lloyd. Universal Pictures, 2008.

Mandel, Debbie. *Addicted to Stress: A Woman's 7-Step Program to Reclaim Joy and Spontaneity in Life.* San Francisco: Jossey-Bass, 2008.

Marc, Dr. [Marc Lawrence]. "Britney Spears: Weight Gain to 160 Pounds?" October 2007. www.celebritydietdoctor.com/britney-spears-weight-gain-to-160-pounds (accessed February 1, 2010).

Maslow, Abraham H. *Toward a Psychology of Being.* New York: John Wiley and Sons, 1998.

McBride, Karyl. *Will I Ever Be Good Enough? Healing the Daughters of Narcissistic Mothers.* New York: Free Press, 2008

McGraw, Phil. "Marriage and Divorce: The Statistics." Dr. Phil.com, 2009.

McMurtry, Larry. *Terms of Endearment.* New York, Simon & Schuster, 1999.

Mean Girls. Directed by Mark Waters. Paramount Pictures, 2004.

Mermaids. Directed by Richard Benjamin. Orion Pictures Corporation, 1990.

"Michelle Obama Tells Girls School Is Cool." UPI.com, April 3, 2009. www.upi.com/Top_News/2009/04/03/Michelle-Obama-tells-girls-school-is-cool/UPI-22641238759685 (accessed February 1, 2010).

Mikel, Lyn Brown, and Carol Gilligan. *Meeting at the Crossroads.* Cambridge, Mass.: Harvard University Press, 1998.

Miller, Matthew, Dorothy Pomerantz, and Lacey Rose, editors. "The Celebrity 100." Forbes.com, June 3, 2009. www.forbes.com/2009/06/03/forbes-100-celebrity-09-jolie-oprah-madonna_land.html (accessed February 1, 2010).

Mona Lisa Smile. Directed by Mike Newell. Columbia Pictures, 2003.

Mooney, Jake. "Women, Haircuts and the Price of Self-Esteem." *The New York Times,* February 15, 2009, New York edition, CY1.

Mosher, William D., Anjani Chandra, and Jo Jones. "Sexual Behavior and Selected Health Measures: Men and Women 15–44 Years of Age, United States, 2002." *Advance Data from Health and Health Statistics* 362 (September 15, 2005).

MSNBC.com. "Caroline Kennedy: Book's Claim 'Nonsense.'" Associated Press (May 18, 2009). http://today.msnbc.msn.com/id/30806637/.

National Alliance for the Mentally Ill, 3803 N. Fairfax Drive, Ste. 100, Arlington, VA 22203.

National Campaign to Prevent Teen and Unplanned Pregnancy, 1776 Massachusetts Ave. NW, Suite 200, Washington, DC 20036.

National Center for Health Statitics, Centers for Disease Control and Prevention, 1600 Clifton Rd., Atlanta, GA 30333.

National Committee on Pay Equity, "The Wage Gap Over Time: In Real Dollars, Women See a Continuing Gap," 2008, www.payequity.org.

National Eating Disorders Association, www.nationaleatingdisorders.org/information-resources/general-information.php#facts-statistics

National Institute of Mental Health, 6001 Executive Blvd., Room 8184, MSC 9663, Bethesda, MD 20892–9663.

National Survey of Student Engagement. 2007. *Assessment for Improvement: Tracking Student Engagement Over Time—Annual results year 2007.* Bloomington, Ind.: Indiana University Center for Postsecondary Research.

Nichter, Mimi. *Fat Talk: What Girls and Their Parents Say About Dieting.* Cambridge Mass.: Harvard University Press, 2001.

Nome, Valerie. "Martina McBride Shares Recipe for Happiness." http://www.okmagazine.com/2009/03/martina-mcbride-shares-recipe-for-happiness-12706/

Northrup, Christiane. *Mother-Daughter Wisdom: Creating a Legacy of Physical and Emotional Health.* New York: Bantam Books, 2005.

Oates, Joyce. *We Were the Mulvaneys.* New York: Plume, 1996.

OK! Magazine, reports in August 18, 2008, issue on "Adolescent Oscars," Miley Cyrus, and the Jonas Brothers.

OK! Magazine. "Britney's Teen Sister Jamie Lynn Spears Pregnant—Babies, Jamie . . ." December 18, 2007. http://www.people.com/people/article/0,,20167059,00.html/.

OK! Magazine. "The Truth About Which Stars Are Really Pregnant." March 23, 2009.

"Parents' Expectations, Styles Can Harm College Students' Self-Esteem." *Science Daily,* August 17, 2009. www.sciencedaily.com/releases/2008/08/080815130429.htm (accessed February 1, 2010).

Parker-Pope, Tara. "School Popularity Affects Girls' Weights." *The New York Times,* January 9, 2009. http://well.blogs.nytimes.com/2008/01/09/school-popularity-affects-girls-weights/?scp=1&sq=%

22School%20Popularity%20Affects%20Girls%E2%80%99%
20Weights%22&st=cse (accessed February 1, 2010).

Pipher, Mary. *Reviving Ophelia: Saving the Selves of Adolescent Girls.*
New York: Riverhead Trade, 2005.

Plott, Michéle, and Lauri Umanski. *Making Sense of Women's Lives:
An Introduction to Women's Studies.* New York: Rowman and
Littlefield, 2000.

Popenoe, David. "Debunking Divorce Myths." Discovery Channel: Discovery Health (2010): 1. Web.

Pretty Baby. Directed by Louis Malle. Paramount Pictures, 1978.

Quenqua, Douglas. "Friends, Until I Delete You." *The New York Times,*
January 29, 2009. www.nytimes.com/2009/01/29/style/29iht-
29facebook.19771424.html?scp=3&sq=Friends, Until I Delete
You&st=cse (accessed February 1, 2010).

Rich, Cynthia. "Ageism and the Politics of Beauty." In *Making Sense
of Women's Lives: An Introduction to Women's Studies* (317–321),
edited by Michele Plott and Lauri Umanski. Lawrenceville, N.J.:
Collegiate Press, 2000.

The Real Housewives of New Jersey. Bravo TV, 2009–.

Sax, Leonard. "Where the Girls Aren't." *Education Week,* June 18,
2008.

Sex and the City. Created by Darren Starr. HBO, 1998–2004.

Sexual Assault and Relationship Abuse Prevention and Support,
http://www.stanford.edu/group/womenscntr/publications.html

Shallow Hal. Directed by Bobby Farrelly and Peter Farrelly. Twentieth Century–Fox, 2001.

Sheindlin, Judy. *Beauty Fades, Dumb Is Forever: The Making of a
Happy Woman.* New York: Harper Paperbacks, 2000.

Shellenbarger, Sue. "Raising Kids Who Can Thrive Amid Chaos in
Their Careers." *The Wall Street Journal,* June 10, 2009, D1.

Shipman, Claire, and Kazdin, Cole. "Teens: Oral Sex and Casual Prostitution No Biggie." *Good Morning America* (May 28, 2009). http://
abcnews.go.com/GMA/Parenting/story?id=7693121&page=1.

Silverman, Stephen M. "Chastity Bono Undergoing Sex Change."
People.com, June 11, 2009. www.people.com/people/article/0,,
20284698,00.html (accessed February 1, 2010).

————. "Dina Lohan: 'I'm Not a Party Mom.'" People.com, March 21, 2007. www.people.com/people/article/0,,20015629.00.html (accessed February 1, 2010).

Simmons, Rachel. *The Curse of the Good Girl: Raising Authentic Girls with Courage and Confidence.* New York: Penguin Press. 2009.

————. *Odd Girl Out: The Hidden Culture of Aggression in Girls.* New York: Harvest Books, 2003.

Simons, Janet A., Donald B. Irwin, and Beverly A. Drinnin. *Psychology: The Search for Understanding.* St. Paul, Minn.: West Publishing Company, 1987.

Simpson, A. Rae, Ph.D. *Raising Teens: A Synthesis of Research and a Foundation for Action.* Harvard School of Public Health, 2001. www.hsph.harvard.edu/chc/parenting/report.pdf.

Simpson, Mona. *Anywhere But Here.* New York: Vintage, 1992.

Slatalla, Michelle. "Nostalgia, with a Stop Button." *The New York Times,* September 3, 2009, New York edition, E2.

————. "How I Became a Soft Touch." *The New York Times,* February 19, 2009, New York edition, E2.

South Carolina Department of Mental Health. n.d. Eating disorder statistics. www.state.sc.us/dmh/anorexia/statistics.htm (accessed February 1, 2010).

StarMagazine.com. "Britney Hits Rock Bottom!" October 4, 2007. www.starmagazine.com/news/13036 (accessed February 1, 2010).

Steinem, Gloria. *Outrageous Acts and Everyday Rebellions,* 2nd ed. New York: Henry Holt, 1995.

Stockett, Kathryn. *The Help.* New York: Amy Einhorn Books, Putnam, 2009.

Sullivan, Emmet, "Sarah Palin's Teenage Daughter Pregnant." People.com. www.people.com/people/article/0,,20222767,00.html Update Tuesday, September 2, 2008, 06:00 AM EDT. Originally posted Monday, September 1, 2008, 01:30 PMED.

Sweeney, Camille. "A Girl's Life, with Highlights." *The New York Times,* April 3, 2008. www.nytimes.com/2008/04/03/fashion/03SKIN.html?scp=1&sq=%22A%20girl%27s%20life,%20with%20highlights%22&st=cse (accessed February 1, 2010).

————. "Never Too Young for That First Pedicure." *The New York Times*, February 28, 2008. www.nytimes.com/2008/02/28/fashion/28Skin.html?pagewanted=1&sq=never%20too%20young%20for%20that%20first%20pedicure&st=cse&scp=1 (accessed February 1, 2010).

Tannen, Deborah. *You're Wearing That? Understanding Mothers and Daughters in Conversation.* New York: Ballantine Books, 2006.

Tears and Laughter: The Joan and Melissa Rivers Story. Directed by Oz Scott. Davis Entertainment, 1994.

Thériault, Jocelyne. "Sexual and Non-Sexual Intimacy in Romantic Relationships During Late Adolescence: The Role of the Mother-Daughter Relationship." *Electronic Journal of Human Sexuality* 6 (February 3, 2003). www.ejhs.org/volume6/motherdaughter.htm (accessed February 1, 2010).

Tilly, Charles. *Credit and Blame.* Princeton, N.J.: Princeton University Press, 2008.

Trachtenberg, Thea, and Imaeyen Ibanga. "Mom Has Plastic Surgery to Look Like Daughter." *Good Morning America* (May 12, 2009). http://abcnews.go.com/GMA/story?id=7560860&page=1.

Traffic. Directed by Steven Soderbergh. Bedford Falls Productions, 2000.

Traister, Rebecca. "Katie Couric: Reports of Her Demise Were Greatly Exaggerated." Elle.com, March 19, 2009. www.elle.com/Pop-Culture/Movies-TV-Music-Books/Katie-Couric (accessed February 1, 2010).

U.S. Census Bureau. *Custodial Mothers and Fathers and Their Child Support, 2005.* Available at http://www.census.gov/prod/2007pubs/p60-234.pdf.

U.S. Department of Health and Human Services Office on Women's Health, 200 Independence Ave. SW, Room 712E, Washington, DC 20201.

U.S. Department of Labor. *Women in the Labor Force in 2008.* Employment and Earnings. 2008. Bureau of Labor Statistics. November 2007. http://www.dol.gov/wb/factsheets/Qf-laborforce-08.htm.

University of Central Florida. "Parents' Expectations, Styles Can Harm College Students' Self-Esteem." *ScienceDaily,* August 17, 2008. http://www.sciencedaily.com/releases/2008/08/080815130429.htm.

Violence by Teenage Girls: Trends and Context. (NCJ 218905) May 2008. OJJDP Girls Study Group Series.

Walters, Marianne, Betty Carter, Peggy Papp, and Olga Silverstein. "Toward a Feminist Perspective in Family Therapy," in *The Invisible Web: Gender Patterns in Family Relationships.* New York: Guilford Press, 1988, 15–30.

Wedding Crashers. Directed by David Dobkin. New Line Cinema, 2005.

Wells, Rebecca, *Divine Secrets of the Ya-Ya Sisterhood.* New York: Harper Paperbacks, 2004.

Whelan, Christine B. *Why Smart Men Marry Smart Women.* New York: Simon and Schuster, 2006.

Wilson, Eric. "A Museum Gala Where High Cheekbones and Higher Hemlines Rule." *The New York Times.* May 5, 2009, New York edition, A23.

Wiseman, Rosalind. *Queen Bees and Wannabes: Helping Your Daughter Survive Cliques, Gossip, Boyfriends, and Other Realities of Adolescence.* New York: Three Rivers Press, 2003.

Wolfe, Tom. *The Bonfire of the Vanities.* New York: Farrar, Straus and Giroux, 1990.

The Women. Directed by Diane English. Picturehouse Entertainment, 2008.

Woodman, Marion. *Addiction to Perfection: The Still Unravished Bride.* Toronto: Inner City Books, 1982.

Woolf, Linda M. "Effects of Age and Gender on Perceptions of Younger and Older Adults." www.webster.edu/~woolflm/ageismwoolf.html (accessed February 1, 2010).

WOWT-TV. "Teen Charged for Putting Stillborn Baby in Trash." The Associated Press, April 20, 2009.

Acknowledgments

✳

To the women who have shared their deepest struggles and personal victories with their daughters, I offer a heartfelt thank-you. Their voices are the soul of this book.

I remain grateful for the support, guidance, and expertise of Jennifer Enderlin, my amazing editor, and Alice Martell, my wise agent.

In alphabetical order: At St. Martin's Press, Meg Drislane, Rachel Ekstrom, Sara Goodman, John Murphy, Sally Richardson, Matthew Shear, Dori Weintraub. For input: Lori Ames, Meredith Bernstein, Brondi Borer, Gail Clott, Susie Finesman, Brit Geiger, Cindy Land, Meryl Moss, Frances Sayers, Jane Shapiro, Judy H. Shapiro, Judy Smith, Cynthia Vartan. Jennie Ripps, my muse, Robert Marcus and Neil Rosini, lawyers, Christine Florio, Dabz Fulton, Angela Marius, Sona Quigley, Alexis Segal, for their assistance. In academia: Carol Camper, Lewis Burke Frumkes, David Linton, Magda Maczynska at Marymount Manhattan College, Suzanne Murphy at Teachers College, Columbia University. In Hollywood: Jon Avnet, Charles Busch, Sally Robinson, Bruce Vinokour, Ellyn Williams. The professionals who have contributed their thoughts to this book: Leslie Bennetts, Ronnie Burak,

Anna Fels, Jeanette Friedman, Barton Goldsmith, Claire Owen, Seth Shulman, Brenda Szulman, Christine Whelan.

My parents, Selma and Herbert L. Shapiro, my in-laws Helene and Ted Barash, and dearest friends.

Jennie, Michael, and Elizabeth Ripps, my precious children. Lastly, Gary A. Barash, my loving husband, always.

Reader's Guide for
You're Grounded Forever... But First Let's Go Shopping

1. The author chooses ten "challenges" that mothers face with their daughters. Which of these resonate for you and why?

2. The author writes in her introduction that 70 percent of mothers feel that they haven't set enough limits with their daughters. Do you believe that this has been a big issue for you with your daughter?

3. Do you view yourself as the kind of mother who pressures her daughter to be a certain way? Or do you believe that your daughter's individuality is what matters most?

4. What do you think the author is warning against regarding mothering daughters today? Do you believe that you have impact in these instances?

5. Discuss why it is so difficult to teach daughters appropriate values. Do you believe that the culture (media, celebrities) has more sway than you have as a mother?

6. The author found that the majority of mothers feel more burdened raising daughters than sons. Is this your experience?

7. Do you feel that you've overemphasized some aspect of your daughter's life (her weight, her friends, her achievements)? Has this been helpful to her or a hindrance?

8. Of the author's ten "challenges" that we face as mothers, what scenario causes the most tension between you and your daughters?

9. The author investigates a daughter's female friendships in terms of trust, rivalry, and competition. Do you feel that you've been a model for healthy female friendships yourself?

10. Define the author's take on encouraging a daughter's self-esteem. What do you think makes this so complicated between mothers and daughters?

11. The author writes that many mothers find it hard to reason with daughters between the ages of thirteen and seventeen. Have you found this to be the case?

12. What are your thoughts about the author's advice when it comes to a daughter's love life? Are you willing to express concern about her partner or the relationship, if need be?

13. Are there parts of this book that you would recommend to a friend when she is immersed in a trying time with her daughter?

14. What has this book taught you? Is there any chapter that has been particularly illuminating?

15. The author believes that mothers are the first and lasting role models for their daughters. In this way, mothers wield great influence. Does this guide help you as you face ongoing issues with your daughters?

HONEST, PROVOCATIVE, AND REAL
Dissect the Difficult Challenges
of the Modern Woman

"Susan Shapiro Barash shines a light on the complicated feelings
and questions we seldom discuss but feel so powerfully."

—RACHEL SIMMONS, AUTHOR OF *THE CURSE OF THE GOOD GIRL*